What Then Will This Child

Turn Out To Be?

An Introductory Handbook
for Foster Care and Adoption

*Jackie
With all
my love —
Dan and His
& Georgann
Thank you
for your
encouragement!
8-18-16*

Georgann Lemaire

With articles by Dan Lemaire MFT
Fetal Alcohol Syndrome
Attachment Theory
Adoption in the Bible

African American male soccer player on cover -
www.dreamstime.com

epub formatting – www.ibookservices.com

Georgann's website – www.georgannlemaire.com

authors' photo on website – www.lemairephoto.com

What Then Will This Child Turn Out To Be?

All Scripture quotations, unless otherwise indicated, are taken from The Holy Bible, New King James Version (NKJV)®, copyright© 1982 by Thomas Nelson, Inc., Publishers. Used by permission. All rights reserved. www.harpercollinschristian.com

Other Scripture references are from the following sources:

Scripture quotations taken from the New American Standard Bible®,

Copyright © 1960, 1962, 1963, 1968, 1971, 1972, 1973, 1975, 1977, 1995 by The Lockman Foundation. Used by permission. (www.Lockman.org)

Scripture quotations marked NIV are taken from the Holy Bible, New International Version®, NIV®. Copyright© 1973, 1978, 1984, 2011 by Biblica, Inc.™ Used by permission of Zondervan. All rights reserved worldwide. www.zondervan.com

The "NIV" and the "New International Version" are trademarks registered in the United States Patent and Trademark Office by Biblica, Inc.™

Scripture quotations taken from the Amplified Bible, Copyright © 1954, 1958, 1962, 1964, 1965, 1987 by the Lockman Foundation. Used by permission (www.Lockman.org)

The formatting for this book was done by ibookservices.

In order to insure the privacy of the foster children, I have ALWAYS used fictitious names and jumbled or invented portions of their stories. There were several adults that I could not contact for permission to use their names in this book, and so I have contrived other names for them.

HUGE THANKS go to my last minute proofreaders—two of my friends who are fellow foster and adoptive parents, Diane Harper and Bob Needham. I am enormously appreciative of their willingness to do this favor for me, and the scope of their combined corrections was astounding and humbling. Yet the final responsibility for accuracy, errors, and omissions is mine.

To our loving Lord Jesus, with thanks for His bountiful grace and mercy to all of us all the time and never ending. Thank You for working all things together for good.

To Tim, Steve, Mark, and Danny—who are steady, hardworking men and are forging ahead, fulfilling their dreams and their destinies. You are awesome!

To Jessica, Jill, and Shelley, whom we cherish, and who love our sons so well. You are bright lights in our lives.

To Quinn, Caleb, Mandy, Nathan, Luke, and Emery Rose, our kids' kids, who bring us joy and laughter. It is so much fun watching you in your stages and sharing this life with you.

To every person named and unnamed in this book who gave David and Dan and I a cup of cold water...thank you for standing with us for whatever length of time. We remember you, and it all counted for our refreshment.

To YOU, the reader, we expect that your own odyssey will bear your unique stamp and we wish you well ...and we pray for Jesus' anointing on your adventure.

To Joan McEachin, my dear friend, who was the first to read our manuscript and who wrote her comments and corrections with a flourishing script and sweet margin notes that sparkled with encouragement and praise. Our gratitude!

My deepest thanks go to Jackie Calabrese, my dear friend, who proved to me forty years ago that Jesus Christ cared about me personally and loved me just the way I was. I credit you, Jackie, with showing me the way of salvation and introducing me to the Lord Jesus.

AND TO DAVID, who is brave and enduring. You will be secure, because there is hope; you will look about you and take your rest in safety, you will lie down with no one to make you afraid, and many will court your favor. (Job 11:18-19 NIV)

CONTENTS

Part III - Our adoption experience, with insights. 92

To the reader:
Hello!

Our foster care and adoption journey began in 1987 when I awakened one morning to realize I had had a vision about newborn babies. I lay in bed, thoroughly intrigued by the very clear visual images and by the feelings of excitement and joy that filled me full of hopeful expectation. I was preoccupied by a sense of awe, knowing I had experienced something supernatural.

In the vision, I saw two babies in blue hospital gowns in the forefront, and beyond them many, many more babies superimposed over each other, seeming to go on and on into the heavens.

I knew how I felt—elated and excited. But I wasn't sure what to think about it.

When I told Dan about it, he laughed. I was homeschooling three of our sons (our oldest son was in public school that year), babysitting friends' children, and active in our homeschool group and in our church. How could I possibly take on more children?

When I told a friend about the babies, she laughed! I stopped telling people and proceeded cautiously, but steadily, asking the Lord lots of questions, getting some interesting answers, and seeking Him in my Bible reading.

There was a long waiting period—six years of dialoguing with the Lord about what the vision meant practically, yearning for it to come to pass. Then we understood God's intent, and the babies came into our family as we began foster care. It was a mystery until He chose to reveal His intention in His perfect timing.

In the years that we were foster parents, we partnered with God in caring for very needy people—orphans in their distress. Orphans because their own parents were unable to care for them for various reasons, in distress because they were homeless and helpless.

One little boy, David, our first foster child, was released to us by his father during a visit arranged by the social worker. He told us that he approved of our adopting his son. With our sons, we agreed to be committed to David for life.

Years later, when David's far-reaching issues got the better of him, life became very hard for Dan and me. We had to 'step up to the plate' and keep going in our responsibility to parent him. We had made a commitment to God and to David, and we needed to see it through. It was the hardest thing either of us had experienced.

But life was very hard for David also. Because his brain cells were damaged, his inner world was in a muddle. Because his brain was not functioning normally, he had trouble with his schoolwork and his relationships were skewed. Anxiety and flash anger became his constant companions. This must have been a very frightening way to live.

David hurt our feelings a lot, and we hurt his feelings a lot. He caused us pain by being defiant and by using stinging words and by acting out. We wounded him by saying **no** to many of the things he wanted to do, and by not really understanding the depth of his deficits because of Fetal Alcohol Syndrome and his insecure attachment style.

There was a lot of disappointment on both sides.

Because of the Christian training he had gotten in our home and because he had a relationship with God, David developed a conscience. So when things became very difficult, especially in his teenage years, he usually told us he was sorry soon after his rudeness or some episode of anger. Often he would write us a note of apology. We would always accept. And he would always accept our apologies for our impatience with him. There were several tumultuous years in our home. Now they are in the past.

We will not be writing in depth about specific instances of David being mean, aggressive, irrational, manipulative, intentionally hurtful, and disrespectful. We will not be focusing on his misdeeds. We don't want to re-live it, and we have decided it would be rude to reveal a time in David's life over which he now feels remorse.

These days we are on the phone almost every evening with David. He is 21 years old and living in a group home a few miles from where we live. We take him to church every Sunday. On Mondays, I take him to his therapy appointment and afterward we go out and grab some tacos. He and Dan hike the local hills or go mountain biking on a weekend afternoon. We make sure to go to his Special Olympics sports tournaments, and we spend all of the holidays together.

As the years have gone by and he has been in therapy groups with other kids his age, he has realized that our boundaries were for his protection. He has also realized how good he had it in our home compared to most of his peers' experiences. As he has become more stable through medications and years of counseling, and because of ours and others' prayers, he has become very grateful that we have been his parents.

Our intent in writing this book is to relate our story so that people considering foster parenting and adoption can see inside of the adventure, albeit through our eyes and our own personal experience. Our desire is to provide a straightforward adoption story. We want to caution against any superficiality in making the serious decision to adopt.

When the judge grants an adoption, the child is issued a brand-new birth certificate, and his original birth certificate is negated. His biological parents' names are nowhere to be seen on the new document. It is the adoptive parents' names that are shown. That is how our culture and our legal system view adoption, and that is how God sees adoption. It is a done deal.

We are excited to share our story and our enthusiasm with you. The Bible says: *We are His workmanship, created in Christ Jesus for good works, which God prepared beforehand that we should walk in them. Ephesians 2:10*

You are His workmanship. You were created for good works.

Are those good works in fostering? Are they in adopting?

We pray that reading our story is part of how you will know.

A travelogue can be in the form of slides, or a movie, or lectures, or a book. It tells about the places visited and the observations and experiences of the people who are traveling.

Consider this book a travelogue of our fostering and adoption journey. We will be pointing out some of the more intriguing features that you won't want to miss and giving credit to some of the craftsmen who contributed their expertise to the building up of a boy. We will be attempting to give you snapshots of our family life and cautioning you about places that you will want to avoid. We hope to cultivate your interest in putting your confidence in Jesus Christ for your pilgrimage. He has been faithful, committed, and unwavering in His loyalty to us and to David, and we believe He will be faithful and committed to you.

Sincerely,
Georgann & Dan

P.S. from Georgann

Jesus is my blue skies.

Life has so many cloudy days, dismal days—in the weather outside, and in the weather inside me! Having a melancholy temperament can be a bit of a battle.

By the time I became a born-again Christian at age 29, I had veered far from my roots and was living a very worldly life. When I came back to my childhood faith, I said like Mary Magdalene: *"From that day on, I became His follower. I wanted to do what pleased God."*(1)

With that decision to live to please God, everyday after was unfortunately not full of sunshine! But whatever was going on, when I turned to Him, I found complete acceptance and a place of refuge. And that changed the color of everything.

Now when I wake up, instead of looking inside myself or looking ahead to what the day holds, I look at Jesus and say something like: "You are never condemning me, love is always flowing out of You for me, it's going to be a good day, and I thank You in advance for living Your life through me!"

Introduction

The reality about foster care and adoption is that the precious foster babies, toddlers, elementary school kids, and teenagers in the foster system already have many strikes against them. They have physical, emotional, and mental ailments on a continuum from 'mild' to 'extraordinarily severe' and going on into 'hopeless'.

They have moved into the orphan category as their parents have moved out of their lives through being snared by a variety of difficulties, which may include alcohol and drug abuse, mental illness, homelessness, disinterest, gambling, death, and other things.

Assisting these children would be a daunting and impossible task, except for the fact that we have the opportunity to partner with the Lord in it. The God of the Bible cares deeply for the orphan and the needy, calling Himself a father to the fatherless. He has active compassion and the power to help and heal. He offers restoration and He offers hope. He uses <u>people</u> to bring acceptance, optimism, and practical assistance to these rejected children who have been placed in the helping homes of foster care.

Jesus walked by faith, always in very close touch with His Father, talking and listening, praying and obeying. Navigating through fostering, if you choose this work, will be a journey of faith, perhaps more of a 'faith walk' than you have yet experienced. There will be many unexpected turns. It will be a time of reliance upon Him.

We can say: God has been with us. He has directed us. God has held us together individually and as a married couple. As we have come before Him, He has spoken to us through His Word and in our hearts. He has comforted us. He has been real. As caretakers, we have been enveloped in God's protective care in this profession. I relied on, "He gently leads those who are with young," experiencing that He kindly shepherds those of us who are shepherding the lambs. Hindsight has proven it, even though there was a struggle getting through it.

One morning, years ago, when our son David was 12½ years old and we were all very frustrated, bordering on 'going crazy'—I went to my Bible, and when I got to this verse, I knew I had heard from the Lord:

And all who heard them kept them in mind, saying, "What then will this child turn out to be?" For the hand of the Lord was certainly with him. Luke 1:66 NASB

This verse refers to what people were saying about John the Baptist, but the Holy Spirit was making it personal to me for David.

By the time God gave me this verse for David, we had spent quite a bit of time at our wits' end. We had been to court because David had been taken to jail. We had failed at teaching him to read and write, not fully understanding the extent of his learning difficulties. He was confused and unhappy. We were bewildered and miserable. And yet, we had experienced so many encouragements and seen so many interventions of the Lord that we knew that God was invested in David's life and certainly must be accomplishing something extraordinary.

Life holds many challenges for every family because we live in a fallen world. For the Christian adoptive family who has taken the bold and heroic step to bring someone else's child into their circle, a kind of bravery is called for that will show itself in the fray. It is there inside you, waiting to be called forth. It is called the strength of the Lord.

Be aware that the darling foster child you embrace and draw into your heart will grow up and change. You need to be prepared for that because if you make the decision to adopt, you cannot change your mind! You MUST keep going. If you choose to step into adoption, you must be strong, or be resolutely committed to becoming strong. [read about Covenant in Part VI]

It is good to remember that we have an invisible enemy who is working overtime with the intended purpose that the adopted child will never find his place in your family and in God's calling.

I want this to be a realistic book so that you, the reader, will know that you have been forewarned, that you have heard the grim realities as well as the euphoric joys associated with this job. I want this to be a prophetic book so that you will be assured that God is the God of hope and healing, and that He will be with you every step of the way as you set your sights on Him and depend upon Him. I want this to be an inspirational book so that even after being apprised of some of the potential risks and the hard facts, some couples will decide they will take up the challenge to care for orphans—temporarily in foster care, permanently in adoption, or both.

Perhaps you feel forced into adoption because one of your relatives cannot parent your niece, nephew, grandchild, or your little brother or sister. Proceed with caution, especially if you are single, and particularly if you do not have a support group.

Take your desire to foster and/or to adopt to the Lord and spend significant time with Him about it. Do not make the decision lightly. If you are married, your husband or wife must be on the same page and deeply committed to the same depth that you are. Beware of trying to push and pull someone along in fostering or adoption. You need a team player, not a lagger. For you it might be a noble cause, but you don't want to find yourself standing alone in it, or worse yet, opposed in it.

If you are finding by reading this introduction that your interest is waning, then be glad that you are not a foster parent who has already fallen in love with a desperate child and adopted him, and yet was not fully committed, and is now headed for a crisis.

If you find that your interest in becoming part of an extremely important rescue work has not diminished but seems to be increasing—keep reading! Something inside of you is rising to the challenge. Perhaps it is the inspiration of the Holy Spirit—**keep reading!**

Be careful that what is happening is not just your competitive nature revving you up to prove to yourself and others that you can do this. That will not prove to be a lasting motive, because this is a serious job, and a lot more is at stake than dragging your family over the finish line!

One important factor to consider as you are making the decision to adopt or to enter the foster care system is --do you have friends who would be supportive and who would believe in what you are doing?

We had several wonderful families come alongside us. One family was made up of Mark & Melissa and their three daughters, Rachel, Rebecca, and Leah. We loved them and trusted them to do respite care for our foster babies. They went through some soul searching about becoming foster parents and they made the decision not to become foster parents. The service they rendered to us in our fostering years was exceptional. By babysitting David and our foster children they afforded Dan and I some very needed date nights, which helped us stay on an even keel. Their girls got to be involved in doing good works for the Lord and they all got their 'baby fix' as they fed and cuddled our little ones.

And we had others who staunchly supported us and to whom we are indebted: Bob and Janet, Brett and Diane, Jeff and Jinny, Dave and Kathy. These couples did many hours of respite care for our children.

They stood with us in some difficult situations, and were invaluably helpful to us. Three of the couples also became foster and adoptive parents. We reciprocated by being their encouragers and by doing respite care for them.

In other words, you can be involved and your family can do an immeasurable service for a foster family by praying for them and by giving them some time off to re-charge. It is a good way to get your family's feet wet and 'test the waters' to see how it goes. It can help you make the decision about adopting or becoming a foster family.

For some of us, I believe fostering and adoption is a mandate. I was not seeking God about foster parenting; He came after me. And in spite of the challenges, I am so glad He did. The real sense of fulfillment I received while fostering continues to dwell inside me, ten years after retirement, and is precious, comforting, and satisfying. I know that I came alongside some desperate little lives and stood in the gap for them. We have so many God-testimonies to go along with parenting 52 foster children.

And David, the foster baby who became our adopted son—he is a unique individual, and a dear son. As we watch him growing and maturing, we truly wonder, *what then will this child turn out to be— for the hand of the Lord IS certainly with him!*

Our friend Bonnee said that we were the perfect parents for David and that others would not have continued with him. That is God's grace to give this boy a chance at life. We look at our friends who have adopted, and we can say the same thing about them. They have given love and stability and family bonding to children who were, and continue to be, desperately in need of these things.

It has been a challenge, and I have whined a lot! But, because it was so clearly the Lord's will for us, both Dan and I would do it all again for Jesus, even though much of it has been extremely painful, and even though we do not yet know the end of the story.

Our walk with God on earth is by faith in Him. Do I bail because life becomes hard? Or do I crowd closer to Jesus for the duration?

In the pits and on the mountaintops of fostering and adoption, I have reminded myself: better this faith walk than a lot of other things I can think of. I just want to please Him and be about His business. And who knows? *We may all be very surprised at what this child just might turn out to be!!!*

Part I - Our Early Experiences

Did you happen to see the original "Cheaper by the Dozen" movie starring Clifton Webb? Or "The Seven Little Foys," starring Bob Hope? I saw them as a very impressionable teenager, in the 1950's, and the fun and challenges of having a large family resonated with me. I tucked the romantic fancy somewhere deep in my subconscious and went on with the task of growing up.

After college, being an elementary school teacher provided a mother-hen vocation for several years. I retired and got married, and Dan and I had 4 babies before our 6th anniversary. Nurturing and raising-up our stair-step sons was very gratifying, and gave me incredible heartfelt joy, and something deep inside me was satisfied.

Yet, the girlhood dream was revived when God gave me the vision of babies. I carried the vision for six years, as we brought up our four wonderful sons, lived in several different U.S. cities, went to Bible School, and pastored a church.

When I was 48 we began foster care. When I was 50, the adoption process was completed, and David, our first foster baby, became legally ours. We retired from foster parenting when I was 60. We had parented 52 foster babies and elementary-school-age children over a twelve-year period. I guess we've had about four-and-a-half dozen children under our care. Interesting what a little vision can give birth to.

Foster parenting is a care-giving profession. It provided me with the feeling of being needed during the years when our own sons were growing up and becoming independent young men. I was able to continue in my nurturing mode with the foster babies, which really suited me and would have stifled the boys. Because of fostering, I did not fall into the trap of over-mothering them.

What we did far exceeded my childhood daydreaming. Have you carried a dream of helping children? Does your heart have room to include the motherless and fatherless that are arriving daily in your county's Child and Family Services? Read on, and perhaps you will be inspired to begin your own fostering journey.

How our family came to this

Dan and I got to know each other in a church in Reno. (In our pre-Christian days we had each graduated from college, married and divorced.) When we met I had been a Christian for three years and Dan was a new Christian. Our friendship became enduring love, and we were married within a year. We spent the first six months of our marriage in Germany in an English-speaking Bible School, and returned to Reno. Seven years later we drove across the country with our four sons and attended a Bible School in upstate New York. We came back to the west coast and Dan pastored a church in San Francisco. We eventually settled back in Reno, Dan's hometown.

For several years we considered bringing another child into our family, because of the vision I had from God. It is such a big decision to alter the dynamics of one's home life, and we took it seriously. We involved the boys in some of our discussions, and all four of them were excited. When our sons were 9, 11, 13, 14, we began the application process with Washoe County to become foster parents.

It was 1993, and the paperwork seemed extensive. We could understand that there was a well-thought-out procedure in place that would eliminate people that had no business caring for children, so we plugged away at it. Dan and I spent a few weeks working through the many pages of questions and gathering our references and debating if we really wanted to become involved in this government agency. There were background checks, fingerprinting, and interviews. We completed stage one, and moved on to stage two.

At that time the orientation class was a one-day seminar. It was held at Children's Cabinet on Rock Blvd. It was not required that Dan attend.

I remember being very favorably impressed by the presenting team of George, Alice, and Michelle. I had been apprehensive about becoming part of 'the system', but as I watched this close-knit threesome interact, heard their relaxed presentations, and began to understand the requirements and the reasoning behind the rules and regulations, I got excited about joining this group of people that seemed to be truly dedicated to their cause of placing needy children in safe homes until other arrangements could be made for them.

During part of the orientation, two long-time foster parents had been invited to talk about their personal experiences with DCFS

(Department of Child and Family Services). They were Pam G. and Janet M. Pam especially was very outspoken about the challenges of working with the system, with social workers, and the rigors of the 24/7 (24-hours-a-day-7-days-a-week) job. Pam was a Registered Nurse and specialized in medically fragile babies and toddlers—always caring for two or three of them at a time. Janet worked with babies and also with school-age children. She shared that every year her family had their family portrait taken, and whatever foster children were in their home at the time, they were included in the photo. Years later, I visited her home and saw many walls full of framed family portraits hanging proudly around the room. Year-after-year, Janet's own children were surrounded by various sized temporary visitors that they had brought into their family fold. Pam's and Janet's stories of the needy children, many of whom were physically and mentally challenged, their tales of difficult parents and of the often-tangled bureaucracy were laced with heartwarming antidotes. As the years went by, I became better acquainted with these veterans and learned a lot from them.

The consequence of these testimonies was that we listeners were hooked. We wanted to join up and embrace the challenges they presented. We wanted our own walls of photographs and our own stories. We wanted to be used in helping needy children whose parents were so embroiled in their own issues that they could not raise them at this time.

The climax of the day was observing a movie about an older couple who had adopted a baby born with Fetal Alcohol Syndrome. The boy had been an endearing child, a troubled teen, and an unmanageable adult. The story was depressing because it did not use actors; the actual individuals were telling their story, and it was a story of hopelessness and despair. I still remember the heaviness I felt. It was right then that I determined not to take any babies that were FAS (Fetal Alcohol Syndrome). I knew that the challenge of 'hopeless' was way beyond the scope of my abilities. I believed that I could not take someone in the 'severely damaged' category with all of my other responsibilities. I left the meeting encouraged on one hand, but deeply troubled on the other. How much control did I really have over who came into my home? Who would make the decision about what baby we would get? Would the worker listen to me and consider my opinions? Could I muster up being assertive, or would I end up being passive and consequentially, overwhelmed?

Our home was inspected and evaluated for child safety and recommendations were made. Our water was tested because we lived outside the city limits and our water was from a well. We purchased fire extinguishers and smoke alarms and began to collect baby furniture and supplies. And we waited.

<u>David arrives</u>

We had passed the interview and the home inspection; the system was ready for us. In our house there was a lot of excitement and a readiness to get on with this! Waiting became so difficult.

Michelle, the state worker who was our liaison, had a baby in mind that she felt would suit us perfectly. The baby was David, one week shy of 9 months old. She told us his story and our hearts went out to him. She explained his estrangement from his parents, his desperate need for stability and for a family who would be devoted to loving and caring for him. I'm not sure when she told me that he was Fetal Alcohol Effect (FAE). That category is not used anymore, but it meant that there was definite evidence that his mother drank in her pregnancy. David had not been officially evaluated.

By this time I had come to trust Michelle. She did not offer to let me meet David, and I did not ask. Dan and I prayed, and I relented from my boundary of "no FAS children." David's social worker was Hayley. Hayley had taken a special interest in David from the first time she had met him. Even later when the case transferred to another worker, she stayed connected with us through the years.

This is what I wrote about David's early history:

Perhaps they lived at the Tip Top Inn on South Primrose Street. The cheap weekly motels abound in that area of Reno. David's Dad and Mom had some time to get organized before they picked up their newborn son from the hospital. Strep septicemia and jaundice had delayed little David's release. But on July 6, 1993, they brought him home wearing blue jammies and a knitted cap. He was 15 days old. His stay with them was short, less than a month, because it was interrupted by a visit from the police and a CPS worker. A neighbor had called about the ruckus in room #8. They both went to jail, and the social worker took David to an emergency shelter children's home across town called Safe Haven. Safe Haven was a place of temporary residence for children who, removed from their biological parents for various reasons, were waiting for foster care placement.

David was probably a little confused by now. A God-given awareness in his brain would be telling him that he should have been bonding and attaching to that familiar woman who had carried him in her body for 40 weeks. But what David experienced was a random succession of caregivers feeding and changing him in the hospital and then at Safe Haven. However caring and diligent and warm they were, these men and women were no substitute for mom. The required nurturing for human development had been interrupted at birth when David was put on an IV and taken to NICU (Neonatal Intensive Care Unit). Mom's visits to the hospital helped keep a connection between them and the attachment could have been revived and sustained, but her lifestyle choices to continue in drugs and alcohol further damaged the attachment process.

After 19 days at Safe Haven, David was placed in a foster home where he would stay for 6 ½ months. He was one of several young children.

Later, when David was evaluated by a local Pediatric Psychiatric Neurologist, the doctor strongly advised that David be moved to a foster home where he would receive attention as the only baby.

David was diagnosed as severely failure-to-thrive. It was not certain if he could see or hear very well, because he was so unresponsive.

The doctor's appraisal was given just about the time we entered the system. We fit the doctor's prescription! We were an older couple, in our late forties, with a delightful family, and all of us were anxious to help a baby and give him lots of attention and affection.

We were really ready for this. We had had family meetings, we had purchased baby supplies, we had prayed.

In retrospect we saw that the Lord had used four families to give us empathy and tenderness for opening our hearts and our home to a little person in need.

Bruce and Diane, a couple in our home church, were involved in foster care for over ten years. During the time we knew them, Dan and I were both fascinated as they juggled their own five children (three of whom were adopted) and what seemed like a never-ending parade of adorable newborns.

A few months after we left Reno and moved to upstate New York, we got a call from Sheri that she and her husband Eddie had taken in three children who had been rescued from homelessness on the streets of Reno. We highly regarded our friends for opening their home to do the round-the-clock care and for wrapping these little ones up in their love. It might have occurred to me at the time that I might do the same thing; I don't recall, because I was deeply involved with our sons' homeschooling, babysitting other children, taking classes, and helping in our church. In addition, we were living an itinerant lifestyle and would continue to do so for a few more years.

After finishing Bible School, we headed back to the west coast and visited our friends, Carl and Suzann, and their three children. We discovered that they had adopted a mixed-race toddler, Noah. Hanging out with their children had a deep effect on our boys' hearts. Maybe it was because Jan, Jeremy, and Eva were infatuated with their new baby brother. Jeremy in particular doted on sweet Noah, and our sons joined with him in making up games, keeping him occupied, laughing at his antics, carrying him about the house.

While living in San Francisco, we became friends with Matthew and Myra and their three children. Their youngest, Jimi, was adopted from Korea. I was still enamored with the puzzling baby vision I was carrying, and delighted in confiding everything to Myra. She empathized passionately with my dilemma and prayed with me. As we disclosed more of our individual captivation with having more children, we realized that each of us was praying that Jesus would leave a needy baby on the doorstep! Those of you who have yearned for a baby will understand that kind of maternal desperation.

These families were special friends whom we loved and admired. They were devoted to their newest members. As we put all of the puzzle pieces together later, we realized that spending time with them had helped us all to be able to picture ourselves enlarging our own family. We did not have to convince our children to do foster care. Jesus took care of it. His ways are high above our ways. He was so faithful to arrange the preparation for His will.

David's arrival date in our home had been postponed for a several days because he had a cold and Michelle and Hayley wanted him to arrive healthy. It was agony to wait. On March 15th, I read my 'scripture of the day' displayed on the window ledge of my kitchen sink: *For the VISION is yet for an appointed time, but at the end it will speak and it will not lie. THOUGH IT TARRIES, WAIT FOR IT, BECAUSE IT WILL SURELY COME. Habakkuk 2:3*

I was shocked and uplifted, amazed that the verse was so pertinent! I'm sure now that it came with an infusion of the Holy Spirit that gave me the assurance from the Lord that I find I need every day in my walk of faith. It confirmed to me that what we were doing was a product of the VISION God had given me years before. It verified that the vision was VALID and acknowledged that it was SLOW IN COMING, and it included the assurance that it was ABOUT TO BE FULFILLED! I took heart, and almost exploded with joy. I thanked the Lord as I danced around the kitchen and then I proclaimed it to the rest of the family. And we continued to wait.

I was so ready to step into mothering a baby again, and especially a baby who needed me so much. Two days later, on March 17, 1994, St. Patrick's Day, Michelle, and Hayley, brought David out to our home. I wasn't there when they arrived because I had to make a last minute run into town for a wall heater that we needed to install in the baby room. When I pulled into the garage, Mark and Danny burst through the kitchen door with huge smiles. "Mom, hurry inside! He's just what we wanted," they cried out excitedly!

What joy filled me as one of the ladies passed our baby boy to me. He was light skinned, mixed-race, and had black hair. He pushed against me with straight arms as I tried to snuggle him. As little David attempted to get his bearings, every face looking back at him was aglow—two very relieved social workers and a stubbornly loving family.

On David's mind on his first day with us

Recently I thought about what might have been going through David's mind as he left one foster home for another:

This is a very long ride in the car with Hayley and her friend. We are getting farther from the other house where I have been staying. They packed all my stuff and Hayley put it in the back seat with me. It's just a couple of plastic bags of clothes and some formula, but it's all I've got. She and her friend are talking and laughing and are very happy in the front seat. I'm sleepy....

Now we are at another place.

Who are all of these people? Why are they smiling so much? Who is 'Mom' that they keep talking about?

It is too much effort for me. I feel a little confused.

Has Hayley moved me AGAIN?

What is happening? Would someone please tell me!

Now 'Mom' is here and someone is putting me into her outstretched arms. Are there tears in her eyes—whoa—wait! This is pretty crazy, and I am going into overload! I better push her away so she doesn't get too close.

Why is everyone laughing and smiling so much?

Hey Hayley!!! WHERE ARE YOU GOING? YOU ARE THE ONLY STEADY PERSON THAT KEEPS COMING BACK TO ME! NOW YOU ARE CHANGING MY LOCATION AND LEAVING ME!

I was many days in the hospital, and I got tired of the IV in my head. I could tell all those guys were pretty worried about me at first. And then I left the hospital and went with a man and a woman to a small dim room. I felt some connection to them because they came to see me in the hospital, but then when they took me with them to the small room sometimes they yelled and got pretty rough, things crashed, and I felt afraid.

One day there was loud knocking and more shouting and more people— somebody put me in a car and took me to another place.

I never saw the hospital again, and I did not see that room again, and I did not see those people again for a long time.

Sometimes when I get hungry and I have to wait, I try to get someone's attention, but they don't come. And my stomach hurts, and then I get mad and I really scream. That usually gets me something to drink. If they hold me while I eat, it feels good usually. But a lot of times they put me down to take my bottle, and I feel alone and like I'm a bother. But I eat and then I sleep.

At this place, these people look at me and smile all the time. But I will probably be going to another location, so I will not let them get too close. It's sad to feel good feelings and then just go to another location.

After Hayley and Michelle left that day, the adventure we were on went up a notch or two. We finally had our baby. David was placid, sucking on his hands, looking around at us or just staring into space. We went into our large living room and put him on a blanket on the floor. The boys all lay down around him and we captured a great picture, which revealed the pure joy we all felt.

<u>David thrives</u>

David was not a strong-willed baby, and we were not inflexibly trying to fit him into some mold or into a structured schedule. We were determined not to try to make drastic changes in his life right away. I like the analogy of the 'dance'—we watched his cues, he watched our responses. We tried new things and according to his reactions, we tried them again the same way, or we tried them a different way. The common practice at this time was to put a loudly crying, over-stimulated baby into his crib and close the bedroom door and leave him for a while. We weren't totally against that, but we hoped that we would not have to resort to that method of calming him.

We really did hope that with our family's love, and with God's help, we would make the difference David needed in order to get some significant healing. We, as a family, hoped to make up for the chaotic time David had had in utero, with alcohol and possibly drugs affecting his formation. We wanted to reverse the effects of his abandonment by his parents when he was just a few weeks old. We ached to pour our love into his life and to fill him up with it.

We knew that in his previous foster care experiences he had been well cared for, but we wanted to be even more attentive, sensitive, and responsive, because we wanted to see big-time developmental changes. We wanted to help David break out of the failure-to-thrive syndrome and see him flourish. We wanted him to have a normal life.

I believe we accomplished some of our goals, but there came a point where it became clear that our love was not all that was necessary to bring David into more satisfactory health and well-being. It became apparent over the next few years that he had severe attachment issues and very serious fetal alcohol syndrome. There came a point where those two things in his experience and in his physical makeup, blocked his ability to receive love and to have trust in his relationships with us as parents. The attachment issue also meant that he would lash out at us, especially me. (The articles on FAS and Attachment are in Part V)

When Hayley and Michelle placed this needy little boy in our care, we knew that David was suspected to be FAS, that he was severely delayed in his development, that his parents were unable to take care of him, and that we were a Godsend to the foster system. We also knew that God was with us, on our side, and would help us in every way.

<u>In the beginning</u>

One of the strongly encouraged disciplines that had been promoted at the orientation was to keep a daily diary of the child's behavior, his eating habits, his milestones, his appointments, and his visits. I had watched my friend Sheri's determination and her success, in keeping her spiral notebook diaries. I set myself to follow her example and do this expected task for the system, which I was now so happy to be a part of. I am glad I did.

David continued to 'straight-arm' us when we, or anyone, held him. We later would realize that this was indication of his difficulties with attachment.(Attachment is discussed in Part V)

He would also turn his head from side to side with his eyes opened, the way a person does when they watch the cars on a train go by. This was dizzying to us, but we found out that this head motion was somehow stimulating to his brain. He would do it several times a day when he was bored or when he was flooded with too much input.

At first, David did not respond to our voices, and he did not track us with his eyes. We could see why doctors wondered if he had sight and hearing problems. He was very unresponsive. The only thing that got any reaction at all in those early hours when he arrived in our home, was tickling his cheek lightly with a koosh ball, and then he would giggle and squirm. [A koosh ball is a brightly colored toy ball made of soft rubber filaments (strings) attached to a soft rubber core.]

We were very concerned. We were not even thinking of adoption in the beginning. We were just trying to help this little boy survive and cope with what life had dealt him.

That first day, David was able to roll over from his back to his stomach, reach out and grab a toy he wanted, and then easily roll back over onto his back to play with what he had grabbed. That first day he did a lot of head shaking, and he also 'arched' his back often. My husband remembers that the 'arching' looked very unnatural, as if something was alarmingly wrong with him, like a spasm or a mild seizure. When one of us carried him through a doorway on his first day with us, his arching resulted in him smacking his head on the door jam, and he cried. It was almost a relief to know that he could cry and feel pain. He had been so flat and unemotional.

The diary of David's first seven months

As I mentioned, Sheri had modeled keeping a diary, and I was conscientious about journaling for seven months. I am adding this to the story to show how our attentiveness paid off and to give you an idea about our daily lives once we added our new member to our family. The material in *italics* is taken directly from my journal. Where I have recently added comments, they are in regular type.

So beginning on day 1, here we go:

3-17 We enjoyed David so much. We put him on some blankets on the living room floor, and he rocked on his hands and knees a long time, then lay on his back and kicked and squealed and sucked on his fingers and his hand. My friend, Sally, came over to meet David with her daughters and their friends. There were four girls and a baby David's age. There was a lot of activity and laughter, and he got a lot of attention.

I rocked him for 20 minutes at bedtime. He was still, wide-eyed and looked at his left hand a lot. Put him down in his crib and he went right to sleep.

Love to our family, meant rocking and snuggling a baby at bedtime and then putting him into his crib. David often seemed restless and squirmy as if he wanted to be laid down. It seemed that David did not understand this language of love, so at those times we did what he was used to and laid him in his bed at bedtime and did the rocking and snuggling at other times of the day.

3-18 David slept all night. He was awake about 6:30am, and I could hear little noises. About 7am, I held him and gave him his bottle. He kept refusing it. I prayed, and he took it then without much further prompting.

During breakfast I held David, talked to him, kissed him. Finally a small smile appeared. The boys played with him on the blanket. They imitated him rocking and cooing. (On our homeschooling breaks from our studies) *they gave him lots of attention. He was the center of everyone's interest.*

By the end of the day, David was smiling easily, comfortable and relaxed in the swing for 20 minutes, not stiff. Not arching much. He received many hours of attention from the boys. They took turns feeding him his bottle on the futon as he lay on his back.

As I said, David was not keen about being held for his bottle feedings. I was very disappointed. I laid him in his playpen and propped the bottle.

3-19 Saturday, David's first ride in the car with us. We went to baseball practice. He enjoyed riding. Marsha, my sister, *called and encouraged me to get him used to being held for his feedings, which I began to do immediately. He is rolling over easily both ways and rocking on his hands and knees.*

3-20 David enjoyed lots of attention at church. Slept through the message. Didn't smile, but didn't resist physically. Not pushing me away as much as he used to when I hold him. Not arching. He holds his head back—but often rests his head on my shoulder. Now for each feeding, Dan or I hold him. He is beginning to relax.

That night we were all ogling and cooing and tickling him. He acted very serious, as if he was trying hard <u>not</u> to smile. About 15 minutes later as I was changing him,<u> he</u> initiated beginning laugh sounds. He had laughed previously a few times, but never initiated.

3-21 He rested his head on my shoulder as I burped him. His head was on my shoulder for at least 2 minutes. <u>A first.</u> Later he lay in the playpen in the kitchen where we were doing schoolwork, bouncing, laughing, chewing on his hand, and making noises. I felt he was responding to my affection by laying his head on my shoulder. I felt he was initiating communication with us by getting our attention with his noisy activity in the playpen.

We had a very large kitchen in that house, and his playpen was near the kitchen table where we did our homeschooling. His noises were his way of getting our attention directed on him instead of on the English lesson. And of course he was much more interesting than <u>English Grammar.</u>

We tried attaching a 'sassy seat' to the kitchen table for mealtime. He liked it, and we decided that it brought him right into the family circle and that it was better than using a high chair.

David is enjoying his bath more. He is able to hold his full bottle for short periods, but if it drops to the side he is not able to recover it. Some nasal congestion today.

3-23 He pulled a half-full bottle out of his mouth, looked at it, returned it to his mouth and continued eating. He had his lunch in the 'sassy seat' when we ate our lunch. He rolled over two times in succession, and was able to hold his own bottle as I cuddled him during his feeding. He grasped a penny on the floor and picked it up. This was indication of appropriate fine motor skills.

3-24 *After our Special Children's Clinic appointment, I began feeding David small amounts of thin rice cereal. He acted curious about it. Tasted it. He was not very interested. He had lots of active play on the living room floor with an audience of six.*

Special Children's Clinic is now called Nevada Early Intervention Services. Pediatricians, social workers, speech pathologists, audiologists, developmental specialists, nutritionists, physical and occupational therapists, and family specialists staff it. Services include comprehensive evaluations, service coordination, and infant and toddler intervention. www.health.nv.gov/beis.htm

3-25 Not as interested today in the rice cereal and juice. In the swing he reached out to grab and hold the pole and stopped the swing. He turned in the seat to pull on the plastic back of the seat.

4-4 David's first tooth poked through. He has become a smiley boy, happy, relating to all of us. Today we tried Gerber's applesauce. He was only semi-interested.

I had heard that premature babies and developmentally delayed babies could have challenges with nipples and spoons and textures and flavors, and that if their foods are not pureed in the blender to a fine consistency, they are just not interested.

4-5 After being set in sitting position by us, he sat easily on the futon. He was bent slightly forward and using his hands for balance, the way Diane Duncan (his case manager) had showed us at the Special Children's Clinic appointment. He was able to regain his balance when he would start to topple. We all applauded.

4-7 David had to have a CAT scan at the hospital. The nurse who was going to sedate him was busy, so another nurse said, "Let's try to do the scan without sedation." David did really well. He was not perfectly still for very long but it took! Tim had come with me and strolled him while we were in the hospital and at the grocery store. Several people gave David attention and compliments on his smile and his good disposition. In the stroller, David sat straight up and leaned forward without the seat back supporting him.

Another front bottom tooth poked through today.

Foster children may have lots of examinations in order to discern the length and breadth of their problems.

David was relating to a one-year old girl in the hospital, very interested in her. He was also very taken with Jannie, 9 months old, our neighbor's little girl. They visited us again today.

We felt both of these interactions with these other babies were very positive. He seemed to be coming out of his shell and becoming interested in life and people beyond his small sphere.

4-12 I had gone out of town the previous day with friends to a homeschool conference. When I went into David's room the next morning to get him out of his crib, *he seemed to have no recognition of me. We had such a strong bonding—this causes me concern that there is the larger problem of fetal alcohol syndrome. I had hoped that the diagnosis was incorrect and had felt so encouraged by all of David's progress. We continue to pray for healing and this week I am putting him on several national prayer chains.*

There was another phenomenon that was probably happening. We experienced it over and over with our foster babies in the succeeding years. When we would leave a baby with a friend, the baby would reject us when we returned by giving us a cold shoulder. It was their way of showing disapproval at being left behind! We found out it is also a symptom of an in secure attachment, which will be discussed later.

Another front bottom tooth poked through.

4-13 To get at some toys which were out of his reach, David scooted and pulled himself along about 5 inches in forward position, rather than turning on his back and arching and rolling to reach these objects. Wow! We thank God!

This morning I held him as we did our schoolwork because he got very fussy and frustrated. He got into the "hyper" mood that we have seen him in twice before—he could not relax. It was as if someone had turned his speed dial up a few notches—he would smile at our words and attention, but then become agitated, over-stimulated. Put him in his crib, he was there 15 minutes and got a little calmer, but then started again. He was quiet on the 35-minute drive to church but was wound up at church. Dan walked him in a darkened room and talked and sang to him. [We were discovering that he could not self-regulate, or recognize his own agitation, rather he was swept along with it in an ascending spiral.]

4-14 David was agitated again. Tomorrow after breakfast we will try having one boy with him (doing his math) on the futon or living room rug. Danny did this the first several days David was here and Danny got 100% on math and David was happy and quiet.

David spent about 45 minutes in the stroller, both inside and outside, entertained by watching the scenery. All the boys love to push David in the stroller, and today Steve pushed him through the house, then outside on the front patio, past the rabbit cages, with David wearing his Giant's baseball cap. David sits up in the stroller and holds onto the front bar. He tires after a while and eventually lies down.

A long morning nap (10-1) seemed to help greatly. Our days have been very busy. David became agitated at dinnertime. Dan had one boy playing with him at all times for the remainder of the evening. He calmed down and was content.

We had decided that having one of us with David when he is excited is better for him than having the whole crew of us around him.

4-15 Mark 'lured' David forward and David was scooting beautifully, pulling himself along to grab the toy Mark was tapping on the ground. David repeated his pre-crawling for the rest of the family—we cheered and clapped for our boy.

David has been standing when the boys hold him upright. His legs have become stronger.

Today Tim pulled him to a standing position several times where he stood happily for several minutes.

Remember, David was 9 months old and could not sit alone (which is a 6-month developmental skill) and could not crawl. He could only scoot for very short distances. That is why every single inch of progress was met with such enthusiasm. And that kind of enthusiasm was the encouragement he seemed to need to believe he could progress in each endeavor.

David began the game—'drop the toy and watch my brothers fetch it for me.' Of course we thought he was very smart to figure this out and we were very encouraged.

4-17 We have had David one month today. Dan easily fed David little bites of barley cereal. The boys applauded each time, and he looked wide-eyed at them. We thought he was going to go for it and finish it off, but after about 1 tablespoon he was done.

David loves to pick up tiny pieces of sock fuzz or lint off the carpet. There was lots of kicking and scooting across the floor. Good report from ear doctor today.

4-20 We realized that we've made the cereal too thick. We thought he could handle it, but we need to go back to puree. The thick stuff seems to be too much for his system.

We were encouraged by Special Children's Clinic to persist in offering solids, even though he was so resistant. I think our kindness in our persistence helped him decide that he would work with us. He wanted to please us.

Special Children's Clinic suggested that we use the brown nipples on David's bottle, rather than the clear ones, which are for newborns. David did not complain or resist.

Later, in my experiences over the years with other babies, most would balk at a nipple change, and all would show distinct preferences.

Special Children's Clinic (SCC) was a wonderful resource for me. I had not mothered a newborn for 9 years, and, more importantly, I had no knowledge of ways I could help our developmentally delayed boy and bring him along into more skills and abilities. David had been referred by the hospital discharge doctor to the Clinic within days after he was born. He had already been evaluated by SCC before he came to us, and was receiving therapy weekly. We also saw the nutritionist, the hearing specialist, the caseworker, and the pediatrician regularly. It meant lots of appointments, lots of waiting in waiting rooms, but the quality of professional expertise we received made it all worth it.

4-21 David has been very congested the last three mornings as he wakes up, and he has been waking up at least once each night for the last few nights.

David was a good sleeper normally.

4-30 I made a list of David's progress since the last reporting on the 21st. It seems like a lot of progress in just 9 days.

eating 1-2 TBL barley or oatmeal cereal per day consistently

still teething vigorously

enjoying mashed bananas
learning to bang a spoon on the table.
banging two rattles together vigorously
playing games more often—looks back to see if we are watching his antics

initiating playing peekaboo 3x in his car seat
doesn't understand pattycake – yet
splashing his hands in his bathtub – first time

*we have been feeding him earlier dinner, so he would not have a bowel movement while sleeping, because he had such a bad diaper rash. Also no feedings in the night; just patted him and sang and prayed him back to sleep.

*he still gets stroller rides outside each day

*he takes morning and afternoon nap, 1-2 hours in length

*we put our two very large living room pillows in David's playpen (for an easy fall) and stood him up so he could hang onto the rim; he likes to chew on the plastic and look around

*enjoying the swing now

*becoming more social. He calls and wants people around. He is not as interested in just lying in the playpen and playing alone, which is a good sign

5-5 Gerber's- stage 1 pears
5-7 Gerber's- stage 1 squash
5-5 Nutrition appointment at Special Children's Clinic

Weight 16 pounds 8 oz. The little weight gain is attributed to his being ill and being on antibiotics. Lana recommended infant acidophilus.

5-19 In last 2 weeks we have seen lots of milestones:

*sat up alone 2x
*says "Ma"
*waved "bye bye" for the first time today
*when I am carrying him, he holds himself up with a straight back so I can hold him with one arm—he doesn't flop forward. We are doing exercises to strengthen his back.

*starting to make his way around the kitchen floor to get to the kitty food and the Tupperware cupboard

*set a mirror on the floor in front of him at dinner tonight [like they do at Special Children's Clinic]. He likes looking at himself.

6-1 In the last two weeks:

*says "bye" and "bye bye" and waves
*waves "hi" sometimes, and says "hi"

*says "ba" for bottle

*says "ummm" after almost every bite of food and claps for himself sometimes, since we don't clap over his eating anymore

*can play pattycake, and he does the "roll it roll it" part with his arms!

*I worked with him on pulling himself up in his crib one day a few times, and a few days later he pulled himself up to the living room ledge.

The living room was a large green-carpeted room, with two steps, like what used to be called a sunken living room. Along 3 walls was a smooth wooden ledge about 10 inches high and a foot wide. We were never sure what the purpose was in its original design, but David would pull himself up and go hand-over-hand along the ledge and practice walking around the perimeter of the room. It was a built-in gym course for him.

6-14 In the last two weeks:

*David has been pulling himself up at living room ledge. Now he 'walks' along the ledge (holding on to it), and while he is doing that he reaches for toys that Timmy moves along just out of his reach. Or else he just looks around and reaches for the electrical outlets (covered). He often will lose his balance but will hang on and recover, or fall and get up again and move on. He pulls or pushes items off the ledge, looks at them, sometimes tries to reach them. He does not like to step on the heater vent and cries for help!

*swims in the tub, and we no longer put the smaller plastic tub inside the big tub. He splashes wildly and loves the tub. He never wants to get out!

*Special Children's Clinic last week: He had good balance as Diane held him on his tummy on the large ball. He was very cooperative for 35 minutes or so, and then tired out.

*Yesterday he was in crawl position. I kissed him goodbye and waved to go; he shifted his weight, lifted his arm, and waved at me with one free hand!

*WIC – weight 17 lb. 14 oz. Excellent, I thought! Iron 11.5 The nurse said the 11:5 was fine, but six months ago his iron measured 13!

*WIC – Women, Infants, and Children (WIC)– is a government agency that provides supplemental nutritious foods and nutrition education to pregnant women and to infants and children up to the age of five. Again, it meant monthly or bi-monthly appointments, and lots of waiting room time, but we felt it was worth it to receive the groceries and some child raising tips. The boys, and the babies, and I made several good friends among the nurses and staff, which alleviated the boredom and brought us all some fun interactions. www.washoecounty.us

*Still loves stroller rides and people—but will not wear his Giants' cap anymore.

*He's practicing 'uhoh' – it comes out 'uhuh'

*We are making it a special point now to take his hands for grace—not hold hands around him, and we all very clearly say "amen!"

*He loves his big brothers. Does not try any names or act interested in names. They all play various games with him.

*David is still enchanted with the cat. Grabs her fur and tail. Has not learned how to pet her. Kitty is patient, so are we.

*Loves the cardboard bricks. Loves to knock down his brothers' towers. Rolls them, bites them—the bricks, not the boys! When he sits on a brick, he carefully maneuvers himself, and often falls off, surprised but okay.

*likes to pull things out of the diaper bag

*rarely arches [when he does we say, "don't do that David" or "no" and put our hand on him and he stops arching]

*rarely shakes head from side to side (yet intermittent head shaking continued through age 16 when he was bored or distracted)

*rarely studies his hand
*wakes up smiley some mornings
*sleeps through most nights
*persistent in exploring
*plays well alone
*pretty bored with all sucking toys; wants to get around, roll around, and army crawl around [Regular crawling is on hands and knees, tummy off the floor. The army crawl is when a baby pulls himself

along with one or both arms, while dragging his tummy on the floor.]

*bats a ball around with his hand and chases it
*does not like lumps in his food—tried small curd cottage cheese—no
*tried regular applesauce—no. Fine when pureed
*crawls off the futon slowly and wonderfully on his tummy, front first
*talks and chatters when exploring
*whoever is one-on-one with him imitates his actions and his chattering

6-16 Went into David's room at naptime to see if he was asleep yet—he had pulled himself up and was standing up in his crib! Smiling! What a smart boy!

6-17 For about 1½ - 2 weeks I have been working with David on "uhoh". Now he says "uh!" at the appropriate time.

7-1 Diane at SCC, weighed David: 18 lb. 16 oz.

8-5 David is 13+ months
*David sits quietly as a book is read to him—a simple baby board book.

*He is very active. We barricaded the hall so that the kittens would be out of his reach. He is careful and sweet to them 98% of the time, making little high-pitched noises (like mewing).

*He pulls up at the piano and plays it, sits under it at the foot pedals, pulls books off the stereo stand, pulls himself up at the fireplace hearth and the barricade; opens the hutch in the dining room and the drawers in the kitchen.

*He helps pull off his clothes when I am undressing him.

*JUST learned to throw up his arms and say "all done" – the TONE is "all done" – the words bear no resemblance! The timing is appropriate.

*He will try any new thing to eat and likes almost everything.

*Lately: he likes gingerbread & whipped cream
        mashed pinto beans
        mashed mac & cheese
        mashed chicken & fruit
        apple juice, undiluted
*We gave him a straw at Janet Needham's suggestion; he chewed on it, didn't sip with it.

*He waited totally patiently for Tia (our new little girl) to have her bath when her turn was first.

*He learned not to bite-- after she had bitten him hard 3 times while they were in the stroller!

*David plays well with Tia. They are interested in each other. Often take a toy from each other over and over.

*David wants to please us—he is VERY social.

*In the swimming pool, he is a fish. He lets Tim whirl him around on his back in circles, and take him under.

10-24-94 We are so behind in this journal!
David is one year and four months old. Tia Maria came to us in July. She is two months older than he is, and she has no developmental delays.

*David is so alert, loving, outgoing, full of grace, full of joy, eager to learn, attentive.

*He would say "ock" for sock, so we are working on "sssss." He tries, thinks hard, does it, and, when we prompt him, he becomes sweetly shy about showing someone else what he can do.

*He loves the magnets on the fridge.

*Tia Maria has been in her crib in his room, which is the baby room, for 2-3 weeks now. At bedtime or naptime, as Dan says: "they 'talk' for a while, but quickly run out of things to say, so go to sleep!"

*They go down for 10am nap and 7:30pm bedtimes at the same time. Get up at 6:30am (she could sleep longer but the schedule would be ruined).

*David crawls really fast. He can stand up by scooting over to a wall, the fridge, a door, then spreads his legs far apart, pulling up. He gets a BIG smile, of PRIDE in his success.

*He loves to play & pound on Aunt Vanna's piano. One day when two mattresses were stacked on the floor near it; he stood up on them and was waist high to the keyboard, which I'm sure was more fun for him than his "fingertip" concerts.

*Dave's in the high chair, Dan feeds him usually. Tia is in the sassy seat, I feed her.

*We just began to give them a saucer or bowl and their own spoon and food, while I feed them. It distracts them and although it is messy, mealtime is more pleasant, and they are eating more. Both are totally off Gerbers.

*What will David do when his friend Tia leaves? They move around exploring the kitchen, family room, TV area, living room, Dan's office, and the rest of the house when they can!

*My prayers for David: that he is sealed in the Sprit because he is in our household, in God's protection, safe, on the course to fulfill all His calling and walk in all of the good works God has already prepared for him to walk in.

David's words at 15 months:

Mama
Dada
Tadun (Tia)
bye bye
kitty
book
bath
uhoh
all done
poo poo
peek-a-boo
'side [outside]

January 20, 1995
David's words at 18 months:

[not in any order]
bye bye
hi
bath
kitty
mama
dada
hot
cold
uhoh

all done
all gone
ba [bottle]
giggy [blankie]
more
poo poo
pee pee
Tim
Steve
Mark
Danny
thank you
juice
please
book
sit down
cracker
cookie
banana
Steve added to the list:
cool

owl
car
baby
teeth

January 20, 1995,
DAVID'S SKILLS:
itsy bitsy spider*
patty cake*
kiss
jargon* (baby talk)
peek-a-boo*
[*he initiates these skills]

DAVID CAN POINT TO:

eye
ears
nose

tongue
hair

Weight: 21 lbs 8 oz (Jan. 19, 1995, Dr. T, pediatrician)

David was a patient of Dr. T's before he came to our home and we continued with Dr. T until David was a teenager. Dr. T and his staff (Cheryl, Renee, and Cindy) never wavered in their professional, faithful, friendly service to David and to me, and to our many other foster children. When a foster baby already has a pediatrician, it is often advantageous to the child to continue with that doctor. When you find a doctor and his staff who are not prejudice against your foster children, but welcoming them and respecting you for your service to them, you have found a goldmine! Thank you, Dr. T, for esteeming us, and for your caring and sensible doctoring of all of our children.

What David might have been thinking during these weeks with us

At this place I don't sit and be alone. Somebody is always in my face and smiling and saying, "David, David, look!" "David, David, here's a toy and this is how it works." "Let's go out in the stroller, David." That's fun. We look at the furry things in the cages. Sometimes I touch them. I like the wind blowing in my face. Sometimes I get a fast ride; sometimes I get a long ride.

It's pretty strange. It's feeling pretty soft here, pretty warm, pretty fuzzy. I expect Hayley will be moving me to another location soon, so I need to protect myself because at the next place I may be set aside, and the lonely feelings will come back strong. But there's a lonely place inside of me even if there are people around. It just doesn't go away.

Even though it's feeling real nice here, some hard place inside of me is sure it won't last. I'd better listen to that and protect myself. It will be safer for me.

Then there were two and three

David's very rapid transformation had stunned us. At nine months old he had come to us with vacant eyes and weak head control. He rocked his head to calm himself, and stiff-armed people who tried to snuggle or get close to him. He was severely delayed in his physical development, in his eating development, and in his social development, BUT he had significantly responded to our consistent love and attention. He had relished our encouragements, and he had begun to thrive.

By the time he was about fourteen months old, he was eating well, staying free of ear infections, outgoing, and friendly. He was making good progress in communicating, playing well alone, and very responsive to our love and our efforts to teach him new things.

Dan & I remember thinking, "Hey, we can do this! We like doing this!"

We probably realized that one of the very best things we could do for David at that time was to provide a playmate his own size.

We called our social worker, Wendy. Our case had transferred from investigative to 'ongoing' and Wendy was our worker. We told her we were ready for another baby. She presented us with the stories of two babies, both who were in desperate need of placement.

Adelyn had a cleft palate and the need for surgery was acute. She needed to be in a stable home environment with foster parents who would be committed to taking her to many follow-up doctor appointments and to therapy. There would also be special feeding challenges. We did not feel competent to do medical care of that nature, and our home was 20 miles out of town, so that the numerous trips would have interrupted our homeschooling schedule.

Tia Maria has been mentioned earlier in our story, and she was the baby that we decided to take. We cannot divulge the serious thing that Tia's parents did. But when the police went to the home to arrest them, there was little Tia. She was taken directly to Safe Haven. She needed a foster home because her parents would be incarcerated for a long time. In the meantime, the workers in the foster system would be searching out her family members to determine if one of her relatives was interested in raising her, and then doing an evaluation to see if they were qualified to take her. A family placement would keep her in the nucleus of her biological family and that was the goal. The search was on, and meanwhile Tia needed someplace to live.

We were torn between choosing between the two needy babies, but we felt that Tia would fit into our family routine. That we had made the right decision was confirmed years later when I met the woman who had stepped forward to take Adelyn. She and her husband had adopted her. We invited Adelyn to David's 5th birthday party, and we had a great time getting acquainted. She was a pretty, perky, well-adjusted little girl.

Tia came into our home and into our family, a darling little girl with big dark eyes and black wavy hair. She had a strong personality, and we met with some resistance as we tried to acclimate her into our home and into our routine. She had spent several days in Safe Haven, so besides being plunked into yet another set of new surroundings, she was still adjusting to being separated from her parents. She was fearful and angry for a short time. We probably talked funny and our food was probably different from what she was used to. She did not have any of her familiar toys, clothes, or routine. And surely continuously on her mind was, "Where's my mommy?"

The atmosphere of our home was loving and accepting. We had routines and regular family mealtimes together at our big dining room table. David had recently been enjoying the high chair, so Tia used the 'sassy seat' hooked onto the kitchen table.

Tia was progressing steadily in her motor development. Therefore, she was a great model for David, and became a wonderful friend for him. Very soon after she arrived they would set out on crawling expeditions around the living room and family room of our large open home. They climbed up and down the living room ledge, they fought over toys, and they shared toys. They loved riding in the double stroller around the property. Tia did not need the services of Special Children's Clinic, but she went with David and me to the appointments and got to play with their cool toys.

One evening after the little ones had eaten their dinner, we put them on the floor with some toys and continued our meal and our conversation. Somebody realized that it had been quiet for a while, and we looked across the room, only to see that David and Tia had opened a bottom drawer and gotten out a large plastic jar of Vaseline. They had smeared it on their faces and hands and they were having a great time in the goo. Our kitchen was not as childproofed as we had thought it was! We have a real cute picture, which we took time to snap before we cleaned them up. Everyone had a good laugh over it, and they enjoyed all the attention.

A few months after Tia had arrived, desperate social workers called us, and we were asked to take Freddie, a toddler for whom we had done a few days of respite care [giving a temporary vacation to his foster parents]. His foster parents, who had greatly loved him, were retiring, and he needed a temporary placement while an adoptive family was found. Freddie was a sturdy boy with light blond hair and a sweet, cooperative nature. Developmentally he was doing very well, which was another perk for David. Now he had two active friends to keep up with and mimic.

We were very surprised by this request to take another child. Our foster care license was officially changed to allow us to take three children under 18 months. We found out later that this was a not uncommon measure resorted to when a child needed a placement and the social workers felt that the foster parents would be competent to handle three little ones under 18 months.

The baby bedroom was a very large room, and easily housed three cribs and three dressers, the changing table, and some of the babies' equipment. Their toys were in the huge living room, which had become the baby playroom. We had moved into this large ranch house without much furniture, so the living room was empty except for a futon, which the babies crawled on, jumped on, and played on. Our couch, chairs, and TV were all in the family room.

Dan's and my bedroom was next to the baby room. I can remember hearing early morning baby noises, and when I would open their door, they would all be standing in their cribs baby talking to each other happily. This was a busy time and a special time. Lots of people were praying for us.

Two and three moved on

Tia Maria, I am very happy to report, was placed with loving family members who adopted her. The transition was very awkward. The relatives were from out-of-state and both had full-time jobs. We met in the DCFS parking lot, talked a little bit, transferred Tia and her belongings to their vehicle, and they were gone! Our darling girl was confused and anxious, and, of course, we were confused and anxious! Dan and I experienced more than a moment's loss, but we had to trust the Lord and we soon got immersed into our busy lives.

The couple, Max and Ella, who were caring for Tia, called us after a couple of weeks, and we soon got the sense that they were very responsible and committed to their niece and had a lot of love to give her. We communicated occasionally by mail for several years—they sent us pictures of Tia and described her as being a very loving little girl. They told us of her love for school and sports and her pets. We could not have been more pleased with everyone's excellent adjustment. Even though they were an older couple, they were exceedingly happy that they stepped out to take Tia into their hearts and their home. I wonder how many of their friends and our friends prayed for the success of this placement.

Normally when a baby or a child goes to another placement, there is a transition that happens which takes weeks and even months. This is so that the baby can adjust to the new adults who will take over her care, and so that the adults can get to know the child and ask the foster parents questions about the child's food preferences, the routine she is used to, her habits, doctor visits, therapy appointments, etc.

Freddie's story was a tragic story of parental rejection, too sad to revisit. Neither of his biological parents was in the vicinity, but he had a devoted grandmother, Nana, who came to visit him at our house. She brought toys for all three of the little children to play with, clothes for Freddie, and occasional treats for our extended family. Freddie was very fortunate to have this connection with his biological roots. Nana knew she was blessed that our home was open to her visits so that she was able to bond with her grandson and keep up on his progress.

When Freddie was chosen to be adopted, he had a long and successful transition into his new home. Jim and Joanne were a neat couple who had not been able to have children, so had decided to adopt. We liked them very much, and they spent a lot of time in our home getting to know Freddie. We met at a doctor's appointment, so they could meet his pediatrician, and they hung out at our house and played with him. They lived in Reno, so after the initial adjustment, they began to take Freddie home for short periods of time. And then they would take him overnight. They kept in touch with us for years. Then, as often happens when couples adopt, they experienced two successful pregnancies, and Freddie became a big brother as their family increased.

Tia and Freddie left within a few weeks of each other. We had already started the paperwork for adopting David, but it was a long process in those days. We took in another toddler, Dandre, who was a very sunny boy. He and David had a lot of fun together in our big living room and family room. After two more months we accepted into our home the most adorable girl, Jaelynn. When Dandre left a few months later, David had Jaelynn for one-and-a-half years as a daily playmate and friend. She was small and delicate, so he learned to be a gentle friend.

Finally, I got my first newborn, Keifon, through an adoption agency. This darling baby captured <u>all</u> of our hearts, even though we only got to keep him for two months. We connected with his adoptive parents who were overjoyed to be adopting Keifon. Their plan was that someday, when they explained his adoption to him, they wanted to include our family's part in his life's journey to get to them. They took numerous pictures of us and they asked for a letter from me to put in his baby book, which I sent them. I saved a copy of the letter and found it in Keifon's file.

Dear Keifon, We were blessed by the Lord to take care of you from January 2 until March 9. We had planned to go to southern California to visit my Dad, but changed our plans at the last minute and decided to stay home. We received a call that a darling little newborn boy needed a place to stay while he was waiting for the paperwork to be finalized so that he could go to his forever family. We were very excited and felt that this was the hand of the Lord. We loved you like you were our own little baby. Mark and Danny asked if they could call you Keifon, and we all decided that that name sited you well. You brought us lots of joy! You always quieted when we picked you up, even if you were hungry or wet or had messy pants. Our friends at church and the checkers in the grocery stores would ask us each week how you were doing and they loved to look at you and cuddle you. I would always say that it was our joy and pleasure to be able to take care of you and have you in our family....

This work suited us. We felt fulfillment in stepping into these babies' lives in their time of need. Dan was working out of our home in those early years so he was available for helping me in the daytime when I needed him, which often meant late nights working on drafting projects in his office.

Dan and I and the boys worked well together, but eventually there came a time when our sons' interest began to wane, the initial novelty having worn off. We worked hard at juggling everyone—driving the boys to their activities and the babies to their appointments.

This is how our lives went for twelve years. We took a few short breaks to regroup and refresh and go on road trips. I think it was the best thing we could have done for David, especially because we lived in a rural area with no close neighbors till David was nearly 3 years old. Since I had made the decision not to send our kids to preschool but preferred to be a stay-at-home mom, it was the absolute best thing for David to have live-in friends! We made sure to reinforce to David that he was staying—that others might move in and move out, but he was ours and we weren't letting him go.

Part II - Things we learned while fostering that might be of some help to the reader, intertwined with our continued story

<u>Thoughts about attachment and abandonment</u>

Something that I have anguished about is the confusion that Tia and Freddie and all the other foster kids will probably deal with all their lives.

Tia had lived in the chaos of her parents' home where verbal, substance, and physical abuse were happening. When she was nine months old, the authorities intervened, and she was liberated from that dangerous household and deposited at the Safe Haven, where she would be kindly cared for. After several days she was brought to our welcoming home where she stayed for eight months. However, one day, in the blink of an eye, as far as she understood the situation, she was transferred to her aunt and uncle's vehicle and driven away from everything familiar, never to see any of us again! She was too young to understand any of this but old enough to be impacted by it. A person is affected by abandonment on some level at any age.

Freddie was taken from his mother at birth, because she might have injured him in her confused mental state. He was in a loving foster home until he was almost a year old and then the couple was forced to retire for health reasons. He became part of our family for several months, and then after a good transition, went to his adoptive home. Again, he was too young to comprehend these shifts in living situations and in caregivers.

As these children in foster care grow up, how will they process all of this change and disruption in their lives? Do they have a chance to securely re-attach to their biological parents or making a sound attachment to their adoptive parents?

I will refer to the foster babies as 'she' to avoid using 'he/she.'

The foster infant thinks the foster parents are her parents. The foster parents perform all of the necessary functions to keep the baby alive, such as cuddling, receiving nourishment, and having a place of security.

In the second half of our fostering experience, over a six-year period, I picked up 26 newborns from the hospital nurseries, usually within a day or two after their birth. As far as they knew, Dan and I were their mommy and daddy. Dan and I did everything for them that loving parents would do. We took them into our hearts and tended to their needs. I have ached over the confusion that must undoubtedly reside in the infant's mind when at some point she would be reunited to her biological parent or eventually be taken to the couple who would adopt her and raise her. Deep inside her was the awareness that something was not right, that someone was missing, and even "someone left me behind."Yes, someone was missing—her biological parents and her foster parents. When a baby has had this experience, particularly early in infancy, it can become abandonment issues. Abandonment issues become an undercurrent of fear that she will be abandoned again. Even in a secure home, or much later in a marriage relationship, the adopted child will live with the anxiety that the persons around her may inexplicably leave or abandon her. This is part of the issue of attachment. It can result in much confusion and despair and often is never resolved. (See the articles on Attachment in Part V)

June is an adult friend of mine. She was separated from her mother at birth and placed in a pre-arranged adoption home where she was welcomed and cherished. Yet she confided in me that she had never reconciled her mother's rejection of her. June was a beautiful woman, successful, effective in her job and in her relationships. And yet the abandonment issue tormented her every day. *"Why did mom let me go? Was something wrong with me? Did she love me? Where is she now? Will I ever meet her?"*

For an infant or a child up to at least five years old, I think there must be a horrible hole of fear and confusion about "what happened to mommy and daddy?" and "who are these guys anyway?"The young child's understanding is so simple, and the problem is profound. Mommy and daddy may make a few months of attempts at working their case plan, but if they fail, they are gone forever. Does that separation ever get resolved in the baby's heart and mind? Is that hole in her heart ever filled?

Children who are older can understand the words: "Your mom and dad were taken away by the police and somebody else has to take care of you for a while." They have the mental understanding to process their thoughts and feelings and begin to deal with reality. With patient help and by living in a secure place with loving people, they can hopefully eventually make the best of their situation. Older children can understand: "Daddy did a bad thing and has to be in jail for a long time. We are looking for another place for you to live. We are finding a safe place for you."

But for the newborn, in the pre-verbal stage, how she is nurtured in the foster home has a profound effect on the development of her brain, particularly in areas of what is safe and who is trustworthy. Sudden changes in caregivers can give rise to a sense of abandonment and distrust in the longevity of caregivers. Depending on the individual child, changes in caregivers may or may not be severely traumatic. Interestingly, studies show the most important issue is the quality of the nurturing, and that is where the foster parent comes in.

The foster parents can make sure they say the baby's name to her often. They can talk and sing to her during diaper changes and clothing changes, and while holding her, and while giving her a bottle. They can speak soft assurance that things are working out for her. They can speak hope into her life, and affirm that God loves her and that they love her. Babies need lots of cooing, and smiles, and singing,

It is fine to use swings and jumpers, but spending time holding her or carrying her in your arms provides bonding. Carrying her in a front pack or a backpack at times during the day also encourages bonding, if she likes it.

As our family experienced with David, it took some time and trust building for him to welcome physical contact. When we would get a newborn, I did not immediately pass her around to all of the waiting arms of my friends who were anxious to snuggle her in church or in our living room. I wanted her to bond with me primarily as mom, and then I would share her. We learned in our foster training classes that babies who bond with the foster parents have a better chance of bonding and receiving love when they go back to their biological parents or when they meet their adoptive parents than those who do not

We had large kitchen islands in both of the houses in which we did foster care. When I was homeschooling or cooking, we kept the baby on top of the island in some type of secure baby holder. We would also have the bassinette downstairs during the day so she could be in the middle of our activity, and then we carried it upstairs to our room at night.

The idea is not to treat her like a little lump! Lots of warm interaction by all members of the family will help her feel loved and accepted.

As to how this confusion about attachment gets resolved, we don't know if it ever does. We have had to recognize it for what it is in David's case, and realize that it may always be an issue with David. The primary attachment person in a baby's life is the mother who gave her birth. David was separated from his Mom for the first two weeks of his life because he was ill and in the hospital. Then she left his life and disappeared. He was at Safe Haven for almost three weeks. That means that during the first five weeks of his life, he was without that primary attachment figure, Mom, who is the single most important person in his life. What if almost every time he was changed or fed during those months, there was a different woman or man caring for him? He came to us at almost nine months of age. Six of us worked hard at bonding with him, and he thrived for years. As his brothers began to leave home, he continued to do pretty well, though he sorely missed them and all of the attention they gave him, and then he hit puberty. That's when we stopped foster care to spend more time with him as he floundered.

Now, fast-forward to the present day. When we drop David off at his group home, we often see a silent question on his face: **will they ever be back?**

That is the haunting question of abandonment—*Will they be back? Will I see them again?*

A good word for foster care and how it works

During the twelve years we did foster care, we saw a few positive re-unifications, some very good adoptions, and lots of hard work done by lots of people to make these possible. We took care of 52 foster children, from one day old to 12 years old. We dealt with over 40 awesome social workers, dedicated administrators, and lots of great support staff. We worked with several of the social workers in more than one foster case. We also dealt with two private adoption agencies and their social workers. We cannot speak for the system today, but in our tenure (1994-2006) in Reno, NV, and for us, it worked quite well. Yes, we saw some mistakes happen, we saw some trusts broken, and we came to know of some tragic incidents. We grieved over these.

The foster care system in the United States is an attempt to meet a concrete need in our society. It is in place to intervene when children in the community are in a dangerous living environment. We met a large number of professionals that we felt were doing a conscientious job. We met scores of foster parents who took their role in children's lives very seriously and worked sacrificially to help the children in their care.

When a call is received at the social services office that a child is at risk, the situation is evaluated. The call may come from a neighbor who has heard yelling or gunshots or from a concerned family member who knows her daughter is neglecting her child and the boyfriend is abusive. If the decision is made to send an investigative social worker to the home, as it was when David's parents were causing some commotion, he assessed the circumstances of the home, the condition of the adults, and the well being of the child. The worker discusses the case with his supervisor and they determine whether or not to remove the child from the home. If they do remove the child, she may be temporarily taken to Safe Haven, but as soon as possible the child (or sibling group) is placed in an approved foster home. A report is written and the worker goes to court with the county's attorney to bring the case before the judge. If the judge approves, which he usually does, this makes the foster home placement legal.

Once the child is in custody, Nevada's primary goal is to re-unite children to their parents if it is at all possible. In our experience during the years we fostered we saw that a lot of effort was expended to try to help this happen. Attempts are made to contact the parents, to keep in contact with them, and to get them into a case plan that will enable them to get their children back. They are monitored by the social workers to make sure their behavior is consistently appropriate for parenting.

Another important goal of social services is to keep the brothers and sisters of a family together. Two years ago our friends, Dave and Kathy, who are in their early 40's and seasoned foster parents, heard about a sibling set of 8 children who were going to be separated into small groups in hopes of making them more adoptable. Efforts to get them adopted as a group had failed. Dave and Kathy stepped in and added a bunch of very awesome kids to their family. That gave them a total of twelve adopted kids and one biological son. Their book, *The Bain Event*, is in the suggested books section.

Our friends, Jamie and Sara, both 45, went on to adopt five more children after they adopted Kilie, which added to their two biological children, gave them 8. At the time of this writing, they have the children in charter schools and are juggling a full house.

Having a large family suits both of these couples. They are full of love and commitment to their kids, and they have close relationships with the Lord. The investment they are making with their children is very impressive.

Getting back to the foster system: the biological parents sign the case plan, which they have gone over with the social worker, agreeing to do their part in fulfilling all the requirements that social services has determined are necessary to re-gain custody of their child/children. The goal is to complete their case plan in a year, but there are a lot of factors that can lengthen or shorten this process. The case plan may include required attendance at meetings for Alcoholics Anonymous and/or Narcotics Anonymous. It may require anger management classes, parenting classes, job training, securing and holding on to a job for a certain length of time, regularly attending visits, meeting the foster parent at therapy appointments and doctor appointments, etc. In most cases we do not know whether the reunification was successful or not. It is something you have to let go of and put into the Lord's hands.

Because parental re-unification may fail, the foster child's extended family is contacted. Relatives who are interested in raising the child must submit to extensive background checks and interviews. The process can be long and tedious, especially since the social workers have thirty other clients' cases to work with. This means that a foster family hoping to adopt their precious foster child can have a very long and arduous wait. And there is the very real possibility of heartbreak for them if one of the family members steps forward and passes all of the tests for acceptability, and the foster child goes to live with them. The foster parents will have to relinquish the foster child that they have grown attached to. We have seen it happen many times, and it is devastating. That child is not soon forgotten. Not only the foster parents and their children, but also their extended families have loved this child, invested in her, prayed for her, and bonded with her. It is always traumatic.

Many of the biological parents fall through the cracks because of their addictions and inability to work their program. But we felt that the worse tragedy would have been if their children had gone down with them. That is why we believe so strongly in children being taken from a dangerous home situation and being placed in foster care. Landing in foster care, they have a chance at life. Will they be scarred? Will they have a hard road? Probably. But the scarring and the hard road are redeemable.

Is the foster care system perfect? No. It is made up of human beings. Nothing made up of humans will be perfect because there are no perfect humans. There are rules and regulations and laws and courts—but they are still monitored by humans. There are people in the system doing their best and there are undignified people in the system who slip in and bring wreckage, whether it be a social worker bending the rules, pleading ignorance, or covering something up-- or a foster parent who hurts a child in his care. As a foster parent, you will need to be transparent, and you will need to be vigilant. If you have concerns, you can speak to the social worker or his supervisor or you can write letters to judges. When we had strong opinions, we tried to get to court when our children's cases came up, but that is not always possible, in fact it might be very difficult, and the foster parent is not always welcomed with opened arms.

It is important to report any injuries your foster children may have sustained in your home. That can be embarrassing because it seems like it will sound foolish or foolhardy or neglectful. But it is important to get a reputation for being open and honest, and not someone who hides things or suppresses information.

This is a side note, and it is embarrassing, but our pediatrician's office manager, Renee, nicknamed me Calamity Jane because of all of the unusual reasons we came into the office. One toddler put a dried bean up his nose, and another one swallowed a watch battery on purpose. A child who is an attention seeker will bring many opportunities for you to get attention that you would rather not have. I believe it is better to face up to the humiliation rather than hide something that may have serious consequences later.

There are people who may not become foster parents, but whose calling in life is to speak on behalf of foster children. Every child needs an advocate, and it might be you. There is an organization called CASA, which stands for Court-Appointed Special Advocate. CASA workers are court-appointed volunteers "who get to know the child and everyone involved in the child's life: parents and relatives; foster parents, teachers, medical professionals, attorneys, social workers, and others. They use the information they gather to inform judges and others of what the child needs and what will be the best permanent home for them." www.casaforchildren.org

All over the world, unwanted children are killed or abandoned by people whose lives are in turmoil. We do not want to think about what happens to children in countries with no political humanitarian structure. In America we have an organizational framework that brings in many of these ostracized children.

During our years of fostering we met devoted men and women who were dedicated to the goal of keeping children safe and re-uniting families when possible. We saw them exhibiting integrity in working with foster parents and the biological parents. I can remember only two social workers that I felt were probably not well-suited for social work, and we were able to work with both of them for the good of the children (although I remember experiencing some real heartaches when we disagreed with their evaluation of a situation and their decisions). They both moved out of the system.

The challenge of fostering

The challenge of fostering comes with a warning: fostering can become an addiction. Once we passed the stage fright of wondering if we could actually parent a houseful, we became passionate about helping children in need. Their situations were desperate and the pool of foster parents was usually inadequate for the crisis of cases.

My close friends Janet and Diane had the same compassion for the children that I did. Our husbands were often able to pull us back to reality --"but, honey, we are bursting at the seams!!" But when we shared the baby's tragic story and need for immediate placement, Dan or Bob or Brett would often encourage us to call the worker and accept the child. Our three families routinely found ourselves very stretched, as did most of our colleagues. Our own children would joke about our homes being group homes (though at times it wasn't very funny to them) and our families shared a special camaraderie. We all went to the same church and it was vital that we had each other for support, encouragement, and consolation.

Sibling groups and school-age kids

In four instances we took siblings. Siblings are two or more individuals having one or both parents in common.

*Meri and June, two little girls, ages five and three, were with us for a few weeks. They were very sad and clung to each other. They were so withdrawn and anxious that they never could relate comfortably to us, and I heard that they had many foster placements.

*Joey and Prissy, a four-year old boy and his baby sister, were with us for a short time until their grandparents obtained custody of them. Although shell-shocked about being separated from their parents, they acclimated well to our home life. We had several visits with their grandparents and extended family before they were transferred into the grandparents' home.

*Juan and Patricia, who were eight and six years old, were with us from Thanksgiving till the end of the school year—seven months. Their foster mom was diagnosed with a terminal illness, so they were dealing with losing her, whom they loved very much. Because we had done respite care for them, their social worker felt that going to a familiar place would ease their trauma. She called us and begged us to take them in to our home, we could not say no. They were very happy to be in the safety and warmth of our home, although they were anxious and fearful they would never be reunited with their parents.

*Meredith and Benny, who were 10 and 12, were left unattended by their parents and were picked up by the police. They were in our home for almost a year. They really wanted to be reunited with their family, although they were pretty traumatized by the events of their parents' lives.

As I said, one of the goals of foster care is to keep families together as often as possible. Brothers and sisters can be a comfort and a support to each other at a time when their lives have crashed around them.

Surprisingly, we found that sometimes the children would rather be in the familiar chaotic and abusive environment with their parents than in the new place with strangers. This was hard for us to fathom. With us they were safe, which I would think would be priority #1 for a child. But they were not with their own mom and dad. They were fed regularly and had clean sheets and washed clothes, but what had the police done with mama? Dad shouted and was mean when he got drunk, but what was jail like and was he okay? If mom and dad were in jail, what about all my stuff? Would we all ever be together again as a family?

In going through my files to write this book, I found a note that exemplified the confusion that was resting in a six-year old girl's mind. One night at bedtime, which is a good time to spend a few minutes with an anxious child, Patricia opened up to me. Patricia said she was going to miss me when she went home. She had only been in our home for two weeks, but she was feeling safe and welcomed. She was in the fantasy that she would be going home any day, which was not going to happen. We chatted a while, then she felt comfortable to ask the question that was haunting her: "Do you get dead in jail? Someone said they blindfold you and tie your hands behind your back and the police kill you. My Mom's been in jail three times before this and I always worry."

How heart wrenching is this? Patricia was developmentally delayed and still stunned from being separated from her Mom. She truly did not know what was happening to her mother. We had her brother also, so I know that was a comfort to her. I was able to soothe her fears and help her feel secure that her Mom would be okay in jail. I did not give her any assurance about seeing her Mom again because I had no assurance that she would, and that would have been giving Patricia false hope.

The rest of the story is that when Patricia's Mom got out of jail and decided to begin reunifying with her children she was expected to have three or four visits a week with them, speak to each of them every evening for 10 minutes, call and apologize to each child when she had to miss an appointment. The social worker wanted her to display consistency to prove she could handle her children on her own. He also wanted her to re-build her relationship with them, which had been shattered. In this case, I remember that we notified the kids' schoolteachers and the principal and cautioned them not to let the kids leave the school with anyone but the bus driver or me. The concern was that Mom would try to sidestep the intensive process of reunification and abduct her children.

As it happened, Mom got overwhelmed or distracted (we will never know) and just disappeared from our lives. Soon after that, Juan and Patricia went to another foster home. Juan and Patricia stayed in the system for many years. As usually happens, we lost track of them.

Our elementary school age children spent almost eight hours each day away from home. They were at school or being transported to and from school. When 3:30 came, I had been working with our own four sons on their homeschool work much of the day, plus giving attention to a foster baby and David. So to then turn my attention to helping the foster children with their homework while also having to make, or at least supervise, dinner preparation—was very difficult.

Babies and toddlers

After a few years of fostering, we decided to not take school-age kids or sibling groups, but to focus solely on babies and toddlers.

Caring for newborns that I was able to pick up from the hospital at birth was really satisfying for me. I would get a call from a social worker, who would fill me in on the baby's sad history. Normally the mother had been breaking the law taking drugs or alcohol or both, which necessitated the baby being brought into protective custody.

Another criteria for social services removing a baby from her mother, was that if the newborn's mom had other children in the system, the newborn was automatically placed in foster care. The mother would be set on a course to win all of her children back into her custody by working through her case plan.

Excitedly gathering newborn jammies, booties, a blanket, and my infant car seat, I would drive to the newborn nursery at one of the two major hospitals in town. The baby's mom had already said her goodbyes and was in her hospital room or had been released. I did not meet the biological mother until later at the visits in the social services office.

There were papers to sign with the baby's social worker and the hospital social worker. I collected as much information about the baby from the nurses that I could. I always took a pad and pencil, knowing I would not remember the Apgar scores, birth weight and length, and other details that the pediatrician would be interested in later. I also noted the baby's feeding schedule and was usually given some formula and the favored pacifier.

Sometimes the baby was born addicted to heroin or recovering from mom's meth abuse or had other substances in her system. I was delayed day after day in being able to pick up Katie from NICU (Neonatal Intensive Care Unit) because she was withdrawing from heroin. I made it a point to visit her several times during her hospital stay so I could talk to the nurses about her. I wanted as much information as I could get, in order to be able to care for her appropriately. When I finally got her home, she was a difficult baby for about a week, but as she became free of the drugs in her system and its effects in her body, she was able to be cuddled and soothed. (I also had people praying for her healing.) Katie's mom was determined to re-gain custody of her daughter. She went to NA (Narcotics Anonymous) meetings, and got a job; she went to counseling, got an apartment, came regularly to visits, passed the random drug tests. After many months, she was awarded custody of her little girl. Of course, we rarely know the rest of the story. But in this case, we heard that mom moved out-of-state. One day she left Katie with her sister and did not return after a few days to pick Katie up. The sister called the police and the foster system was involved again. We never got used to the tragic events. We would have our time of grieving and move on. When you know you are doing what you are supposed to be doing, God's grace is there to help you recover quickly and pick up where you left off.

I knew I had done my best for Katie. I had to trust God for her life. We found that a short time of grieving over the heart-rending sorrow that we would see in our foster babies and foster children's lives—and in our friends' foster babies' lives—was imperative. We were not really able to move on in a healthy manner unless we spent some amount of time bringing closure. This is why a husband and wife being on the same page and sharing the responsibility of the babies is so important. This is also why having friends who also were foster parents was important. We needed each other to process the sadness, rejoice in the joyful things, and laugh at the absurd.

<u>Our home as a temporary place</u>

I had a definite conviction that this temporary care giving was my purpose for this season of our lives. I felt that we were rescuers, and that our job was to provide immediate care to the child and to be her interim parents until she was reunited with her parents or her extended family or was adopted. I never felt that we were to adopt a houseful, and I did not feel we were to take back into our care children who had been in our home who had failed placements.

Dan and I believed that foster care was a way to be a blessing to others in need as well as being a blessing to our family.

One huge perk was that our sons who are now 30, 32, 34, 35, saw first hand the devastation that comes from falling into the pits that our foster babies' parents had fallen into. For years they heard stories of lives ruined by drugs and alcohol. They held babies who were the innocent victims of their parents' promiscuity and substance abuse. I think this helped them make some serious decisions about their own lives and goals.

Our rule

I made a rule for myself, which my husband agreed to. Once a child left our home, we would not take her back if she came back into the system because her placement with her biological parents failed.

My reasoning was that we as a family had done our part. We had given the child our best. We had worked hard at bonding with the child. We had made an honest attempt to work with the parents. We had invested ourselves. When the child went to another foster home or back to her parents, and that placement failed, I was very sorry that it happened, but we had moved on and we were usually caring for another child who needed us. Several of our friends would take the child of a failed placement back into their homes. Often the child had been neglected or physically abused while away in the other living situation. A couple of our friends found that the routines and dynamics and relationships that were established in their home were jolted and rocked and often wrecked when a child was returned to them. It would have caused me too much agony and heartbreak to try help that child again. An experience confirming that boundary happened with a sweet baby named Jamar.

Jamar's parents, Duane and Nicole, were nice people to work with. It was surprising and yet very encouraging to see them working so hard to restore their family. Their history together was sporadic, their lifestyles were quite unconventional, and their list of past offenses was pretty extensive, so we all marveled that they stayed completely faithful to their case plan and week by week met their goals. They each got a job, they got an apartment, and they were genuinely loving toward Jamar. Their reunification took almost a year, and seemed like it was going to work. But very soon after he was returned to their home, they fell back into their old ways, and Jamar was once again placed in protective custody.

Jamar went to a new foster home and the foster mom, Mary, contacted me with the news of the sad story. She had known Jamar as sunny and cooperative when he had been in our care. He had been one of our most consistently even-tempered and loving children. After a few weeks in his parents' home, Jamar became explosive and inconsolable. He was put on heavy medications, which left this normally good-spirited boy in a bleary-eyed daze. Mary did not have much hope for his full recovery. I don't know what he went through, and it is heartbreaking to think of him even now. I know caring for him would have been too tortuous for me to cope with, had he been returned to our family. I saw very clearly that I was only a partial hero! I was not able to go the extra mile into the depths of despair with this precious boy. I could only go so far.

My husband went back to school in his mid-fifties to get his Master's degree and then earned his MFT (Marriage and Family Therapist) license. He says that an important part of self-care is knowing what you can emotionally bear to undertake, and using that to establish personal boundaries.

And that is what foster parents must figure out individually, as a couple, and as a family.

There are people who would be capable of coping with Jamar's tragedy, and I applaud you.

I thanked God that my boundary was in place and prayed that Jamar would recover fully. I was thankful that my boundary had spared my family from the emotional upheaval that bringing him back would have provoked.

With clear boundaries, coping is easier and standing firm is easier. Even if someone is pleading, if I hold on to my boundary I will not give in to my emotions and make a mistake I will possibly regret.

I think it would have been worse if I had taken Jamar back and found that his chaos in our household was causing insurmountable problems to our family. I would have had to ask that he be removed. The wait time for his leaving might have been months, until another home was found. It would not have been good for any of us.

Another story about sticking with a boundary involved an adorable and needy little girl that two people in our family wanted us to adopt. Dan and I had decided that especially because we were older, we would only adopt one child. We are very thankful that we did not budge from that boundary.

Scenarios of biological parents' problems

These are some of the scenarios in which our foster children's parents were entangled:

*homelessness
*drug users and drug dealers (meth, heroin, crack, marijuana)
*pimps and prostitutes
*murderers
*severely mentally challenged
*alcoholics
*a mom who disowned her baby within minutes of giving birth, claiming, "she is not my baby!"

*a mom who called a taxi for herself after giving birth, leaving her baby in the hospital; she disappeared and was never found

*a mom who was bi-polar and had attempted suicide twenty times

*moms who were on meth their entire pregnancy

*a mom who gave birth in a public restroom on her break from her job

*moms who drank alcohol during all or most of their pregnancy

*most moms had no pre-natal care

*mom and/or dad in jail/prison

We had a couple of moms in the Step-2 program, which can be live-in or outpatient. When a woman is in Step-2, based on her good behavior, she can have her baby with her. The mission statement is: *Step-2 is a comprehensive substance abuse and treatment program that provides women and their children suffering from chemical addiction, poverty, and domestic violence the opportunity to rebuild their lives.* www.step2reno.org

When the mom is in Step-2, the foster parent keeps the baby until the mom shows that she meets the requirements of the Step-2 program and her social services case plan. The baby is then transferred to the mom's and the program's care.

Termination of parental rights

When a child is taken into custody by social services, the child's social worker will make several attempts to contact the biological parent by going to the last known address and by placing an ad in the local newspaper for six weeks. The ad contains identifying information for the child and the birth mother, as well as information about the date, the time and the place of the court hearing. If the biological parent does not come forward, her parental rights are terminated by default. Social services also puts out a notice for all unknown fathers when paternity is not clearly established.

There are several requirements that have to be met before the parent's rights are legally terminated. Basically, they have either abandoned the child and/or they have failed to remedy the circumstances that brought the child into foster care despite being given time and supportive services to help them do so.

David's mother may have moved out of town, because she was not located in the required time limit. Her rights were terminated and she lost custody of her son.

Relinquishment of parental rights

A parent may also relinquish his rights, which is what our David's father did. Our social worker, Hayley, had contacted Louis to tell him that she had a family that wanted to adopt his son and he told her that he would like to meet us. We met Hayley in a nearby town one fall morning. After a friendly interview in which Louis told us about himself, and asked us several questions, he signed off on his parental rights and thanked us sincerely for raising his son.

We saw Louis a few times after that first visit. Dan took David to spend time with his father three times. David was two years old and was intrigued by the soda pop and candy machines in Louis's apartment complex. Louis had anticipated his son's curiosity and had some coins ready. He let David make his snack choices, put the coins into the machines, and buy his own treats. Louis wrote to us three or four times. They were good letters, always asking about David and thanking us for bringing up his son.

<u>Open and Closed Adoptions</u>

We wanted David to meet his father, and we were glad we did. We would have liked him to meet his mother, also, but the system lost track of her early on. David has had more problems emotionally, regarding his mother, perhaps because he never met her as an older child. Each family needs to decide whether they want their adoption to include having a relationship with the biological parents, and if so, to what extent.

There are various ways of explaining the types of adoption, but you will probably be offered a choice: 1) closed adoption, or confidential adoption, means that even if the adoptive parents and the biological parents have met, usually their contact is through an agency or an attorney; 2) semi-open adoption may mean an exchange of letters or pictures; 3) open adoption may mean there is open contact between the adults and possibly the adoptive child.

The boundaries need to be clearly set by the adoptive parents. We suggest caution in the beginning, because you can always decide you want your child to have more contact, but you may not be able to get the biological parents to agree to less contact.

<u>Scenarios of our foster children's issues</u>

*HIV positive baby--it was our choice to take this baby after we were informed about her condition
*physically abused children and babies
*verbally and emotionally scarred children
*a baby with heroin in her system
*babies testing positive for meth, cocaine
*pre-term babies (10 weeks, 6 weeks, 4 weeks pre-term, and others)
*babies with scabies, eczema, broken bones
*FAS babies
*babies with serious allergies

When we were asked by Piper, the Foster Care Liaison, to take the HIV positive baby, I was in a dilemma. When she called me, she said, "When this baby's case came up in our meeting I thought of you and Dan." I called a friend of ours who lived in San Francisco and asked what she thought. She said, "Well, Jesus was with the lepers, and I guess you can be with this dear baby who needs you so much and may not be able to be placed very easily." We prayed and we took him. He was one of the sweetest babies we ever had. We never regretted the decision.

We had two real preemies--a baby girl who was ten weeks premature and a few days later we took a baby boy who was six weeks premature. I'll call them Valerie and Johnny. Both were newborns that I picked up at the hospital when they were healthy enough to be released. Both were drug and alcohol affected. It was like having twins! Johnny was normal size, but Valerie was extremely petite. We put a crib downstairs in the living room. At night we put one baby at each end of the crib. We placed a sleeping mat on the floor, and we had a schedule: After their 10pm feeding, I would go upstairs and sleep for 4 hours, and Dan would try to sleep on the mat, but would be on call as the babies needed him. At 2am my alarm would go off, and we would switch places after feeding and changing them. We were living an adventure, and it was very fulfilling to give ourselves away so that these little ones could make it. Of course we were exhausted, but we believed so much in what we were doing and wanted to help.

Remember, there are usually not enough foster parents to cover the need. The social workers pleas for help were hard to ignore. We had also been thinking about helping the needy and the orphans for six years, so to be in the thick of it was a blessing. It was a set-up by the Lord to help us to learn about giving and loving.

We had Valerie for two-and-a-half years. It was thought that because she had been on life support as a premature newborn, she had not mastered sucking. This is not uncommon for extreme pre-term babies. She had serious feeding challenges during the entire time we had her, and when she was two years old a feeding tube was inserted in her stomach. That was probably the most traumatic event we experienced as foster parents. She was so tiny, and very underweight, that it had become a life or death medical condition. The operation was a necessary procedure to save her life. Adding to the concern of her surviving the operation, I did not feel adequate to cope with the special feeding routine, but I was trained at the hospital, learned the feeding technique, and Dan and I did well with it. It was a very stressful experience. Valerie was adopted about eight months later, with a good long transition. We visited with the family several times, and last we heard (years ago) Valerie was going to school every day on a school bus, and her mom was a strong advocate for her education.

We kept Johnny, the other 'twin,' for several months and then because his mother had rehabilitated, secured a job, passed random drug tests, and had kept up her weekly visits with him, she was reunited with Johnny. Amy worked very hard to get her baby back. I still remember the anguish I felt as the social worker picked Johnny up from our house. He was a very sweet boy. I was happy for the reunification (which is the goal whenever it is possible), but my heart really hurt. All I could think of was—he thinks I am his mother and that I am giving him away! I had my good cry, and Dan commiserated with me. We took another baby as soon as possible so we could move on.

Attachment is about unconditional love

My husband and I made sure to form a strong emotional bond to the newborns. We had learned in our foster parent training classes that if a baby makes that strong bond (attaches) with the foster parents, there is a much greater likelihood that she will be able to attach to the adoptive parents or form a re-attachment with her natural parents, so we attached. We loved those babies, and they learned what love is all about.

The experience of unconditionally loving someone is pretty amazing. It is the experience of giving yourself away and not expecting anything back. It is also the experience of loving the lovely and the unlovely. It is loving and caring for someone who is screaming and cannot be mollified—when her anger, anxiety, drug withdrawal, is out of control. It is loving the little toddler who comes with a skin disease, it is cleaning bright-red crusty bottom rashes, and it is carrying the bradycardia backpack for a baby with breathing problems.

It is the experience of loving when you know that the baby will not remember you. Soon, after she leaves your home, she will forget to look for you. You will not even be a conscious memory. That kind of love is marvelous to give. It is like the love that Jesus is always pouring out upon us. Even though we do not return His love in the measure in which He gives it to us, even though we ignore Him, forget to say thank you, and get too busy to read His Word and fellowship with Him; in spite of our inconsistencies, His love is always pouring out. We can draw on that love and give it away.

I remember one baby that was very unattractive. Part of the reason was because her eyebrows were very dark and heavy and always set in a serious frown. I had picked her up from the newborn nursery and I soon learned from the social worker that her mom had been on heavy psychotic medications during the entire pregnancy. No wonder little Camille was sad and serious. To be fed heavy meds throughout her in utero (in the womb) experience was tragic! My heart went out to her and I was determined to overcome my superficial feelings. I decided to call her Camille-Beautiful-And-Lovely. I introduced her as Camille-Beautiful-And-Lovely and always referred to her that way. As far as I was concerned that was her name. I decided that she was beautiful deep inside and that a lovely personality was emerging! This helped me a lot. I hope that somehow it helped the forming of her self-concept and that instead of getting negative and rejecting vibes from me, she felt my sincere acceptance. After we'd taken care of Camille-Beautiful-And-Lovely for a few months, an adoptive home was found for her. I have a vivid picture in my mind of her adoring adoptive parents focusing all of their love and attention on their long-anticipated sweet little five-month old. It was love at first sight.

The perks of foster care

In foster care it is best to have no expectation of the baby or the young child thanking you or loving you back or giving you a present for your efforts to take care of her. It is a experience of loving the needy child unconditionally.

I landed at Wikipedia for a definition of unconditional love: "In psychology, unconditional love refers to a state of mind in which one has the goal of increasing the welfare of another, despite any evidence of benefit for oneself."

There is the boon of a paycheck, which does help pay the mortgage and buy the groceries and the gas. We were extremely glad to see every check that hit our mailbox.

The appreciation, or the reward, for this job primarily comes in the form of endorphins. Endorphins are a group of neurotransmitters released within the brain and nervous system, which have a calming effect and give a boost. "Endorphins are among the brain chemicals known as neurotransmitters, which reduce our perception of pain and act similarly to morphine and codeine, leading to feelings of euphoria. "www.medicinenet.com Endorphins are natural hormones that combat stress. Several things we do can release them: smiling, laughing, exercise, eating certain foods, listening to music, and other things. www.wikihow.com/release-Endorphins Endorphins are also released when a person does volunteer work or helps people, like doing foster care!

Along with the pick-me-up of endorphins, appreciation came from our family, our friends, and the checkers in the grocery store.

My Mom and her sisters had been in foster care in their teens. I knew that as I was growing up, but that season of their lives was not discussed because the memories were too painful. I remember as a child feeling grateful that there had been a place for the Henry girls in the 1930's after their parents had died, but I don't remember any identification with wanting to be a foster parent.

Unfortunately my Mom was not alive to meet David and our babies, but her sisters were. My aunts, Ginger and Virgi, marveled at the work we were doing, and enjoyed our visits to southern California. They were proud of us for adopting David and loved hearing our foster babies' stories. My Dad was apprehensive that we had embarked on a strenuous childcare vocation in our 50's, but he was also gratified by it. Dad had a special relationship with David when David was young. David was sweet and attentive to his grandfather, who shared his chocolate bars and his recliner with him.

As we navigated through the twelve years of fostering and adoption, my sisters, Marsha and Connie, consistently stood solidly by my side. We talked on the phone several times a week during particular seasons of stress. Though they often felt I had a mountain of responsibility on my plate, they were fully supportive of me, always compassionate, and always ready to listen to whatever was on my heart. I depended upon their validation and felt undergirded by them.

Dan's family—his mom and dad, his brother and his wife, and his aunt, were also very caring, kind, and sympathetic. They were always interested in hearing about our new foster children and always made them feel welcome at our holiday family gatherings. Dan's brother and his wife and Aunt Yvonne had ready arms for snuggling a baby while I took a little break from mothering and made Thanksgiving gravy. Papa, Jean, and Bebo always gave David an open-armed and openhearted reception, and made sure to plan activities to entertain him during our visits to them.

We had many close relationships in our church family. Friends gave us clothes and baby equipment, babysat, encouraged us, and always showed a keen interest in the children. We never felt anything but love and support from them. We are indebted to them for their prayers for us and for the children.

I had made friends with many of the checkers at WinCo supermarket, and several of them looked forward to meeting our newest foster babies as we shopped each week. They stopped their duties to admire the babies and always had kind-hearted words for our sons and the older foster children as well as benevolent curiosity for the steady steam of babies we brought in.

Applause also came from the social workers. I valued their esteem very highly because I respected them very highly. They were very thankful that they could rely on us to do our job, and they expressed that to us often. We came to have a reputation of having a safe home, being easy to work with, and being responsible. Our foster children only occasionally missed their medical and therapeutic appointments or their parental visits. We could be counted on to provide regular feedback about the children. We were interested in the children's lives and in the progress of their case plans, and we were supportive of the social worker's efforts in the child's life.

Foster care is strenuous and demanding. It requires an attitude of self-giving and a continuous outpouring of love and physical energy. I feel that God had built me up in my spirit and in my commitment to live a sacrificial life during those six years of waiting for it to come to pass. I relied on that foundation of personal relationship with Him and faith in the Word of God that He had built into me. My footing was on solid ground. I'm not saying I didn't falter and cry out to Him for help—that happened constantly, but I knew that I was 'called' by Him to the task, and I made use of all my resources.

My husband was a tower of strength. He figured out early on that the enemy would try to tear down our marriage by dividing and conquering. So we worked hard at our relationship. We came through all of the ups and downs, and there were many in the twelve years, even stronger and more devoted to each other. Praise the Lord.

Remember: seek God about doing foster care or adopting, endeavor to stay on the same page with your husband/wife, be prayerful about everything, respect your own children, and have a strong support group of people you trust. Please don't launch out on your own because you think it's a good idea or because your heart breaks for the poor little children.

When you work with older children, a fringe benefit is that they just might remember you. Christopher came to our front door one day, and David and I did not recognize him at first glance. When he introduced himself, the recognition was instantaneous! He said he had driven past our street many times and had finally gotten the courage to come to the door to see if he was remembering correctly where we lived and to see if we still lived there. He was 19 years old. The last time he had been in our house he was eight years old. He came in and visited with us for a half hour, and it was great to hear that he had graduated from high school, been involved in sports, and had his driver's license. He said he was debating about joining the military. It was so good to connect with him. That was seven years ago, and we have since moved from that house. What impacted me and brought me joy, besides the fact that he wanted to look us up, was that he was clear-minded, healthy, and really cared about his dad, his mom, and his siblings. He had a future before him and the real probability that he would not commit the same mistakes that his parents had made.

It was such a boost to welcome this young man into our lives once again, even for just a short thirty minutes. I believe I heard a gentle "well done" from the Lord, and I felt heartened about the 50 other children who had been with us. I had sealed the door on that part of our lives, and opening it and taking a peek inside reinforced all my positive memories.

A strong family foundation is necessary

We were a strong family unit going into fostering. We had been through some special adventures together, which I believe had bound us into a tight-knit troop. We had traveled across the United States when the boys were two, four, six, and seven, camping out, staying in motels, sweltering in Needles, California, basking in the spray of the falls at Niagara. We were re-locating to upstate New York so that Dan could attend a two-year Bible School missions program. We lived there for two-and-a-half years, one of our happiest seasons as a family.

From New York we drove a tiny motorhome (perched on a Toyota pickup) to the Carolinas, to visit Dan's grandfather and several of my relatives, then made our way back to New York to say our final goodbyes to our friends there. We pressed on through an early snowstorm to see Dan's Mom in a Chicago suburb, and then headed for Castle Rock, Colorado, driving in yet more inclement weather, and staying with friends for several days. We stopped for a short time in Reno, and then drove on to San Francisco, where we stayed for almost a year.

After the SF earthquake, we went to Pasadena and lived in the US Center for World Missions for a few months and then our friends, invited Dan to be the Missions pastor at their church. After about a year, the pastors in the San Francisco church we had attended called us and asked Dan to pastor their church because they were heading out to pastor another church. Dan met with the denomination supervisor, we prayed and sought counsel. Sensing the favor of the Lord to make the decision to live in the City again, we went back to SF, where we pastored the Foursquare church located in the downtown Civic Center area for one-and-a-half years.

After seven years away, we were ready to settle down, raise rabbits, and give our sons opportunities for lasting friendships and reunification with family and friends. Home meant Reno, Nevada. We rented a sprawling house out of the city limits in the high desert, and planted ourselves back in our home church. It was there, in church, that God made the vision plain, and we began foster care.

Settling in, I was happy to continue being an at-home mom, homeschooling the boys, cooking real food, baking muffins, and baking birthday cakes.

I was not a back-to-nature mom—gardening, canning, making our butter, sewing our clothes, and spinning our wool.

However, we had all our meals together at the dining room table, the boys did their chores, Dan and I prayed over them at night, we knew all of their friends, listened to all of their adventures, and we laughed together.

We spent all of the holidays with our relatives in Reno or with those in southern California. Our best friends were the parents of our kids' friends, and in those days our church was one of the hubs of all of our lives—Sunday morning, Sunday night, Wednesday nights, and youth groups.

When we started foster care, our sons were 9, 11, 13, and 14. I could see the Lord's wisdom in having us wait until they were older. They were homeschooled and we were in close relationships with other homeschool families and with the families in our church. Our sons' initial enthusiasm for the foster kids did wear off. We tried to be sensitive to their needs and not be continually overcome with the needs of our foster children. We sought to keep our kids' activities going strong, and we continued homeschooling them. During the first six years that we did foster care, Dan worked at home in his drafting business so he was involved with teaching them math and science, raising rabbits, camping, driving them to their sports practices and games, as well as to swimming pools, and to friends' homes. I focused on reading, language arts, Bible, homeschool group activities, as well as doing the foster kids' parent visits and doctor and therapy appointments. The boys helped with cooking and baking cookies, had a few chores, took care of feeding the animals, and had occasional Saturday weeding projects.

At one point, as teens, our sons all got guitars and worked diligently at teaching themselves to play, after some initial instructions from Dan. Danny was in some punk bands with his friends and they practiced in the garage. Tim and Steve started off in the garage, got serious about the hobby, and played in bands together consistently for many years, until just recently. Steve was sometimes in two or three bands at one time.

Tim, Mark, and Danny took up snowboarding and became instructors at Mt. Rose for a few winters. By that time Tim was able to drive them to and from the ski resort. Dan taught them all how to shoot, and they all took hunter safety class with him. They went on some hunting trips with Dan and their friends.

One thing that worked for us: every Friday for a few years we had a pizza and movie day—while the school-age kids were at school and the babies were napping. This was our family time together and it was fun for all of us.

We met for family meetings, sometimes associated with the pizza party afternoons, to keep in touch with what the boys were thinking and feeling. They had an opportunity to voice their gripes and grievances.

The boys were involved in various sports over the years. They worked for our church friends doing yard work and running errands, and then procured jobs in the community.

They were part of a great youth group at church and made many long-term friends. We were diligent to keep those relationships going because we genuinely enjoyed their friends and knew how important good friendships are.

Interestingly, our oldest son, Tim, and his wife, Jessica, did foster care for several years and adopted their first foster child, Quinn, who is awesome. Jessica has written an article in the second section of this book.

Biological parents visiting in our home

One of the main jobs of the foster parents is to get the child in her care to the scheduled visits with the biological parents. Cooperating with this is mandatory. The social worker will try to find a meeting time that works with the biological parents and the foster parent.

The visits are normally held in the social services visiting rooms. Sometimes the social worker will supervise the visit, especially in the initial stages of the child's fostering experience. Often a social services' aide or assistant or intern will be involved in the supervision of the visits.

Many times I was asked to stay with the child during the visit. I normally wanted to be in on the visit, especially if the social worker was going to be doing office work and would not be in the visitation room for the full hour. I always felt protective of my foster children, especially the babies, since I had stepped into the role of the primary caregiver. My challenge was to be friendly and helpful with the parent without being insensitive or domineering.

Our boys met many of the biological parents when we took the babies for visits at the social worker's offices. Several times we invited the parents into our home when it seemed appropriate. I've mentioned Duane and Nicole. We had them over for a barbecue after we had all gone to church together one Sunday.

I've introduced Freddie's grandmother, Nana, whose aim was to visit Freddie in our home about once a month during the time that Freddie was in our care.

We had a dear friend, Linda, whose grandson came into foster care. Her adopted daughter, Maggie, was having serious substance abuse problems and was mentally challenged. Linda requested that two-year old Brennan be placed in our home when he was removed from his mother's care. Linda knew that her daughter would not respect her decisions or her boundaries if she were to take Brennan to live with her, and that she had to let Brennan go to a place where he would be safe and where Maggie could not dominate his life and disregard the rules. Linda, the grandmother, visited Brennan weekly in our home and kept her relationship with him strong. She was a steadying influence in his life. She was very appreciative that we had opened our home to them.

Rather than have Maggie in our home to visit her son, I took Brennan to meet his mom in the social services office.

Brennan was eventually adopted by a family member. The adoption was set up so that Maggie had visitation rights and was included in the family gatherings. We found in this case that the family sincerely wanted their estranged family member restored to the family unit. Brennan's safety was the issue of their concern.

Once in a while, a situation would come up where the social worker saw the biological parents as safe, but I did not. My opinion was respected, and I was never expected to have a visit in my home or at a location other than the social services office in which I did not feel comfortable. A couple of times even though I did not feel completely comfortable, I consented to try meeting a biological parent in a off-site location. I would probably not do it these days, and it might even not be allowed.

Alan came to visit his son, Damien in our home but I was not really at ease, even though my four teenage sons were at home. Alan started ranting and took his anger toward the system out on me and gave me a verbal tongue-lashing. It felt scary to be screamed at, and I felt very vulnerable. The social worker was horrified at the parent's unexpected behavior and that was the last time we set up visits with Alan outside of the social services offices. Damien was an especially sweet baby boy who was adopted by a very loving couple who quickly became attached to him.

Visits with biological families in other places

When Juan and Patricia begged me to meet with their mother outside of office hours because of her work schedule, I relented. We chose a fast-food restaurant, and they happily ate French fries while we all visited. Maria was a very pleasant woman, but she did not seem very attached to her children, which was heartbreaking for me to watch. I wanted to do everything I could to promote their relationship, in hopes that her heart would change, so when she invited us to come to her apartment so she could cook some special meals for the children, I acquiesced. Her place was in a complex where I felt only marginally comfortable. It was a highlight of their lives for the children to spend time with their mom, so we went to her apartment more than once. Eventually, after only a couple of months, Maria faded away and dropped out of their lives. I felt very sad and disappointed, and the children were broken-hearted. I was very glad that I had been able to help them get some very positive memories of several good times with their mom.

In another situation, with another set of older foster children, we went to a nearby community to visit their grandmother. This meant that Meredith and Benny could also spend time with their younger siblings and their aunt and uncle. The situation was not ideal, so we did not go there many times, but I was glad we had made the effort. Unfortunately, things like this can make the foster kids feel homesick which can bring unhappiness and depression. They might remember that their foster parents took them to Grandma's house and that we made an effort to do something that was very important to them. I hope so.

I have to add one other unusual visit. The foster child's parent was incarcerated and she requested that her son come to see her. I agreed to go with some of the child's other relatives on a long drive to a remote prison in Nevada. It was an all day drive, but I was not willing that the child should experience the long journey without me, and I wanted to participate in the experience so I could help him process it. It was a stretch for me to be that brave, but Dan and I felt that it was important for the family reunification process. It was a positive experience, and I never regretted doing it. The family was very grateful. The child was under 3 years old, so she may not have much of a memory of it.

Grief and sadness when a child leaves us

You would think that losing a foster baby or a child to a good placement should be a time for enthusiastic rejoicing. But, in the majority of cases, the real feelings for me were: *"I was Mom to that little baby. Her Mom was unable to take care of her, and I stepped in to feed her, burp her, change her, cuddle her, keep her clothes clean, encourage her development, pray for her, get up with her night after night, take her to visit the doctors, the therapists, and her relatives. I gave her the quality care I gave my own children. I am experiencing some real pain!"*

Oops! Did I say that?? Yes I did, and my feelings meant that the attachment really happened, which was the goal, and now it was a bit of a struggle to get disentangled emotionally.

I felt very glad for the child to have a good placement, yet I keenly felt the heartache of the parting. There was a moment's loss. The worst part, as I mentioned before was:

The baby thinks that we are "Mommy and Daddy" and she will feel some abandonment and loss over this. Her little psyche has become attached to me, and my ways, just as I have become attached to her.

How did I cope? I told myself that I was the adult. I was the adult that had stepped in to rescue a very needy little person whose own mother was unable to take care of her. I was convinced that it was better for the baby to not be with her alcoholic or mentally challenged or homeless mother at this time. I believed in the foster care system. I hoped and prayed that if reunification was inappropriate or impossible, something else would work out for the baby. I did give my opinions to the social workers, and I did write a few letters to the judges, but if I did not agree with the final decision, I had to let it go. I only had so much power and control. And, I was also sure of my calling. I was to rescue babies, love them as my own, pray, trust God, and let them go.

Knowing that there would be another needy infant in a few days, hoping I would not have to wait very long, helped me get past the pain of loss. Looking at my wall of photos in our bedroom made me very happy.

When the little one was going to what we felt was a good adoption situation, we could only rejoice. Our baby would have her very own parents. If her birth parents were stuck in their addictions and could not work out their program then it was awesome for the child to have a place to go where people really wanted her and would be committed to raise her as their own.

Honestly, we did not attach as closely to some of the children as we did with others. One baby girl, about 6 months old, was with us less than 12 hours. Her Mother was a teen and had been picked up on the streets with her baby on a bitterly cold winter night. Janey came to us in a police car, and her Mom was taken to jail for the night. The next morning, the Mom's parents were contacted and they welcomed their daughter and their granddaughter into their home. In this situation, it was very exciting to be used to harbor a sweet little baby for a night because I was a nurturer. When the social worker called me the next morning, I had already called our pediatrician to get the baby physically evaluated and was setting up an appointment with WIC to get the formula. I had gone into autopilot and felt disappointment that we would not be able to provide Janey with more help.

I mentioned the two frightened little girls who were with us for about four months. They would not let us bond with them. They clung to each other, looked at us with big eyes, and kept to themselves during playtimes. They never acted out. They cooperated with us. But I wondered what trauma had put them in this reclusive and fearful state. I heard recently that they had been in several foster homes. They probably aged out of the system, which happens when a foster child turns 18. I believe the county has a program for helping the kids transition into society.

When the child was going into what I felt was a questionable family placement, I was open and straightforward with the social worker. Because I had seen placements work that had surprised me, I gave what input I could and stepped back. I said my prayers, but then I tried not to think about it.

I remember one situation in which my husband and I wrote some letters to the judge. We appealed to him on behalf of the child—we were her advocates. We gave our assessment of the case, and even pleadings, and we had 4 people lined up who were willing to give their opinions on the matter. We were not contacted, and we were overruled. We had to let go. We had felt conscience-bound to let our opinions be known. And, thankfully, the placement worked out very well for the next few years. There came a point where we lost track of the family, and perhaps that is better. You have to let go and you have to learn to live with the unknown. That is another reason I was glad I was in my 50's for my foster parenting experience. I had some maturity and a lot of faith. I was able to live with the loose ends.

Staying sensitive to your own children

Twice we made a call to the social worker that the foster child placement with us was not a good one and requested strongly that the child/children be moved. There can be a personality conflict between the foster child and the foster parent or a personality conflict between the foster child and the foster parent's children. When we saw that our four older sons were losing all of their excellent family spirit because a particular foster child was a continual annoyance to them, and all of our interventions failed, we had to listen and act. I think kids can feel they have no outlet and that they are missing the sanctuary of family life. The discontent simmered over several months, and we tried troubleshooting and making certain changes. It is not a good policy to have a home atmosphere that is full of resentments and bitterness. The social workers do not like to change the foster child's home. Before you make the call, be sure that it is an imperative move. It cannot be done nonchalantly or frivolously.

We had one experience that was very interesting. Our son, David's, younger half-sister, RaeAnn, came into the system. Her social worker was correct in ascertaining that we would want to meet RaeAnn and take care of her. We had some other foster children in our care at the time, so we needed to pass our three-month old baby to someone else so that we could fit RaeAnn into our household. Our friends Bob and Janet happily took Lily, our very sweet three-month old girl, so we could make room for RaeAnn, who was about the same age. We were very grateful to have the opportunity for David and our family to get to know his baby sister.

Because of David's immaturity we decided not tell him at that time that RaeAnn was his sister. He was about seven years old, but he was thinking as much younger, and he was severely emotionally delayed. We had already decided that we were not going to adopt another baby. RaeAnn was up for adoption and it was expected that she could be placed within six to eight months. Our feelings were that when David was older we would be able to explain that we could not pass up the chance to have RaeAnn with us while she was waiting to be adopted, but that we could not adopt her ourselves.

This is what we said to him later, when he was about 12:

Remember RaeAnn? She was your sister because she had the same father. (We had a picture, but he clearly remembered her.) She was so little when she came into the foster care system, and she needed a place to stay while Betty was finding a family to adopt her. We had already decided that we could not adopt any more children, but we were very happy for you two to get to know each other and become friends. So we took care of her for eight months. Remember that your friends Brennan and Cora and Calley lived with us then too? All of you had so much fun playing together. Maybe some day we can visit with RaeAnn. I will talk to Betty about it.

David did not need to have any more information than that. Too much information would have confused him. I did not want him to know the very bad incidents involved with the case, so I had to keep it simple. We talked about it many times and answered his questions as well as we could. A few years later he got angry with us and wanted to know where RaeAnn was living and why he could not see her. As parents, we need to make good decisions for the family and they are not always understood. We were able to reason with David and ask him— "Aren't you glad that we had her with us for a while? Perhaps you will meet her someday. When we feel it is the right time, we will try to make it happen." Just recently we have emailed Betty, the social worker in the case, to request a visit between the families.

Boundaries we observed:

1. Someone advised us before we began fostering: never take a child that is older than your youngest child. Not everyone had this rule. In two families, one of their own children was molested by an older foster child. Consider that foster children may have come from years of abuse and neglect, possibly violence, and probably chaos. They may not have the code of honor that your family embraces. We prayed over every social worker's call before we took a placement. We were proactive to have a foster child removed if we felt our own children were threatened by them or were at risk.

2.   One tradition we developed in order to keep our own kids positive, was having a celebration when a child left—we would have a special dinner or dessert and get a video. We were not big TV watchers or big dessert eaters--so this was a treat. It gave us some closure, and it was a way to reward the whole family for a job well done.

3.   Another very important rule at our house: we did not expect our sons to be involved in the care of the foster child beyond holding the baby for a bottle occasionally, or putting on shoes and socks, or buckling them in a car seat, or strolling them in the stroller. They never changed a diaper. They never gave baths. They did not dress the toddlers or the babies or anyone ever. That was my husband's and my job. They never had to baby sit any foster children while we went on errands. We always took the foster children with us. We did not want to build resentment against the foster children in our sons' hearts by requiring them to parent them. These rules were also for their protection and they were not sliding rules, but were firm rules. Of course the boys were perfectly happy not to be required to give any more care than a bottle-feeding or a spooning of some cereal or pushing them in the shopping cart. We have pictures of our sons' smiling faces as they are giving bottles to babies or holding them while I am fixing dinner. When they lost interest in helping, we made adjustments. They grated the cheese, chopped the veggies, baked the chocolate chip cookies, and Dan and I tended the children.

We believe that it is important for children to be involved and contributing to the family calling and the family function; to be givers, not just takers. But as parents we used discretion and our good judgment.

We did ask our sons to play board games and baseball in the front yard with the older foster children—and that worked for a quite a while. However, when we saw that they were begrudging these requests, we switched our focus to newborn care, thereby relieving them of the responsibility of entertaining the kids.

What we realized was that children are not normally altruistic. Altruism is "the principle or practice of unselfish concern for the welfare of others. www.dictionary.reference.com I believe that altruism is a mature attitude that is acquired. We did not want to kill all of the possibility of our sons becoming altruistic in their adult years by stealing their childhood with our altruism. Today all of our sons care about people and are well adjusted, and I believe they have worked through any resentments they formed in those foster care days.

Coping with the issues of the parents

We tried to treat the biological parents in a friendly manner, without negative or prejudicial judgment. Sometimes it's very hard to stay non-judgmental. Such as:

- when the foster parent believes that the foster child is in mild or serious danger when he is with the biological parents. Even if the parent and the child are in a visiting room at the social worker's office, the parent may be someone who acts odd, or may be acting oddly that day. The foster parent may worry that the biological parent will not be able to handle the baby or will get impatient when the baby gets fussy. Even concern that the parent may be rough when changing a messy diaper, changing the outfit if it gets soiled, or that she may over-feed the baby or force the baby to finish the bottle. These are the sorts of issues that can come up, and they can be emotionally distressing. A foster parent is bonded with the baby/child and is very invested in the child's safety.
- when the child comes back from a visit smelling like cigarette smoke or when the child gets sick because the biological parent was sick at the visit.
- when the child is asthmatic and the parent is a smoker.
- when the biological parent brings candy or cokes and lets the child have as much as they want. Many of us have experienced the biological parent bringing food and presents to try to win back their child's affections. They often will make promises to take the child to Disneyland or buy her a dog when they get back together or get the child's hopes up in other ways.
- when the foster parent disagrees with the social worker's decisions. This can be a problem, because in some instances the foster parent can feel that the social worker is off base in her estimation of the case. The foster parent has to be careful to not ally with the biological parent against the social worker. This can cause lots of problems and is very unprofessional. I had some challenges in this area, especially as a new foster parent.

We tried to treat the biological parents with kindness and with encouragement in our dealings with them:

Remembering my own failings and that if life had been just a little different, the tables could be turned, and I could be the one struggling and slipping and failing so badly.

Remembering that this person is the biological parent of the innocent child and for that reason needs respect—if only to honor the child who had nothing to do with the situation and is the blameless bystander.

Hoping that if the child is old enough and has enough visits with her biological parent, she will eventually 'see' her parent realistically rather than in the protective fantasy that she has imagined. Foster children tend to have a positive view of their biological parents without regard as to how well their parents are behaving towards them. Hopefully the foster parents' personality, habits, and home life demonstrate to the foster child that there is a better way than her parent's way of coping. Hopefully she will want to choose for her own lifestyle the better way of the family that is modeled before her.

When I say a 'better way' I am speaking of a life without drug dependence, domestic violence, alcoholism, physical and verbal abuse, and other things that break up families, hurt people, and are destructive. I mean a family life where all the members respect one another and work hard at being kind and forgiving, and one in which people listen to one another and do not put each other down.

These were our standards; a home life built on respecting one another.

When a parent filed a report against me

I have not mentioned Ross. He was a baby boy, I picked up from the hospital one snowy afternoon. He had had multiple injuries inflicted on his body. I had only been a foster parent for one-and-a-half years. He was three months old. The case was serious, and emotionally charged. My heart went out to the little boy as I was shown a photograph of his injuries taken by an angry nurse when he had arrived at the hospital before his wounds had been tended and before his legs had been put in casts. I was given instructions for medical home care and instructed to take him to follow-up appointments with our pediatrician.

After Ross had been in our home for several months, it was the biological dad who brought the complaint against me because he felt that I had a disagreeable and prejudicial attitude about him. I remember that this was our first case in which a child came to us as a result of obvious physical abuse. Not having dealt with this type of scenario, and having never suffered any abuse myself, I was deeply distressed, and it contributed to a bad attitude towards this person. He picked up on my bad attitude (i.e., judgment) and filed a complaint against me with the social worker. Our social worker passed the complaint on through the channels of the system.

I was extremely nervous when my husband and I were called in for an appointment with one of the administrators, Marlene. I called a few people to pray for us and that brought me some peace. Marlene was a little foreboding at first, but as we spoke she could see that we were not argumentative or armed for battle. We did not try to defend ourselves, but we were reasonable. I wrote in my notes later that I was able to think clearly and speak clearly during the appointment. The biological Dad did not want his son removed from our home. He trusted us and was happy with us as caregivers. He wanted behavior change from me in my attitude toward him. I could do that for the sake of this toddler. I apologized to him when I saw him at the next visit.

Because the administrator had been a foster parent herself, she understood the biological dad's position and my position. She spoke very candidly about what my professional attitude should be and as we talked she knew that I would respond to her admonition. She and I ended on a very friendly note, and we have had a positive relationship ever since. When I dropped my judgmental attitude, the dad and I got along fine, and we had Ross in our care for a year and a half.

During the 12 years we fostered, I had several positive experiences of sticking with a child who had difficult parents and was very glad that I did. Over time, trust can develop. I found that when judgment ruled, love was extinguished. No one likes to be judged, most people want to be accepted.

When we are willing to let go of our own anger and control, healing can happen on many levels. It is important to remember that people can change. Sometimes a tragic event will precipitate deep inner searching. Forgiveness is a healer. I had to let go of my indignation and self-righteousness. I had to forgive the offenders deeply, in the way I prefer to be forgiven when I mess up. Receiving forgiveness can set a person free. I had many excellent relationships with birth parents that expressed thanks to me for how well they could see their child was doing in our care. It was fun to see birth parents relax and their defenses come down when we treated them with respect week after week.

On the other hand, we must be very discerning. My friends and I had some experiences of being afraid that an irate or unstable parent would follow us home from a visit and try to take the child or cause a disturbance. We were careful and prayerful for each other. Thankfully nothing happened to any of us. I believe our safety was another result of the adventure of a prayerful life.

Foster parent/social worker relationships

This was our philosophy and this was what worked out for us:

The child was the central focus in the fostering endeavor. The county had a system which was set up so that children in distress had a safe and secure place to live while their adults were getting their lives together. I, the foster parent, worked for the county and cared for the children in my care as if they were my own children. I considered the social worker to be the authority figure in our partnership. I had a voice in the relationship and it was vital for both of us that we kept the lines of communication open at all times.

There were rules and regulations set into the foster care framework. The social worker also had the courts to comply with and a supervisor that she worked closely with. She depended upon me to provide excellent care for the child. We looked to each other to be cooperative.

This relationship worked best in an atmosphere of mutual respect.

Dan and I worked very hard at respecting the social workers. When we started foster parenting, I was just turning 48. We adopted David when I was 50. We retired when I was 60. We understood the principle of authority. Dan and I did not have the mindset that it was our role to challenge the authority structure. We were happy that someone else had the final authority and the major responsibility for the case. Foster parenting was our job and the social workers were our bosses.

Respect is the Magic Word

We dealt with over 40 social workers in the twelve years that we did foster care. Since we often had several children at a time, we dealt with multiple social workers at the same time.

Most of the social workers had over 30 cases in their caseload.

As I mentioned, I kept in touch with the social workers by phone and by email. I wanted them to know the results of parent visits and doctor visits as soon as possible, so I would leave detailed phone messages, which I often followed up with an email. That was the first way I showed respect. I was saying, "I understand that you are very busy and so that you will understand what is going on, I will accommodate you and do what I feel is my job by keeping you in the loop." I got a lot of positive feedback from this habit.

It is good to remember that as a foster Mom, or Dad, I am not the boss in my relationship with the social worker. Even if I am older than the worker, which I usually was, I did not have seniority in the relationship. Even if I had been a foster parent longer than they had been a social worker (which happened lots of times), I was not the person in charge.

There will be times when the foster parent will have a differing opinion than the social worker. It is inevitable. We are two adults from different backgrounds and with different temperaments, working on a common job together.

One of us, the social worker, is in the office with the paperwork and the court-mandated responsibilities, and the other, the foster parent, is in the home with the child.

One sees the child one to four times a month, sometimes less, and the other is with the child 24/7.

One is very involved with the parents, keeping them on track with their case plan, and helping them fulfill their reunification requirements, whereas the other only sees the biological parents at the child's visits and possibly at doctor appointments.

I certainly have a brain, which I use, and I had my opinions, which I often shared. The very best thing I can do is to be respectful in my interactions. Am I insisting on my own way? Am I barging in with my definite opinions? Do I harbor mean and critical thoughts in my heart, thoughts that will be sensed or will eventually come out? I need to constantly check my heart.

Relationships are always challenging! In my relationships with my husband, my children, my friends, and social services, debates and disagreements will arise. If my standard is respecting other people, things will have a tendency to go smoothly even if I am having a bad day or the other person is having a bad day.

If 'respect for others' is in my personality, or if **I** am having a bad day, at least I will feel guilty and be able to apologize and try to set things right.

At my age, I usually find apologizing easy—I have had so much practice at it!

Another rule, or standard, is working hard to not to take offense. A person who is overly sensitive and who is always offended is very difficult to deal with and ends up being a very negative individual. It is best to try not to take offense, to forgive, to think through it, to come to some rational conclusions, and to move on, hopefully wiser. This is where your support group comes in so you can talk things out.

If communication with the social worker is difficult and you seem to be hitting a 'brick wall', consider making an appointment with the social worker's supervisor. These men and women have had field experience and they also have authority. They can mediate and they can go higher up the administrative ladder if it should become necessary. They may just look you in the eye and say, "I understand," when you share about the difficulties you are experiencing with a social worker. This may mean that they are aware of the worker's personality quirks and are monitoring him.

The foster parent is a very important cog in the machine. (Using the cog as an illustration came from a friend, Linda.)

The online dictionary reads: *a cog is a wheel or bar with a series of projections on its edge that transfers motion by engaging with projections on another wheel or bar.* www.oxfordreference.com

Imagine a machine, which functions because many various-sized cogs are turning in their places.

If my cog has broken teeth on it, which could be thought of as an abrasive personality or defensiveness, it is not going to mesh with the other cogs. If the social worker has broken teeth on her cog, or if the foster parent has broken or bent teeth on her cog, she will not mesh, and the intended functioning of the cogs will not occur. For the fostering machine to work smoothly, the cogs need to be well oiled in kindness and respect, and the individuals need to take care of their malfunctioning parts and work hard at getting along with each other.

As I said, I tried to keep in close contact with the social worker. I would email any changes in the child's wellbeing, as well as the results of the parent visits and the doctor appointments. I consistently emailed updates about the child so that he would be apprised of any possible difficulties before they became major obstacles. No one ever told me I was bugging him. Most were thankful to be kept informed. Even if one had told me I was bugging him, I would have continued so that everything was documented. If questions arose, we could refer to the emails.

Foster children are very needy

Foster children are very needy. They have normal childhood issues compounded by what feels to them like parental rejection and abandonment. The circumstances of children being detached from their parents was most likely acutely traumatic, however it happened. It may have involved a fracas with the police if the parents had to be removed from the home forcibly, which would have left the children confused and frightened. Other policemen might have driven them to Safe Haven in the middle of the night, where they would have been with complete strangers, and probably separated from their siblings.

We found that even if the children were removed from conditions of verbal and physical abuse and extreme neglect which they were experiencing in living with their parents, they were typically devoted to their parents and keenly felt the loss and a sense of destitution. They had been moved out of their home and their familiar neighborhood, and may have had to change schools. They may have lost their relationships with their grandparents, cousins, aunts and uncles, friends, pets, and toys. Everything that they were acquainted with was gone. Even if it was in their best interest for them to be in foster care, the adjustment was going to take time.

If the child is able to go to an approved close relative, it can be somewhat less traumatic for the child. But a relative placement is very often NOT ideal. Those relatives may have their own serious issues, and the child needs to be protected.

In a relative placement, the biological parent may dominate the relationship and it might not be a good arrangement at all. What if the child goes to Aunt Lena? It sounds good, that a dear child would be adopted and raised by her aunt. Aunt Lena has a great job and an upright reputation. But she may be under the control of her abusive sister who is the child's mother.

We had a situation with a baby I'll call Angel. Angel was in our home for two years and we became very attached to her. When a relative was located who fit all of the qualifications for being an approved placement, we were very happy for Angel. We met the relative and liked her very much. After a short transition, Angel went away with her to another state. We heard from the social worker that Angel's Mom, who had never completed her case plan and who had been disqualified from reuniting with her baby, had quickly moved into the Angel's new situation and said, "Thank you very much, I'll take my daughter now!" There is no way that something like that can be foreseen. We had some news about Angel ten years ago, and her situation had vastly improved. What happened after that, we do not know.

The transition into a foster home can take the child a significant amount of time. Everything is new. Sometimes there are cultural differences, such as when Tia and Juan and Patricia came into our home. The food is different, the language is different, and the music is different. But love and patience and time can make inroads into frightened hearts.

As years go by, and a foster child is not placed in an adoptive home or reunited with her parents there might be more than one placement, sometimes several. This is very sad, and no one wants this to happen. As I mentioned, sometimes children are in foster care until they 'age out of the system,' which means that they turn 18 while still in foster care. And that is beyond the scope of this book.

Reasons foster children change foster homes

During the time that we were foster parents, we were aware of these situations which necessitated the foster child being moved to another foster home:

- the foster parent retired
- the foster parent died
- the foster parent developed health issues
- the foster parents moved out of state
- the foster parents wanted to adopt their foster child but were rejected for some reason and moved out of the system, heart-broken
- the foster parents found that there was a clash of personalities—between their own children and the foster children
- the foster parent decided that the child was too difficult for them to handle
- the foster parents' child was molested by the foster child

- the foster parents' child molested the foster child
- the foster parents retired and their foster children were reassigned to other homes in the system
- the foster child got very sick and had to be moved to a home where specialized nursing care could be provided

This list goes on and on. You can see that there are tragic realities that necessitate a child being moved from one foster home to another one. Dismal stories of foster children moved from home to home are, unfortunately, not uncommon. In our family's experience, and in our friends' experiences, the decision to move a child out of our homes was made very carefully.

Part III - Our adoption experience, with insights

The Adoption Process

When David came into the care of Washoe County Department of Child and Family Services in 1994, his social worker, Hayley, was an investigative social worker. Her responsibilities included court appearances to keep the legal system informed about David's case, and locating and maintaining contact with David's parents. She also interacted with us, visiting our home to make sure we were keeping our standards of home maintenance and giving careful supervision to David. If she had seen or suspected anything going on that was dangerous for David, she would have removed him from our home. She made sure we were attending his appointments at Special Children's Clinic and following through with their suggestions. She expected us to keep David's well-baby checks with the pediatrician. Sometimes she came to our home (a 25-minute drive), and often we met her at her office.

When it became apparent that David would be remaining in the system (because neither of his parents were able to take care of him), our case was transferred to another social worker, Wendy, who was an 'ongoing' social worker. Her job was to carry the case until David was successfully reunified with his parents or adopted, according to the court's time limit. If we had not become interested in adopting him, Wendy would have searched for a person or a couple whose goal was be adoptive parents, determined their qualifications, and eventually taken David to meet them. The prospective adoptive parents might have been a foster couple who was hoping to adopt, or someone whose application was in the files of the adoption unit. If the adoption team determined that the person or couple would be appropriate to be David's parents, David would have been transitioned into their home.

We were not going to let go of our little boy! We had all fallen in love with him and already considered him part of our family.

Prior to finalizing David's adoption, we were given access to David's files. We met with Wendy, asked lots of questions, took notes, and were given as much information as she could legally give us.

Unfortunately, there was no information about David's parents' health history. Sometimes birth parents choose not to reveal this information, and that was the case with David's parents.

We were invited to meet with the adoption specialists. They discussed the adoption process, and they warned us that when David reached school age he would probably have serious problems because that was when learning disabilities surfaced. They assured us that counseling would be available to him.

We continued to receive $385 a month from Washoe County through David's 18th year. When we began fostering, in 1994 that was the wage that was paid per child. The checks continued without interruption. We were always thankful for that envelope to arrive in the mail.

We were allotted a $200 allowance to use for our adoption attorney's fees. We were thankful for the stipend and very thankful for the fact that our attorney, a friend, did not charge us any fees beyond that.

Our social workers and the adoption specialists emphasized that there had been many occurrences of adoptive parents attempting to give their adopted children back to the system. It broke their hearts as social workers, and they made sure we understood that the adoption would be a finalized legal agreement. You may be shocked to think that anyone would give their adopted child back, but unless you have walked in the shoes of an adoptive parent, please reserve judgment.

On David's adoption day, our family and the foster children that were in our home, went to the judge's chambers. Hayley, Michelle, and Wendy were all present and ecstatic for David and for our family. Our attorney was in attendance as well. Our three school-aged foster children had just come up for adoption and they had worried themselves almost sick about what the adoption process entailed. We wanted them with us in order to diffuse some of their fears. The judge said some kind words of congratulations and affirmed us in our fostering and adoption calling. Afterwards Dan's brother met us at an ice cream parlor to celebrate our happy family day.

Changes in our family dynamics

We moved into town from the rural setting in our third year of foster care.

Our family was made up of our five sons—Tim, Steve, Mark, Danny, and David and five foster children; Jane, Meredith, Benny, Johnny, and a little baby named Joey. We were looking for a place for twelve of us.

Dan's father believed in what we were doing by taking in the foster children and he supported our plan to eliminate the long drives on Pyramid Highway and move into town. He offered to help us by giving us the down payment for a house, which we gratefully accepted.

We found a 2,400 square-foot house in a good part of town that met all of our needs. It was near social services, near our church, near our favorite grocery store, and near a WalMart. It had a huge backyard with a swing set for David and the younger foster children.

Our sons were growing up, and we were aware that it was time for them to have their own space and their own activities. They needed independence and autonomy. It became difficult to try to meet all of the needs of all the different age groups. Our own children were our first responsibility and we knew we could not lose sight of that.

In our fifth year of fostering we made the decision to take only newborns, although during the next six years we did take one or two older babies who were difficult to place. Our sons had been 'involved' in the beginning, and 'good sports' in the middle, and we liberated them for the remainder of our fostering years.

As the months went on, our foster children were placed in adoptive homes or in relative placements, and we began to receive the newborn babies.

This new resolve excused me from supervising school-age foster children's homework, from going to school activities, and from the parent conference. I was not necessarily adverse to these duties, because when I became a foster parent I was committed to doing what I could for the children in our care. I cared about them and wanted to help them. But when you are pulled too thin, the joy goes away, and working from a sense of obligation can become a strain.

Brothers invested, brothers left home

David's brothers invested a lot of love into David. In the early years they helped him to learn to walk and talk and become a social human being. They played Legos, made cardboard-brick towers, taught him how to throw and catch a ball. They played with him across the street in the schoolyard on the playground equipment, flew kites, and tossed Frisbees to him.

Every one helped and cheered as David learned to ride a bike, roller skate, and skateboard. They read to him, laid out the wooden Brio train tracks, worked on chemistry experiments, set up the slip-n-slide and the above-ground swimming pool in our backyard, built snowmen, took him sledding on nearby hills. They tumbled with him on the grass, went to his birthday parties, and bought him Christmas presents.

When all the boys still lived at home, we went on road trips to my Dad's house in southern California, and visited our relatives there. We journeyed to Disneyland, Yosemite, Sequoia, San Francisco Exploratorium, and Golden Gate Park. We drove north to Oregon and Washington, sightseeing and having family time.

The boys' friends were around a lot, and they seemed to genuinely like David. Dan organized a summer teen event at our church for four years called Impact Reno. We pastored a youth church for four years. David had a lot of socialization and a lot of acceptance. We had challenges when we would say **no** to something he wanted to do, because he did not like to hear **no**. We had disagreements over which of the kids he could hang out with and which ones he could not.

Each year our four older sons spent a week at Old Oak Ranch, a church summer camp. They were camp counselors, and three of them spent entire summers on staff at the camp. In time, they enrolled in community college, obtained their driver's licenses, got jobs, taught snowboarding, played in garage bands, hung out at friends' houses, found girlfriends—and then, for three of them, came marriage and having their own families. David was in Tim's, Mark's, and Danny's weddings.

This happened over several years of course, but little by little the boys moved on, and David had trouble accepting that. He missed them terribly, and spoke in terms that indicated he thought they had abandoned him. He became angry about it. That anger came out usually when he was angry about something else, and then he would bring up the fact that all his brothers had gone away and he was still unhappy about it.

Homeschooling David

We had homeschooled our four sons from kindergarten until they went to community college at 16 or 17. (Tim went to public school one year when we lived in upstate New York.) We never considered that we would do anything else but homeschool our son David.

David's development during these years was complicated by fetal alcohol syndrome. He had been seen at Special Children's Clinic from the age of two months old until he was almost four years old. Then it was advised and expected that he would go to Marvin Piccolo Elementary School with otheralmost-4-year-old graduates of Special Children's Clinic, as well as other special needs children in the community. We had the philosophy that children did better at home with family. Time proved that we made the right decision for our son.

When we began teaching David to read and write, we were of course aware that he learned very slowly, and we knew that he had learning challenges, but we were committed to working with him every day, moving along at his pace. When he was young we had compact teaching sessions. He was very developmentally delayed and his attention span was short. We believed that the one-on-one instructional setting and our patient perseverance, as well as our commitment to his success, would eventually compensate for his learning difficulties. We also felt that all of our extracurricular input into his life would give him experiences that would help him mature and learn.

I helped David with his reading, language arts, penmanship, social studies, and art, and read aloud to David several times a week. We used lots of hands-on learning materials. We used tactile and manipulative resources: clay, sandpaper letters, felt board, puzzles, blocks, and stickers. I came up with various reward systems, games, and incentives, and bought a special reading program.

David's learning happened with lots of repetition and it happened slowly. David would also regress and have to re-learn letters, sounds, and words. Day after day I paid him a penny for each word he could read from our stacks of word cards. I figured he was also learning the work ethic—i.e., work hard at remembering and reading your word cards, and you will earn some compensation. He had a lot of success with remembering, and he cooperated because he was instantly rewarded with pennies. Once or twice a week we went up the hill to WalMart to spend his 'pay.'

Dan found the same thing to be true in math. He made up most of his own work sheets, used real money, and lots of manipulatives. David was a kinesthetic learner so Dan did hands-on science experiments, which David enjoyed.

David had always been interested in all aspects of nature, and Dan explained geological features on their hikes and on our trips, just as Dan's dad had done with him, and just as Dan had done for our other sons.

An interesting thing happened when he was six or seven years old. David began to teach himself to tell time on the standard clock in the kitchen. He would ask the time, or guess the time and ask if he was correct. We were really encouraged by this. He motivated himself, because it was important to him. He learned through his own drive and ambition how to tell time on a standard clock. Digital clocks are more difficult for him to read, even now. Norris Dupree, one of David's therapists, called this spotty intelligence: David's brain worked at times in surprising ways.

David was also an auditory learner, and Dan read some of the classics to David in the evenings—*Treasure Island, Kidnapped,* and *The Chronicles of Narnia.* David listened avidly to these stories and lots of others. Dan read some of the dialogue portions with an English accent or a pirate's voice. David had clear understanding of the stories and asked questions when something was confusing. He could not read them himself but he could listen and comprehend. He had excellent listening skills and picked up big words easily and used them. Later, in academic testing, his comprehension and vocabulary scores were his highest marks. We were really encouraged by this skill.

We had heard that it was when the FAS child reached school age that the deficits in his mental capacity would become very evident. We found this to be true. We had plugged away for years in our daily homeschooling routine, and we made progress, as I said, up to a point. David was still doing second grade work at age twelve.

During his twelfth year is when life became very difficult. He began to oppose us on all fronts, but especially during school. We kept thinking that if we just kept at our patient pace, with our innovative methods, David would learn. It was frustrating to us when, at about the middle of our second grade reading and math curriculums, he just stopped making any progress. (It was soon after this that we sought and found counseling help with John Trentalange.) Subsequent efforts by his reading and math tutors and by professional educators were just as fruitless.

We didn't understand that David had reached the potential of his FAS brain. Today, he is 21, and reading is a challenge for him. It is a great grief in his life and has brought him a lot of heartache.

David's behavior in Sunday School and the Sunday night kids' group, Life Force, was very good. He cooperated in swimming lessons. He was good at the library, but not consistently good with me at the grocery store. In fact, it became apparent that he was good for everyone but us. This is typical insecure attachment behavior. (discussed in the Attachment article in Part VI)

When David decided that he did not want to participate with our plan or our instruction, he was stubborn. He would oppose us and become defiant. We saw this beginning about age seven. Once in a while, when I said **no**—"No you cannot have a cookie, it is time to eat dinner"--"No you can't go with your brother, he is going to work" – he would turn on me and accuse me of hating him. At first it happened once in a while and randomly. Sometimes he would bring me to tears. Several times I called Dan at work. Occasionally Dan would come home and relieve me. By the time David was 12, his accusations were a daily occurrence and increasingly upsetting to me. In this season we took a long break from foster care. One day I called social services and told Kristy that we had decided to retire.

<u>David's relationships</u>

These years were very frustrating for all of us.

I felt insecure about taking David to the homeschool field trips and other activities because I could not count on his cooperating with me. His thinking was very mixed up. Plus he had some significant hygiene issues, which is also an FAS symptom, which were very embarrassing. We tried to give him incentives to wash carefully and brush his teeth, and other things, but he was very stubborn about cooperating, so we were home a lot.

We were happy when he would play with the next-door neighbor girls, but there were often disagreements because he felt they were bossy. Well, they <u>were</u> bossy, but also pretty patient and very nice. They would play with him for a while, on our front porch or in our back yard, or in Marianna's or Lupe's front yards. Very soon they would realize that he could not do some of the projects that involved cutting, counting, reading, and playing school. He would become disagreeable (because he felt stupid), and they would go home or run away from him. He would try to join them again later, but would experience the same outcome. It was very frustrating for them all.

We tried letting David ride his bike in the neighborhood because he insisted that he be able to do it. We learned very quickly that he could not handle the responsibility to stay in the designated area that we lined out for him in front of our house and the houses on each side of us. After he took a few experimental excursions, we gave up on letting him ride his bike without one of us standing on the sidewalk and watching him. We soon realized that David had no discernment about which were good kids to be around and which were not. He was easily led by stronger personalities. This is typical FAS behavior. This is when he began to fabricate fantastical stories that he made sound so convincing we would wonder if they were true. We could not trust him to tell us the truth about his activities when he was apart from us. This is another FAS symptom. We had to keep David in close proximity.

Our friends, Dave & Kathy, had a great idea and set up an adoption playgroup. Unfortunately it was short-lived. I think it would have worked if all of us parents had taken turns supervising the kids while others got a break to do some errands. I could not imagine leaving my difficult child in a room with other possibly difficult children that he might conspire with—or with nice children that he might become angry with.

During this time period David would threaten to run away from home, and one time he took off running across the street and down the block. His brother, Steve, happened to arrive at our house in time to see David bolt. Steve quickly parked his car and took off running after David. Dan and I watched them from the front porch, big brother with his arm around little brother's shoulders, reasoning with him to come home. It was a very touching moment, and David came home.

Trouble!

A few months before David turned 13, he got in trouble with the law. Before the police arrived at our house, we had a chance to talk to him and pray with him. Around midnight, he was handcuffed and taken away. He spent the night in juvenile hall. We emailed our sons, my sisters, Dan's brother and his wife, and two or three friends, and asked them to pray. We went to court the next morning, bleary-eyed after only a couple of hours sleep. Is anyone ever prepared for legal entanglements?

We could not imagine our young, sheltered, troubled son, spending time in jail. We prayed, and took our places in the courtroom, with no opportunity to meet or talk to David's public defender before or after the trial. We did not know the man's name nor did we ever see him again. We were sitting there in shock trying to fathom that David would be going to jail.

We believe a true miracle occurred because David's attorney asked the judge to put David on house arrest since he was young and homeschooled. The Judge mercifully agreed, and after court we were able to take him home with the condition that we would keep him under strict supervision, and in our line-of-sight.

With tears in my eyes I silently thank the Judge who compassionately ruled in a righteous manner many times over the years that David was on probation. David has received so much mercy from the Lord, and we are so thankful.

In the days previous to this event, we had become deeply concerned over David's increasingly disturbing behavior. We had been feeling desperate about securing more intensive family counseling. We wanted to figure out what we were doing right and what we were doing wrong.

We had been searching online for an attachment specialist. We had heard the term 'radical attachment disorder'(RAD) and we wondered if David fit in this category. We needed to understand it and get help.

In our online search, Dan had aphone interview with one therapist whose counseling procedure was to live in the client's home for a couple of weeks in order to observe everyone's behavior. Living temporarily in the thick of the family dynamics he could counsel them and give them advice. After Dan shared our story about David, the therapist candidly told him that he was usually used for much more serious cases of radical attachment disorder (RAD). He suggested we keep looking. We were grateful for his integrity and we thanked God that David was not as difficult as some of this man's clients seemed to be.

New parenting skills from John Trentalange LPC

We continued searching online and found an attachment therapist in Colorado Springs, John Trentalange, LPC (Licensed Professional Counselor). Dan talked to him on the phone a few times, and found him compassionate, and received excellent advice. Another miracle in court that day was that the Judge gave us permission to keep the counseling appointment we had set up with John before David got into trouble.

We drove to Colorado Springs and took with us a young woman who was a friend of our family. Her purpose was to be with David during the hours Dan and I were in counseling sessions with John. After our morning session we would pick them up and go to lunch, then drop her off at the motel, and continue the family counseling with David included.

We made time to have some fun in Colorado Springs. David was hugely interested in airplanes and the military. We went the Air Force Academy museum. We also went to some tourist sites and took turns choosing our restaurants.

Dan and I both took detailed notes on everything John said over the three-day period. Dan and I were learning that our parenting methods had been working against us. We realized that we needed brand new tools for working with our son and holding our family together.

David was pretty confused and upset, still processing that he had been handcuffed, taken away in a police car, spent a night in jail, and was now on house arrest. The upheaval had happened so quickly for all of us—and in that season life seemed to be moving almost out-of-control in the fast lane so that all of our heads were spinning. As I looked back in my journal to write this, I wondered that we all survived the intensity of those days without a breakdown or a blowup.

In my journal, I noted the highlights of our counseling sessions with John:

David can think as an adult at times, yet at other times he functions like a small child.

He has attachment disorder, but not RAD (Radical Attachment Disorder).

He may have anxiety disorder.

John's advice:

1. Make a concentrated effort to slow down, which may mean giving up pastoring your youth church and Dan taking a sabbatical from the university (Dan was pursuing his Master's Degree in order to become a marriage and family therapist).

2. Dan and David and I should bond and connect, taking a break from everything to do it—perhaps closing our church and even pulling back in our role as grandparents in order to focus on David.

3. Homeschool needs to significantly change.

We began to immediately experience defusing of power struggles because, following John's specific suggestions, we no longer engaged in them! That in itself was life-changing. (see the article about John's advice in Part VI)

<u>God's guidance and our decision</u>

While driving home to Reno from Colorado Springs, Dan spotted a billboard advertisement in one of the small Nevada towns that said "TOTAL CONNECTION." He said, "That's prophetic." He felt that the Lord was using the words on the sign to reinforce John's advice to slow down our lives and focus on our relationship with David. We needed to aim for closer connection with David.

The next day while we three were praying together, David prayed: "I want to know more about You, God, and I want You to help me be better." (June 7, 2006, my journal) I believe that was David's true heart. He had been brought up to have a relationship with Jesus and to get along with people and be obedient. He was overcome with his weaknesses and knew he was off-course, but he knew that God was his answer.

In prayer, I got a picture of a scene I had observed when we were in Nepal the previous year. It was of a huge valley between two TALL mountain ranges. The valley was green and lush, with a river running through it. I felt that we three needed to cross over the valley from one mountain range to the other—but there was no bridge! And then I saw, as if in a prophetic moving picture, that <u>as we walked along together in faith with our eyes on the Lord, the board planks of the bridge were miraculously appearing under our feet</u>

<u>with each step</u>. It looked like a mile-long bridge would be needed for the journey across the valley, and we were very high above the valley floor. It was daunting, and I felt a sense of apprehension. What I felt I was sensing from the Lord was that God wanted us to begin walking together and doing what John Trentalange had said: to stop everything to save David. God was assuring me that as we walked by faith in Him, He would be with us and lead us. I did not at that time get any assurances that it would be easy. I felt that it was a step of obedience that was placed before us for our choice.

In another prayer time, I felt like God said, "I am driving you into the desert." I did not feel like He was banishing us, but I felt He was encouraging us to get away, drive away, change our surroundings, and that He would be with us. As Dan and I prayed together, we decided to purchase a motor home and drive into the deserts of Nevada and Arizona for the winter. We would work on building our relationship with David and on holding our family together. We all liked camping and hiking and traveling. Driving away from Reno would remove all the distractions in our lives and we could focus on putting John's advice to the test.

<u>Moving into the motorhome</u>

We had retired from foster care. We closed our youth church within the next few weeks, explaining to our very special group of kids that we needed to work full-time on holding our family together. Dan decided he would take two semesters off from his master's degree program, and we put a down payment on a motor home with money we had in savings.

We knew we needed to take radical steps. We felt that getting out of town and away from everything familiar would put us all in a new frame of thinking and enable us to practice wholeheartedly what we were learning. We hoped to prove to David our love and commitment to him. We hoped to make huge strides in re-bonding and in connecting with David.

Over the next few weeks, we took a few practice expeditions to nearby campgrounds and lakes to get comfortable driving the motorhome and working out the kinks. We went to Topaz Lake, Ebbett's Pass, and Kinney Reservoir. We took longer trips and went east to Dixie Valley, Star Peak, and then took two more short jaunts to

Lahonton and Pyramid Lake. These were very positive and adventurous. All during the fall months, between outings, we worked hard at preparing our house so we could put it on the market. We no longer needed the large 2,400 square foot home. Our sons were on their own, and we had ended our fostering venture.

All the hustle and bustle kept us busy doing projects together and provided some bonding time. As we got the house cleared out and the floors and windows polished, we continued taking our mini-excursions.

Dan got the idea to purchase a unique vehicle for David called a Tote Gote, which is an old-fashioned (1960's) off-road motorcycle. He found one on Craig's List, and he and David worked on sanding and painting it. It was a big machine with top speed of only twelve mph. It was sturdy and the engine was strong. David was going to be able to ride it up and down gullies and on desert trails. Riding it was going to be one of our incentives for good behavior and cooperation in schoolwork. We had had conferences with John about incentives and how to use them. We also purchased a child-sized compound bow and arrows for David. We packed the motor home with our fishing poles, David's tackle box and fish net, our bicycles and helmets, board games, books to read together, and our camping gear. We gathered sheets, towels, pots, pans, food, and all of the other basics for our winter excursion.

John Trentalange came to Reno about six weeks after our trip to Colorado Springs and stayed in our home with us for four days. We received more of his intensive counseling. For fun, we took him to Virginia City, walked around on the wooden sidewalks, gawked at the saloons and gift shops, and stopped to take in the view from Geiger Grade. We introduced him to some of our friends who also had adopted children, and plans began to come together for John to do a seminar in Reno. John has since moved to Reno.

When we talked to our friend, Dave, who was also an adoptive parent and head of an adoption group, about our issues with David, he said that the onset of puberty was proving to be a traumatic period for most of the adoptive families that he worked with. Besides hormones raging, there was a stirring of interest in finding biological parents, and it seemed that repressed memories were surfacing in kids as they were trying desperately to sort things out. It really helped us to find out that we were not the only people in crisis.

Winter in Arizona

When we left for Arizona in December 2006, I followed behind the motorhome in Dan's pickup, which had the Tote Gote strapped into the bed. This proved to be a wonderful break for me—riding alone, recovering from the intensity and drama of David's unhappiness and his acting out. I listened to the radio, and to music and teaching CD's, and I concentrated on keeping in close proximity to the motorhome so I wouldn't get left behind in strange territory. The hours of travel time proved to be a good bonding time for Dan and David, with lots of time to talk, to plan the trip, and discuss the geological features of the landscape. We were not rushing to Arizona to find one spot and settle down for several weeks. The journey was a major part of the adventure. Our traveling goals: a slowed pace, bonding time, working together to set up and tear down our campsite, and finding new places of beauty.

We did a lot of dry camping, which means we would pull off the main highway's two-lane roads onto small dirt roads. We delighted in the desolation of the Nevada and Arizona wildernesses, the silence of the desert, and the awesome sunsets. It was restorative to all of our spirits and something we really enjoyed.

We were attempting to homeschool David daily. We wished later that we had not even tried to put schoolwork in the schedule. David was going to need more specialized learning situation, which we were later able to research and plug him into once we got back to Reno.

What the three-month trip did for our family was to keep us connected. It was a rocky time because we were still on the learning curve of knowing how to parent David, taking into account his insecure attachment. He was a defiant, immature thirteen-year old, thinking as a six or seven year old at times, yet expecting to have the freedoms of an eighteen-year old. We worked on using incentives and rewards to help him control his behavior. John taught us to say calmly, "your behavior is showing me that you are not interested in riding your Tote Gote this afternoon," and he would be given a chance to change his behavior. If he did not change his behavior, if he did not cooperate with us in his schoolwork or in helping us pack or unpack, it meant that he missed riding the Tote Gote for that day. He loved that vehicle, so it was a good incentive which he had a fresh start with every day.

Besides riding the Tote Gote as an incentive, we also used shooting the bow and arrows, watching DVD's, and eating certain fun foods as incentives.

Until this time we had not put David on medications. He was in counseling, and his therapist knew that we were hoping to get through the rough times without meds. We felt pretty strongly about trying to have success without them, but that changed later. There came a point when we realized how important medications were for his stability and his sanity. He got so that he could not otherwise control his behavior. Dan said, "David's attachment-affected assumptions about care-givers and his tendency to be in survival mode gave rise to intense anger or rage which could get out of control and become irrational. He always realized later that he had been irrational, but that did not stop him from going into a rage again the next time he had the same feelings of fear or insecurity."

While we were in Arizona, we would find a location we liked and would stay in that place from one or two nights to a week or two. David loved to go down to a lake or a stream, bait his line, sit in the sand, and watch, and wait. We had a rubber boat, and Dan would row David for hours on a quiet lake, his fishing line dragging in the water. We had campfires where it was permissible and took daily hikes over hill and dale. With the archery equipment, David practiced shooting the arrows into the sides of hills, and a couple of times we bought hay bales and carried them in the back of the pickup with the Tote Gote. When we would arrive at a camping spot, Dan and David would drag the hay bales away from our site, where David would practice. He built up some skill at archery. We were giving him experiences in success in activities other than schoolwork.

We had always had a practice of reading aloud to our sons, and on this trip we discovered the Mrs. Pollifax mysteries from the owner of a second-hand bookstore. Dan and I took turns reading these and other books aloud. We all enjoyed them. I would knit and listen when it was Dan's turn to read. David also loved to play Monopoly, so after dinner and dishes, we would sit at the motorhome table playing until bedtime. We had no TV hookups (we were not TV watchers), but we rented DVD's once in a while or watched some that we had brought with us. This brought opportunities for laughter and camaraderie.

Dan and David spent many hours playing a strategy marble game called Mancala. David became very good at it so that he would often win.

We tried to be near a church on Sundays, and when we were in Quartzite, Arizona, we happened upon an old-time revival. We stayed there for a couple of weeks and went to a few mid-week meetings and to one or two morning meetings. We met a couple, Gil and Dell, and found we had a lot in common. We became friends, and a few weeks later visited them in their Arizona home. They came to visit us in Reno the next summer and we still keep in touch. They, and all of the people in the small church, were very loving to David. Most of the people greeted him warmly, gave him hugs, and even let him help take the collection and assist with the sound system. David was well behaved, fit in, and had a great time in Quartzite. We found a profusion of rock and gem exhibits and great places to hike there.

Dan had a good friend, Dave, a man in his early 80's, in nearby Blythe, California. We visited him and he spoiled us with steaks and apple pie. He was a collector of African art and artifacts and interesting for all of us to listen to. He was in a bluegrass band, and one night we went to hear the band play in the community room of an RV park. Dave took a special liking to David and treated him with respect. He gave David some incredible rocks for his rock collection.

While we were in Arizona, our friend and real estate agent, Fred, got the paperwork together for us to purchase a house in Red Rock, Nevada, which was small rural area 22 miles north of Reno, and 17 more miles from the main highway up a two-lane road. We had spent some time looking for a new place to live before we left for Arizona. David seemed to relax when he was in the desert camping with Dan and when we were hiking the sandy trails in Arizona, so we chose a place with some acreage. We felt it would be good for all of us, and we wanted to continue the family bonding in a quiet setting, with no neighbors David could get into trouble with.

Red Rock for a year

When we returned to Reno from our Arizona trip, we moved into the house in Red Rock, and lived there for a year. It was a comfortable house on ten acres of land, set on a hillside with lots of tall trees and green bushes, as well as sagebrush. It had a spring and a small pond. There was a beautiful sprawling ranch across the road from us, but no other nearby neighbors on all three sides of our place. David was able to take the Tote Gote and ride on the trails in the hills behind the house and be safe.

A good friend of our family, Bonnee, lived with us during that time. That meant that I was not alone with David, which was a good thing, because during this period David was very upset and angry. It was another year before he began taking medications, and we lived in constant tension. Bonnee is a long-time close friend, and a wonderful woman, with lots of wisdom and wit, and she did not let David intimidate her. Dan was away from home long hours each day, having resumed his studies for his Master's Degree.

By this time, we had gotten David an SPCA dog, Alpine, a well-mannered, older black Lab who would run along with David as he cruised over the hills behind our house on his motor bike. David was still in the oppositional defiant mode of behavior and continually alienated us, but the dog was a friend with unconditional love for David. He was an especially nice dog, not a barker, or a jumper, so Dan and I got along with him just fine.

David had a hard time waking up in a pleasant way, so every morning Dan would take Alpine into David's room. Alpine would rest his head on the edge of David's bed and Dan would say: "Alpine is here to say 'good morning', David." Pretty soon David's hand would come out from under the blankets and would rest on Alpine's head, and he would begin to pet him. After a few minutes David was usually up and heading for the shower, and very often antagonism was averted. Without the dog, David would become passive-aggressive and would refuse to get up.

It was during this time that we began several other interventions for David (besides pet therapy). When we had purchased the house, we had not foreseen that all of us would be commuting back into Reno most days.

We had the Easter family gathering at our place, and our sons and Dan's family came and brought lots of food for the buffet. We have a great family picture of the event.

In June, we had a big birthday party for David. I emailed friends and family and church friends, and asked them to encourage David by coming to his 14th birthday celebration. Many people came, and he received lots of gifts, and got a big boost in feeling very loved.

Fast For Word and biofeedback

Dan read a book *The Brain That Heals Itself*, by Norman Doidge, MD. He became very encouraged that David's brain might be able to make up for the damage done by FAS. We considered moving to LA or even to Canada in order to enroll David in a special school for people with learning disabilities.

As we continued researching, we discovered a woman in Reno, Rachel Brown, who was using a computer-based reading intervention program mentioned in Doidge's book. It was called *Fast For Word*, and was designed to help the brain overcome learning deficiencies. David met with Rachel, a very gifted and positive woman, four times a week for almost two years. There was a welcoming family feeling in the large therapy workroom where children of all ages received physical therapy. All of the therapists and other clients were very friendly. It was a good place to be. David did his computer program in one of the side rooms. This program, and Rachel's commitment to David, as well as games they would play, and her genuine positive upbeat banter, helped David's reading skills as well as his self-esteem. Medicaid paid for this, for which we were very thankful.

One of the other things that helped David tremendously was biofeedback with Dr. George Green. From his website: *Biofeedback is an electronic based means of showing how you respond to stress. Biofeedback can help head, neck and back pain, tension, stress, anxiety, ADD, ADHD, rage disorder, depression, and sleep problems.* www.StressLessLife.com

David had about 50 sessions of biofeedback. Dan or I took him two times a week. David excelled in this program. His self-esteem was boosted because of his consistent success and the encouragement he received from George Green. Dan thought that biofeedback was the most effective intervention that we tried in helping David calm himself. Prior to biofeedback therapy, during the years from age 13-15, there would be times when David would stay angry for hours or even into the next day. The effect of biofeedback was that when David had an explosion of flash anger and was irrational, after 15 or 20 minutes he was able to calm himself and think rationally. He was able to apologize and resume relationship with us. This success encouraged us to persevere in working with David without resorting to psychological medication.

Dr. Green had had his own learning challenges in his youth because, as Dan says, "He is a genius", and was misunderstood. He had compassion for David, and they had a great relationship. He is a very gifted and caring man. We only stopped this therapy because we could not afford it anymore. Dr. Green did not take Medicaid at the time, although I have heard that some biofeedback centers do.

<u>Swim team, piano lessons, and Boy Scouts</u>

Besides *Fast For Word* and biofeedback, David joined the local swim team, something our oldest son, Tim, had suggested.

Remember, David was appropriately behaved when he was out of the home—when he was with authority figures that were not asking him to do things that he did not want to do! He was relaxed, polite, obedient, and cooperative with most other authority figures.

He had an excellent coach, Alex, a high school senior. David progressed in his swimming skills equal to or better than his teammates. I took him to swimming every weekday afternoon, and became acquainted with several of the other Moms. I could also knit or read while I was watching David and the other kids in the pool.

We went to two swim meets, one in Gardnerville and one at UNR, and he won some ribbons for his swimming skill. He did well and had a lot of fun.

David and I went to Alex's high school graduation where Alex was the valedictorian. Alex was an excellent role model for David and treated him with respect always—when he wasn't yelling at him to "Go! Go! Go!"

David was given two nice piano keyboards (from Dan's Mother and his Aunt Vanna) when he was young, and loved to play around on them. He showed significant musical ability. He was able to sit at the piano and pick out short pieces of songs and commercials by ear. Over the years we enrolled him in piano lessons at Callahan's and at Carpenter's (each enrollment about nine to twelve months in length). He had two different teachers, who were very patient men. As they worked with David, they could see that he had potential, but David refused to do the homework practice on our piano at home. We believe now that because of the brain damage he had experienced during his Mom's pregnancy, there were just certain things he could not do, like learn to read music. He also could not be self-directed to practice his music at home. When Dan sat with him during a practice session, David resisted Dan's directions and encouragements, and Dan had to give up trying to help him.

David really wanted to join the Boy Scouts. He had a good leader and was part of a small troop of boys. He was very proud of his Boy Scout shirt, his tie, and his badges, and he wore them whenever he could. He went to the weekly meetings for over a year, did good deeds, earned merit badges, and at one time he held a leadership position. Dan attended the scout meetings and went on the annual camping excursion. We cheered for David at the four local parades and followed him around town as he participated in a Civil War reenactment, a colorful and impressive event in Virginia City. There was a fake robbery while we were riding on the train, and lots and lots of explosions as the military battles ensued on the bare desert hills.

Back to jail for two weeks

We had not been able to sell the 2,400-square-foot house, and had been renting it out while we lived at Red Rock. Dan was commuting to UNR, and David and I were on the road daily with his activities and appointments. The rising gas prices, plus the hours spent on the road, caused us to feel that the strain outweighed the benefits of the secluded life in Red Rock. We had also been driving one hour each way to the church we attended on Sundays. We moved back into town into our old home on a rainy blustery day. Two family friends, Danny and Steve, helped Dan and David with the loading and unloading of our furniture and boxes into the rented U-Haul.

David continued to be moody and explosive, and one night we called 911. David was arrested again and went back to our local juvenile hall, which is named Jan Evans. He was there almost two weeks.

Since David's initial incarceration in 2005, we had been having regular monthly appointments in the probation department. We wanted to give credit and praise to the four men who were assigned to David's case over those seven years, but it is not possible to give their names. They know that Dan and I highly esteem them.

Probation officer #3 had been counseling David, Dan, and I. He said that when David threatened us, or postured, that we needed to call the police because more intervention was likely to be needed, perhaps even some inpatient treatment, and that they were looking into other living situations for David. He was concerned with David's bullying and believed that we were being too patient with him.

Posturing in the dictionary (www.dictionary.cambridge.org) means behavior or speech that is intended to attract attention and interest, or to make people believe something that is not true. In this case, David would pull up to his full height, and lean in toward one of us in a stance of intimidation, power, and control.

Because David was acting so imbalanced, speaking hatefully, and making threats, it was during this time that we took all of the knives and sharp objects and locked them in the garage every night.

We went to see David at Juvenile Hall on visiting evenings, which were every 3 days. But we were honestly relieved to have the break from his tirades, which had increased in intensity during the time we lived at Red Rock. We believed that in jail he was safe and out of danger, so we rested at home and had a break. We hoped and prayed that he would prefer home life to jail life, and that this experience would be an incentive for changed behavior.

From this experience David found he really liked the structure and the set routines of incarceration. He earned perks by having good behavior, such as extra TV time and ice cream snacks. But he did not like his loss of freedom or the experience of being locked up.

This was the turning point for us to be fully able to understand that David needed psychological medication. David was evaluated during the time of his detention, and the terms of his release included procuring medication. We made an appointment with a psychiatrist so that David could get a prescription for the impulsive anger outbursts and for mood stabilization. The psychiatrist prescribed Zyprexa. As a side effect, David gained 60 pounds within a few months, which was alarming, but the medication did help significantly with his mood swings and angry outbursts.

Therapy and testing between 2006-2009

David developed a good relationship with his therapist, William Smith. Dan and I also met with William, and he encouraged us that we were doing very well in dealing with our son. He also gave us suggestions about things we could change, and ways to direct and encourage David.

Later, David was evaluated at Mojave Adult, Child, and Family Services. The therapist saw the presenting problems as attachment, anxiety, and anger. We felt she was right on target.

During this time period, we had David tested at the University of Nevada, Reno, in the Ed/Psych Department. He had a psycho-educational evaluation and the results were dismal. We had to take a hard look at David's abilities, and we clearly understood why we were frustrated in teaching him, but more importantly, why he had been so frustrated and angry. He just could not do math beyond addition and subtraction or reading past a middle second grade level. His IQ was very low in those areas, so he did not have very much capability to work with.

Norris Dupree, David's next therapist, recommended further testing. David had psychological/neuropsychological testing, which were administered by Dr. Able in Feb 2009. Those tests were one of the biggest eye-openers of what David's real abilities and handicaps were. Norris had sat under Dr. Able's teaching and knew that she was specialized in understanding the brain and could be very helpful in determining specific areas of damage in David's brain function. We were attempting to determine if he had experienced a brain injury prior to arriving at our home at age nine months, or possibly from the serious bike accident he had when he was about six years old.

Dr. Able also ordered an MRI to see if David had had a stroke. The results showed that he had not had a stroke.

Dr. Able gave us a detailed report of the testing she had administered, and again the news was not good. She concluded from the testing and from her interviews with David that she expected that he would need group home placement very soon. She recommended that we begin to research local placement possibilities so that when it became imminent that he be placed in a group home, we would have already done the legwork. She wanted to spare him, and us, an impulsive placement that might do more harm than good. She said that David would reside in group homes the rest of his life and would not be able to ever function at any level of normal employment. This was a huge blow to us. We had nourished high hopes for David all of this time. This brought us to another level of 'grieving the dream.'

'Grieving the dream' was a term that John Trentalange, the attachment specialist, had introduced us to. Parents have hopes and dreams for their children. Even if their aspirations are not specific, they hope that their child will succeed and be all that they can be. As our children disappoint us, or get into trouble, we need to stop and recognize the sadness we are experiencing and give ourselves some time to adjust our thinking in order to be able to move on and accept the reality of what we are living with. We continued lamenting for David as we faced the truth about his mental condition.

David met weekly in therapy with Norris Dupree for two years. Norris had years of experience with teenagers and had some revealing insights into David's psyche. He told us about an after-school day-treatment program called Koinonia, which he highly recommended. David was admitted, and Medicaid paid. Thank you, again, Medicaid. David attended Koinonia every day from 3:30-6pm. Katy Hartley, the director, was a good leader and administrator and worked with a skilled staff.

Koinonia

Being in Koinonia meant David was in daily interaction with kids his age, male and female. Unfortunately, this meant David had to drop the swim team. This was deeply disappointing for all of us. It took him a while to get over this loss. David had enjoyed being on the team so much and had done very well.

While he was in Koinonia, David had the stability of being under the care of the program's psychiatrist, Dr. Bale. She was a very caring and astute medical practitioner. She adjusted David the Zyprexa dosage and eased him onto another prescription. She watched his weight and conferred with the Koinonia staff about his behavior. In fact, her office was in the same building in which Koinonia met.

David's medication was slowly changed and carefully monitored by the doctor every two months, and more often if necessary. She and the staff of Koinonia, Katy, Mo, Jerry, John, Krista, and Carole, were very dedicated and caring people. We are grateful to each one of them for their investment in David and the other kids in the program. David played basketball with the staff and the students, and he was part of socialization groups and anger management groups. An hour was allotted daily for the kids to do their homework, and they had life skills experiences in grocery shopping and food preparation. They went on field trips and listened to guest speakers.

Each of the kids had a daily home note from Koinonia and that was the cause of some new problems. The home note was to let staff at

Koinonia know how David had behaved at home. David would gain or lose points depending on whether he did his homeschool assignments with us, cleaned his room, and whether he cooperated with us, or defied us.

David confronted me and challenged me about my reports, and it was yet another source of enduring his rage. He would scream at me and intimidate me if I divulged his bad behavior, because he saw me as the reason for losing favor with the staff at Koinonia. He never understood that his consequences were the result of his choices, not because we wanted to be mean to him. This is fairly typical FAS thinking. Because David's brain was damaged, his thinking was not logical or consequential. Even if a mother knows this fact, believes it, and accepts it, it still is devastating to be screamed at and blamed day after day.

Katy and her staff had other FAS students and consequential thinking was taught, stressed, and reinforced daily.

Most people understand that a choice is inseparably linked to the consequences or ramifications of that choice. Even at two years old children are learning this concept. But for the FAS brain, this is often a missing link. So the consequences, if the child does something bad, are seen as somebody else's fault, not as a result a personal choice made. In David's mind, we were the reason he lost points. Very gradually, he has learned fairly good consequential thinking and is beginning to take responsibility for his behavior and accept the consequences. It has taken years and many interventions, but it really is all working together for good.

Surprising testing results

When Dr. Able met with us to share with us the results of her testing and interviews and her diagnosis, she was very kind and gentle with us, which we appreciated very much. She knew of our investment in David, she knew we were in that category of 'hopeful' parents that are not seeing 'giving up' as an option. She also knew that we needed concrete understanding about his real abilities and disabilities from a scientific reality.

We were pretty much in shock over Dr. Able's evaluation. My husband and I see ourselves as intelligent, and we are prayerful. We have a lot of faith in a BIG God. We believed that David's healing would come from ours and others' love and acceptance of him, from prayer (and David had a lot of it), from our hard work in schooling him, and from getting him into programs that could help him with his academics and later with a trade.

From the time we spoke with Dr. Able, we began to prepare ourselves for the fact that we were not going to be able to see David's healing happen in the way we had hoped. We tried to get used to the idea that David would be going away from our care and into the care of others, eventually. We were losing our son, we were losing control, and we were losing the hope of his imminent healing.

In Aug 2009, we were able to follow up on Norris Dupree's, Dr. Bale's, and others' suggestions to have David evaluated by the Fetal Alcohol Syndrome Comprehensive Clinic. This clinic was convened only as funding allowed. There were four women were on the panel: two board certified child psychiatrists, a neuro-psychologist, and a well-known local FAS authority. The evaluations they provided were for the diagnosis of FAS and for assessments in these areas: medical, neuro-developmental, psychological, educational, and behavioral.

We were put on the waiting list for the FAS Clinic, but there was faint expectation that funding would come through for another clinic in 2009. I emailed 30 people to pray about it, and we felt that we received a miracle answer: we were called for an August appointment.

We said a prayer in the waiting room before the test, praying that David would be calm and able to perform to the best of his ability in the testing which would take several hours. Because we pray a lot, sometimes I jot down what each of us says. Recently, I found this in one of my file folders:

David prayed that day: *"Lord, I pray that my brain would be normal, and my heart would be able to forgive my parents for what they did before I was born."*

David speaks often of sadness and recurring resentment toward his parents for their drug and alcohol problems. He knows his brain was severely damaged by the alcohol his mom drank daily. We have told him what social services has recommended that we say: "Your parents could not take care of you because they were having trouble taking care of themselves."We have forgiven them (and we continue to forgive them if resentment arises) and have encouraged him to keep on forgiving them whenever he thinks about the impact they had on his life.

The results of the Clinic were devastating. David was 16 years old. His overall measure of adaptive behavior was much lower. His skills were very limited in all areas of the testing. The diagnoses were many, which I will not relate in order to shield David.

David was diagnosed with FAS 1, the worst level on a scale of five levels, based on documented exposure to alcohol in utero (i.e., in the womb), classical facial features, low birth weight, complex behavioral/cognitive profile (i.e., learning problems, social problems, judgment problems). Some of the recommendations of the team were: life-long placement in a group home, continued follow-up with a psychiatrist to treat and achieve mood stabilization through medications, continued individual therapy for anger management, and to pursue eligibility for SSI (Supplemental Security Income). Men and women who cannot work to earn a substantial living that will pay for their lodging and food and power and garbage, etc., need to have outside help. We knew we could not support David for the rest of his life, in fact with the economy shift, and Dan starting a new career, we had our own financial concerns.

What do people do when a bomb drops like this? Hold on tighter to Jesus and to each other and pray, and after the dust has settled, re-group and then keep going. This is a deeply personal journey that cannot be prescribed or mapped out by anyone else for you if you are in that position. Acceptance is the goal, because life has to go on. Depression, alcoholism, suicide, drug abuse, a life style of anger and blame, are not options.

Life with David was already very challenging, but our foundation was firmly on the foundation of: God called us to this, God is faithful, God is good, God is love, God will show us what's next, God will be there for us every minute of every day, God is working all things together for good, and no weapon formed against us will prosper.

We were committed to each other and to David. We had friends who were praying, a church with caring pastors, a loving congregation, and a network of professional services to access.

Our interventions—going the extra miles

Before I go further, I want to list more of the personal interventions that we made on David's behalf. David hasn't been an assignment or a project; he has been a son and a brother.

We took our responsibility to raise David very seriously. Of course we did not do everything perfectly, and we apologized when we were rude or we made mistakes. But, as his adoptive parents, we have peace that we have given this endeavor our very best effort.

Be prepared as an adoptive parent to go the extra mile. Actually, I mean, be prepared to go extra m-i-l-e-s. If your adoptive child is cooperative and conciliatory, rejoice and be glad!!! If your child is difficult and becomes rebellious, go to prayer and seek the Lord's wisdom, stay in a forgiving mindset, and seek counsel. Even when your child does not appreciate what you are doing, God does. He sees it all. In spite of all your child's stubbornness and lack of cooperation, and in spite of dismal evaluations and reports, there really is always hope with God. A song taken from Lamentations 3:22-23 comes to mind:

The steadfast love of the Lord never ceases, His mercies never come to an end! They are new every morning, new every morning, great is Thy faithfulness, O LORD, great is Thy faithfulness.(2)

Here are some ways we brought David into our 'fold' and invested in him. You will have your own family's peculiar camaraderie and unique traditions. Be assured that all of your loving efforts will build up the child inside. Your child very well may have a family tree that includes people without faces—people who just existed and did not ever have birthday parties or joyous Christmases. She may have a heritage of people that never experienced traveling or cultural events, or American traditions. Your child may only have a legacy of addictions, lawlessness, failure, sorrow, and tragedy without redemption. You get to break the cycle!

We kept in touch with Hayley, David's first social worker, until she moved out of town when he was about ten. We would visit her at her office, traditionally on March 17th, the anniversary of the day she brought David to us. Sometimes we took flowers to her, which brought a river of tears. She was always very glad to see David, and he was always very glad to see her. It was a healthy connection to his personal history. Adoptive children need positive connections to their past because there are a plethora of distinctive memories running around in their minds that are vying for their attention and wanting to pull them down into sadness.

We took David to cultural events—art museums, natural history museums, concerts, and to a ballet. We went to zoos, aquariums, a couple of professional baseball games, Reno's annual balloon races, and the air races.

David attended piano lessons, went to summer swim lessons, played in the oceans and in rivers and lakes. He liked camping, and hiked many miles with his dad in the Nevada hills. He enjoyed exploring caves, sighting bighorn sheep, and collecting rocks. Dan and David flew remote control airplanes in the desert outside of town as a shared hobby.

Dan and David made 3 or 4 trips to Vancouver, BC, Canada, during the time our son Mark was in school there for two years. It was a long drive, but long drives meant lots of conversation, numerous fun food stops, and interesting adventures.

One fall, Dan and David flew to Gilbert, Arizona, to get a pickup than Dan had purchased online. Coming home they stopped at the Grand Canyon and Page Dam.

Our oldest son, Tim, became engaged to Jessica, in 2001. I wanted to have one more family vacation before the dynamics of our family changed forever. We had just received a small inheritance, so we took our five sons to London, three months after 9/11. We stayed in youth hostels and in school housing, and we took trains and busses to other cities, and visited two castles. On Christmas day, while playing on the play equipment in a park, David dislocated his elbow, which was extremely painful. Dan and David and I took a taxi to the hospital, and David and I spent the night there. His elbow was casted so that he could make the trip home without further injury. After he was released we picked up where we had left off in seeing the city, pushing David in a wheelchair all around the Natural History Museum.

Intentionally, so that David could understand how good life is in the United States, in 2005, Dan, David, and I, went to New Delhi, India and Kathmandu, Nepal. We had met Milan and Shusma, a young Nepalese couple, on our London trip, and a few years later they invited Dan to speak at a Pastors' Convention in their church, which was in a suburb of Kathmandu. David was almost 11, and had a great time riding bikes and playing kickball with children he could not communicate with but who enthusiastically befriended him. We took a suitcase filled with WalMart toys (nerf balls, a soccer ball, bubbles, origami paper, puzzles) and played simple board games with the seven kids in the orphanage that Milan and Shusma's church sponsored. David was deeply impacted by the deprivation in which the people of these third-world countries lived, and became more appreciative of the lifestyle he enjoyed in America. This realization has deepened as he has matured, and he often mentions the effect that visiting Nepal had on him.

Dan and David and I took a few weeks off one summer after we had retired from fostering and made time for a road trip. We visited Utah, Colorado, Kansas, Missouri, Iowa, Nebraska, South Dakota, Wyoming, and Idaho. We enjoyed visiting Laura Ingalls Wilder's home, George Washington Carver's home, and the Black History Museum in Denver, Colorado.

David had his dog, Alpine, for pet therapy, for two years. David responded extremely well to having a friendly canine companion. With the dog came the challenge for David to feed him and clean up after him, and for us to be patient and consistent in monitoring both of these activities.

We homeschooled David, rather than sending him away for someone else to teach him. This was a huge intervention, and not everyone was in agreement with it. Friends and professionals thought we should let the experts work with David in the school and 'save ourselves' from the challenge and what they assumed was an impossible task.

In her exit conference with us, Dr. Able told us that she does not usually believe that homeschool is a good alternative to public or private school, but that in our case we had saved David because we had homeschooled him. She said that he had such a good self-concept and such a good rapport with adults because we had homeschooled him. Norris Dupree also supported our homeschool efforts. He said that if we had not homeschooled David that he would have been more confused, more delayed, expelled from public school, in and out of institutions, and in much worse condition.

Sometimes a family must stand against the flow of public opinion to do what seems best for their child.

I also want to report that Dan and I tried to take care of ourselves. I had my wonderful, faithful, loving sisters: Marsha is a very capable marriage and family therapist, and Connie is very compassionate and wise by life! My sisters (and their husbands, Don and Jerry, respectively) were consistently sympathetic, understanding, and sensitive to the ups and downs I was experiencing with David during his teenage years, especially when he was 12-16. They called often, were good listeners, and we got together when we could.

I had many friends who had watched David grow up and were caring and committed to me during his teen years. I had professional counseling sessions with Mary Carlson, and advice from Katy Hartley.

Dan had several counseling sessions with two local psychologists during our twelve-year fostering/adopting experience.

Together we met with four therapists: Norris Dupree, John Trentalange, William Smith, and David Turner. Dan also received excellent and caring support from his supervisors and colleagues in the MFT program when he was a student at the University, and as an intern.

I learned to let people into my personal world. I could not have gone the extra miles otherwise. It is very easy to let discouragement beguile you into giving up. Beware of pretending that "everything is just fine, thank you."

Take every relationship as it comes and be thankful even for the temporary care and prayer you receive. Some people you meet will be politely interested in what you are doing, some will pray and be a support for a time and then gradually fade away. Keep a list of people who will pray, and try not to burden them. Then when an evaluation is coming, or you need wisdom for a big decision, or a calamity arises, send some of them an email for prayer support. Even if each person prays once, that might be 30 prayers that go up to God for one crisis!

During one season, I was extremely weary and yet did not want to offend people when they asked about David. I found I was just not able to confide the latest drama, so I would say, "I only talk about David on Tuesdays." People were always surprised by that statement, but I think they were actually relieved not to have to hear the newest report—and it helped me to avoid reliving the recent events.

Oppositional defiant and suicide threats

During the teenage years, especially 2006-2009,when David was 13-16, we were having lots of trouble with David. He opposed us, and screamed at us whenever we said **no**. With God's strength, through Bible reading, prayer, encouraging one another, and encouragements from professionals and family and friends, we just kept going, hoping&

praying our son would get better. I guess the world would say that we were in major denial. We felt we were **walking by faith in God.** God had initiated the foster and adoption experience with a vision. He had sustained us through all of the good times and the bad times for years, so we proceeded and prayed for wisdom and strength. We relied on Him for love and forgiveness for David. We knew God would never leave us or forsake us, and we kept on going day after day, believing He had a plan and a purpose. As we did our devotions, we asked for words of truth, words of strength, and encouragement to keep on. We prayed for David, crying out for his healing.

Even when David was on prescribed medications, it wasn't a quick fix. The medications had to be adjusted and re-evaluated based on his behavior, weight gain, physical symptoms. We (and his house manager) still work with the psychiatrist to keep his meds balanced as he grows and develops. Meds are not a magic fixer. The correct prescriptions can bring relief for the patient, which brings relief to the caregiver. Ideally, God's healing comes to restore and deliver the person.

We have saved a number of notes from David written on scraps of paper, binder paper, and the backs of math assignments. These notes, written in a childish first- grade scrawl, include everything from apologies to threats of suicide and homicide. We took David to the local mental hospital a few times for suicide threats or bizarre behavior. Even if he was not admitted, the process of leaving our house, driving to the facility, being 'buzzed' through the locked doors, filling out the paperwork, sitting in the waiting room, and having the intake interview, took the edge off, and we all relaxed and we came home. Three times he has been hospitalized at the mental facility for three to seven days for angry outbursts and suicidal ideation.

The situation became dangerous

This is the experience that caused us to make the decision that it was time for David to go to a group home. This was the turning point for us.

David was on probation from May 2006 until Sept. 18, 2013. He was kept on probation because of his anger issues, suicidal tendencies, and violence, etc. We found that for David, being on probation was something that gave him identity and value. It wasn't threatening to him most of the time. Having a probation officer gave him a sense of significance. Each of his probation officers treated David and us with respect and dignity. Each one was able to penetrate David's defensive shell and talk to him in such a way that David could comprehend their concern and their boundaries. He took their authority very seriously. The possibility of incarceration helped David monitor his behavior. As I mentioned before, he had been incarcerated in our local juvenile hall, called Jan Evans, twice. The first time he was there for an overnight, and the second time, for two weeks. The possibility of going to 'big jail' across the street on Parr Boulevard was real, and something he actively sought to avoid.

David made many threatening remarks to us and wrote notes warning us of his hurtful intentions. His probation officer had been preparing David for an action line, advising him that this bullying needed to stop. David had already tried to intimidate Dan by brandishing a knife at him. He had become physically threatening to both of us, once putting his finger in my chest and pulling himself up to his full height, as a means of intimidation. When this happened, something rose up in me and I calmly and firmly told him to never touch me or try to frighten me in that way again. He never has. I told him he could give me hugs only.

The probation officer asked David if he ever thought about hurting us. David said that he often got that thought. The P.O. asked if David wanted to hurt us, and David said that he "really did not want to hurt us." Then the probation officer asked,

"David, do you think it is time that you moved into another living situation?" David said, "Yes."

I was stunned. <u>WHAT?!!</u> David was 16 at this time.

In my journal the next morning, I wrote: *The probation officer talked about David going to a residential home. My thought was "How does that glorify God?" I was thinking of the vision God gave me, and about Jesus coming to me. I thought of the healing prophecies we have received. David going to a residential home??? NOT!"*

But four days later in my devotional journal, I wrote: *David was oppositional and stood up to Dan vehemently over a very small matter. A grief settled over me and I accepted that this is it. It is too much. I told Dan that I realized finally that we have reached our limit AND* (agreed with Dan) *that David does not want our parenting. I felt heavy. Later David was oppositional to me. I told him that we were considering the residential home that the PO mentioned. David said: "You can't un-adopt me." I said that we would never do that, but that things had not been working between us for a long time. He said: "I would probably do better, because I only act bad with you guys. And besides they do fun things in those places."*

I told God that this is not the way I would have done it! I asked Him, "Why couldn't You use us for David's healing?" It felt like failure.

I felt I was to let go and to trust God. But I was not looking forward to walking out the process. Dan said later that a residential home may cost a lot, but we have some savings and could sell the house and move into a small place and focus on each other. At this moment, I just feel relief.

Later, I became angry with myself for feeling relief that David would be leaving, and I felt guilty about it. Then I thought of all the what ifs---- "what if we had not taken so many foster babies, what if we had spent more time with David, what if we had put him on medication sooner?" But then, I thought of the counsel we had received from John Trentalange, and Dr. Able, and Norris, and other professionals who worked with us. They had been patient with us, waiting for us to come to the personal realization that we had done all we could do for David. None of them had ever chastised us for what we had NOT done or for anything we had done wrong.

When we met with Norris, a few days later, he said that he believed in <u>prevention</u>—"because if we do prevention, we will not have to do intervention." That resonated with both Dan and I. Norris reminded us of our conversation with Dr. Able: she believed that David should be in a facility. Norris pointed out that we had tried Koinonia Day Treatment for the last two years, because of our willingness to continue working with David. But on this day he said, "You have done what you can, and I feel it is time for him to be in another living situation."

This decision was supported by my long-time friend, Karen M, who has been a special education teacher for 25 years, by my sisters who were concerned for my health and well being, and by many others. In fact, everyone felt that this decision to let David go to a group home was long overdue.

I am so grateful that Dan and I know beyond a shadow of doubt that we did what we could for David. David was on a course that would lead to incarceration, and we needed to change direction and look at the options.

Dan and I knew that all three of us were at the end of our rope. The most interesting thing to me is that our rope was stretched and stretched and stretched way beyond what any of us thought we could handle. Our testimony is that God was with us in the stretching, helping us, strengthening us, and empowering us.

David would not leave home for about 5 months after this decision had been made.

David leaves our home, age 16 ½

The next step was to select a group home. Remember that Dr. Able had advised us to begin researching homes so that, at this juncture, we would be prepared, but we had not even begun to consider the research, because we had not really 'owned' the idea that David would live somewhere else.

We went to interview Gilbert, the owner of one of the many group homes in our area, who had been recommended to us by someone whose opinion we trusted. We liked him and were comfortable with him. Dan and I met Gilbert and his wife, Birdie, at two of the houses they managed, which had space available for David. Both were middle-income homes in nice neighborhoods.

The house we chose had two other young men living in it. Each boy had his own bedroom. The boys shared the fridge and had their own cupboard space in the kitchen. They shared the TV in the living room. There were staff persons on site 24/7, taking shifts, helping the boys do their grocery shopping and homework, and taking them to doctor appointments. One of them would give David a ride to Koinonia every afternoon.

David would be moving into the master bedroom, which had recently been vacated. It needed painting and new drapes, but I had to tell myself that it was not my responsibility. There was a sliding glass window so there was lots of light coming into the small room. Because he had the master bedroom, there was a walk-in closet and his own bathroom. There was a lock on the bedroom door to lock him in at night and to lock out intruders. That comforted me a lot.

When we left the interview and walked to our car, my body began to shake involuntarily. I began to cry. This lasted for an hour. It was my physical manifestation of grief and loss. My son would be living across town with strangers. They would be supervising him, taking him to his appointments. He would be eating whatever he wanted, watching whatever he wanted on TV, having friends that I did not know and could not approve of. He would be happy—and I had to let go and get real.

I grieved the dream once again as my expectations of David being healed while in our home, fell to the ground.

It seemed that everything was moving very slowly and everything was hurting very badly.

Dan had attended a seminar for fathers of children with disabilities some years previously. He had heard that part of the process of being a good dad to your child is to grieve the loss of the perfect child you had imagined he would be. Dan had not been able to do much of that grieving until we came to this point.

Another suggestion from Norris was that we apply to Sierra Regional Center in order to get more help for David. SRC is *a division of the Mental Health and Developmental Services of the State of Nevada. It assists persons (who qualify) who have developmental disabilities. The organization helps plan and arrange and monitor support services.* www.mhds.state.nv.us They accepted David's case, which has been another Godsend, and another opportunity for grateful thanks to Medicaid.

Our service coordinator has been Robert. Again, we have been blessed with having an excellent working relationship with yet another professional. We communicate well and work together in a respectful and friendly manner. Robert's experience and guidance have been very helpful in making decisions in David's life.

David's treatment team, consisting of Norris, Robert, his probation officer, and Dan and me, decided that it would be good for David to attend high school. We met with the personnel of the school and the special education department, and they worked up a plan for him. The team determined that while David was still living in our home he would transition into new his role as a special education public school student. I would take him to high school every morning and pick him up every afternoon for three-and-a-half months. Then, in December, he would move into the group home and begin taking the school bus to and from school. This plan would give us time to get used to the new life ahead.

While attending school, David had some problems with kids his own age, and he also had some difficulties with the teachers. He had some things in his mind that he wanted to do, which were very inappropriate. He could not do any of the schoolwork, as it was too advanced for him. David had been assigned a Psychosocial Rehabilitation Worker, a PSR, but even one-on-one, how can a person with brain cells missing, understand fractions, contractions, and parts of speech? His PSR worker voiced her frustrations, and he became angry with her. Unfortunately people think, as we had, "if you would just try harder, David."She was now in the same position we had been—the target of David's anger and frustration over his inability to succeed in schoolwork.

A few months later, in one of our sessions with Norris, he said that people take advantage of persons like David. He said that two of the doctors in the FAS clinic said that David was the worst case of neurological that damage they had ever seen.

At the same time, David's behavior in school was giving everyone some concern. This is when Norris realized that David could become separated from his staff in a WalMart, accidentally or on purpose, and just disappear. We could not see him strategically disengaging himself from his staff, but we could imagine him going off with one of our old neighbors or some other unusual occurrence. He did not know his new address or phone number and had always had trouble memorizing. He would not be able to find his house or tell someone how to get him home.

Combined with this potential danger were some serious conflicts with roommates and staff in the residential home and inappropriate behaviors at school. David was making some poor decisions, some of which affected other people adversely. These incidents precipitated Norris' beginning to consider the need for a higher level of care.

Copper Hills and Benchmark

Norris was aware of a lock-down facility called Copper Hills in the Salt Lake City area. He had stories of some clients doing exceptionally well there. We looked into it in consideration that David needed more supervision than he was getting in his group home, more intensive therapy, a more structured environment, and education geared to his learning disabilities.

We discussed this with David's team, who I have mentioned earlier, with the addition of Katy from Koinonia. They all agreed that this was a good move for David. During a court review hearing, the judge in the juvenile justice department approved the plan, and ordered that David complete the program at Copper Hills. Medicaid agreed to fund it. Praise God.

The probation officer offered to arrange for David to be transported to Utah. But we wanted to be part of David's transition. So in August 2010, we drove David to East Jordan, a suburb of Salt Lake City. David was very grateful to have the time together on the long drive. Leaving him at the institution was distressing, not knowing how well he would do, and not knowing much more than the website had shown us about the institution. We had to have 'big-time' trust in God once again. We felt assurance because we had made this decision through consultation with a our team of professionals, all of who were very familiar with the needs of young people in David's situation.

We could not talk on the phone to David during the initial six-week orientation period, but after that we talked to him at least once a week. We were able to visit him every three months. We drove three times across Nevada for the two-and-half day visits.

In spite of high gas prices, motel and food expenses, and loss of income, we made the choice to make the trips because we wanted to support and encourage David. David looked forward to our coming, but for the first two visits he sabotaged his opportunity to leave the facility with us. We had wanted to take him hiking, out to eat, shopping, and to church, but before we left Reno, his therapist called to tell us that David had 'acted out' and gotten into a fight and broken some rules, so that his behavior took his level down to 'restricted freedom.' His therapist wanted to know if we would still make the trip, even though David would not be able to leave the facility. Dan was thinking that it would be detrimental to show rejection of David because he acted badly. We felt it would show our unconditional love by proceeding with our plans, so we went to Plan B: we drove to Salt Lake City, we brought meals from nearby restaurants, talked a lot, played games, and watched a video in one of the family rooms. We were all really glad we had made the 520-mile journey. It was really good to see David and to encourage him.

David had a wonderful therapist at Copper Hills. I had been worried about being judged, but Sharon had walked in our shoes. She had adopted two FAS children several years previously, and had experienced problems with her kids that were similar to what we had experienced with David. Her children had gone into institutions, at ages eight and nine, if I remember correctly. At the time we met her, they were adults and holding jobs, and one was married with children. There was no judgment in her. David was able to relate well to Sharon and so were we. We had 55-minute family counseling sessions by phone every week that David was at Copper Hills. If she was out of town, another therapist took her place.

David had a difficult time in Copper Hills. He was frustrated because he could not do the schoolwork, just as he had been frustrated in the high school special education classroom, and at home. His brain would not perform for him. I don't think he was called 'stupid', but of course he felt stupid. He would be working on first grade math while the other kids were doing algebra and geometry. This was extremely disappointing for us also. We had expected that he would get schooling at Copper Hills that was geared for his needs and abilities. We had hoped that he would make even a small amount of progress in reading and math.

David's treatment team at the facility was made up of his classroom teachers, his section staff, his therapist, the medical doctor, the nurse, and the psychiatrist. While they were conducting their monthly scheduled meetings about David, one of them would call us and we would receive a verbal report from each member of the team about David's health, education, behavior, and medicine changes. We could ask questions of any of the specialists. In the mail we received a written report, which kept us informed and current about David's life.

David had a lot of anger, and a lot of it came out in striking out at people in rages. It was an undercurrent of anger that we felt was contributed to by his biological parents abandoning him, by his failure to succeed at school, by his loss of his brothers as they grew older and moved out of the house, and by his mixed-up thinking abilities. He was also probably angry with us, and the legal system, for putting him in Copper Hills.

The best thing about the two years he spent in the lock-down facilities was the structure. Every aberrant behavior had an immediate and CONSISTENT consequence, with no emotional interference from the enforcer. This is one of the things the FAS brain needs.

As parents we take in all the factors:
he didn't sleep well so he's over-tired,
we were late and we had to rush and he got upset,
his dog is sick so he's distracted,
he didn't have enough breakfast so he's in a bad mood,
his brother couldn't come over and he is sad.
But at a facility, if you break the rule, you get the consequence. If you fight it and scream "unfair" and begin to hit staff, you go into the time-out room and you still get the consequence. If you still do not settle down, staff can restrain you and administer a sedative. That strict level of consistency is just what the fetal-alcohol-brain needs. And that level of consistency is hard for a most parents to give.

David receiving sedation was a pretty alarming for us. We had to trust that his overseers were making good decisions for David. The staff was required to call us every time there was an incident in which David needed to be restrained. In the monthly report there was an account of his behavior and how many times he had been restrained, and how often he had received a PRN.(3) We had the prerogative to have the incidents investigated, which we did twice when we were concerned.

It was very nerve-wracking to have him so far away and under the care of people that we had met only briefly during our visits. David's condition was extreme and was beyond our ability to help him. This was our last resort. We definitely wanted to get services that would help him grow up safely and keep him out of prison, which was destined to be in his future without some very intense intervention. We hoped and prayed that this experience was going to be life changing for him. And in hindsight, we believe that taking this extreme measure of having him live in lockdown facilities was what was necessary to bring about his present level of maturity and self-control.

Copper Hills treated youth up to the age of 18. Because David was turning 18 in June 2011, the exit plan from Copper Hills was that he would come back to Reno. He would not be living with us, but would be going into a group home. Dan and I began counseling in February with David Turner, MFT, in order to prepare us for our son's return.

We were managing with everyday life, but we were not healed from the intensity of those last few years of living with an angry person and from the acute sense of our failure and disappointment. We did not feel able to cope with David's return to the area and the increased contact and involvement in his daily issues that would be inevitable. David has always been 'high maintenance' from the time he was a baby, with lots of interpersonal drama as well as real (and imagined) health concerns. We had a long list of doctors that he was seeing by the time he left Reno for Copper Hills. One of David's means of receiving validation is by being the center of attention. This takes the form of being emotionally upset about disturbances in relationships, a plethora of health concerns, and story telling.

We knew that we needed help processing our history with David and we knew that we needed a fresh starting point. We wanted to get assistance in dealing with the resentments that we realized we were carrying. Boundaries had to be set for our relationship with David so that we could maintain our autonomy and not be engulfed once again in his typically all-consuming urgent difficulties.

David Turner listened attentively, gave us practical advice, and was very encouraging. He had worked extensively with foster and adoptive children and their parents. He thought we were doing better than we thought we were doing! We kept the counseling sessions going as long as we could financially afford them, which was eight or nine weeks.

David did not come home as planned. In the final days before his discharge, because of recent violent behavior, the psychiatrist recommended that David be transferred to the company's psychiatric hospital, also in the Salt Lake area. David's Copper Hills treatment team determined that he was not ready to be released to a step-down facility with a lower level of care, which he would have gone to in Reno.

The day before he was 18, he was driven across the Salt Lake City suburbs to a facility named Benchmark, in Woods Cross. In order to protect David from being subjected to the adult unit at Benchmark, he was placed in a unit with the younger patients. This was a very wise move, as David was developmentally only about 15 and would have been out of place with the older clients.

During his stay at Benchmark, I don't believe he was in any fights. That season of angry outbursts had run its course.

Once again, the Lord had blessed David with another caring and skillful therapist. He and David had a good rapport, and David liked and respected him.

As had been the practice while he was in Copper Hills, David and his therapist called Dan and I once a week for one hour of family counseling. David was able to call us one or two other times during the week, depending on his behavior and his 'level.' David matured rapidly at Benchmark so that he eventually moved into the adult unit during his last few months there, and it worked out very well.

In both facilities, David bonded with some of the adult staff. They listened to him and treated him with respect. He has always related better to adults than to his peers.

We went to see David every three months while he was at Benchmark. The company was able to pay for our travel and motel, which was terrific.

Chrysalis

In August 2012, David flew home to Reno with a Benchmark staff person, after being in Benchmark a little over a year. Robert had counseled with us to determine which group home facility we felt would be best for David. We chose Chrysalis group homes. They use residential homes to house adults with intellectual and developmental disabilities, with a goal of guiding the client in as much independent living as possible. www.gochrysalis.com

Dan and I picked David up at the airport and spent a couple of hours moving his bed and dresser and some of his personal belongings that we had stored for him, into his new living situation. He would be living in a nice house in a neighborhood just five miles from our home. In this home, he lived with three other clients, each in their own bedroom. There was round-the-clock staff. The house manager was Rosie, a smart, experienced, and caring woman. Rosie assisted us in setting our boundaries so that they were practical for us, for her, and for her staff. She was just what we needed. She helped us see that by letting David call us at any time of the day and night with his needs, her authority was usurped. We needed to interact with him at designated times of the day and evening, and he needed to work with the staff on his house problems. It took some time to work this out but it was very wise counsel.

Living in this first home was to be temporary until another space opened up. As it was, David was proactive about this, much to his credit. He moved into another Chrysalis home, still in our part of town, for which we were very grateful. This change in housing worked out very well. David had another mature and caring house manager,

Richard, and, again, excellent staff. Since then he has moved again and has another excellent house manager, Shauna.

Chrysalis has been David's home for two-and-a-half years. He is getting used to making some of his own decisions, though he has had some real setbacks. The structure in the house is not as rigid as in the Utah facilities. We believe that in order for him to mature and to become self-governing, he needs the 'elbow room' so that he can try things, learn to think for himself, and explore possibilities—all within a supervised environment, and that is happening. When he has relationship problems, there is a structure, oversight, a listening ear, and restraint if necessary.

David receives monthly financial stipends from SSI (Supplemental Security Income) and from SRC (Sierra Regional Center). Chrysalis accountants pay from his account his share of the utilities, house phone, garbage, and cable. David receives from his account a weekly food allowance, and shops for his food with the house manager. He prepares most of his own meals, but sometimes the staff prepares family-style meals for the clients, or they have a barbeque. David also receives spending money, which he can decide how to spend, although always with the oversight of the house manager. David has money in his account, and he must receive permission from an administrator to withdraw any of that money. David also earns tokens in a behavior-modification plan. The tokens are turned in for money, which he can spend at the 7Eleven or the Dollar Store or some other approved place.

David calls us almost every evening and we talk to him for about 30-40 minutes. Sometimes he is worked up about a relationship problem or a health issue, and sometimes he asks our advice.

It must be very difficult to live with FAS. We can only conjecture how life with FAS presents its own unique challenges. We have empathy for people with other mental conditions and brain damage on any level, or with any other special needs challenges. We are grateful for the people who are in these caring professions.

We salute Special Olympics, Easter Seals, United Cerebral Palsy (UCP), SRC (Sierra Regional Center), Chrysalis, and the multitude of other organizations that work hard to improve the lives of a wide range of people.

David has been working in the warehouse at UCP five days a week and it is expected that he will soon be transferred to the UCP store. He earns a small salary.

While he has been living at Chrysalis, he has been involved with Special Olympics in basketball, track, and swimming. As the season for one sport ends, another begins, so there are weekly practices to look forward to. At the playoffs, he has received individual and team medals.

SSI

Norris is the one who strongly suggested we apply for SSI—Supplemental Security Income—for David.

He told us that with David's FAS diagnosis he would be considered disabled. With this condition, it would not be possible for him to get a full-time job and support himself. Because of David's attachment issues, it does not work for him to live with us. People who cannot support themselves live on the streets if they do not have government or family help.

When I began the process, I found out that I could not apply for SSI until David was 18. It was slightly complicated because I could not take David into the Social Security offices with me, since he was living in Utah at that time.

If you have a special needs child of your own, or one that you have adopted, make sure to get copies of all evaluations and diagnosis from clinics, hospitals, doctors, therapists and keep everything on file.

To receive SSI, I had to be able to prove through documentation that David was qualified to be on disability assistance.

Because I wanted confirmation that David had been suspected of fetal alcohol effect from birth, I went back to Special Children's Clinic. David had not been a client there for 16 years. I found out that they had stored all of their old files in a warehouse, and they were inaccessible. I did have David's hospital discharge paperwork from when he was born. The doctor had stated: *suspected fetal alcohol effect*. There is a long paragraph about David's mother's being under the influence of alcohol when she gave birth to David and at subsequent visits in the hospital while he was in NICU. This proved that David's condition was from his birth and that his mother had alcohol problems. This information is vital so that your child will receive a correct diagnosis and appropriate services if and when they are needed. This may not seem important when the child is young. But in case you will have need of them, collect all relevant paperwork so that in years to come you will not hit a dead end and discover that some of it is unavailable.

I also had the FAS Clinic report, Dr. Able's report, and the monthly evaluations from Copper Hills and Benchmark.

As a foster parent, keep all documentation on each child you care for. You can pass on to the biological parents or to the adoptive parents relevant paperwork that may be of crucial help to them. Each of our 52 foster children had a file, housed in one of our file cabinets. The files contain my scribbled notes on scraps of paper, extra copies of doctor's reports, social workers' thank you cards, anecdotes, photos, immunization records, travel slips, phone numbers, etc. We have received phone calls months after a child has left our care, asking for immunization records and other details. I was able to pull the file and know immediately if I could help the caller or not.

When I filled out the SSI paperwork, I was deeply comforted with the expectation that David was going to have to have a place to live all his life, unless the Lord intervened to heal him. Dan and I could not keep him with us, nor could we support him in a living situation and pay his bills. David had to have SSI when he turned 18 in order to continue living where he was in Utah, and for his placement after that one ended. I included a mother's personal appeal with the paperwork. I don't know if anyone read it, but I knew David had to be accepted.

We had been told that everyone is initially denied. That happened. But within a very short time we learned that we were approved. Of course, we had made our strongest appeal to God. I had emailed 35 friends and family to pray. I don't know how many did pray (only a few replied), but Jesus moved on our behalf.

SSI clients are re-evaluated every two or three years to determine if the individual's status has changed. Of course, our prayer is that David will be healed and will be able eventually to work and support himself.

The safeguard of guardianship

To secure the guardianship we needed an attorney and a friend had a recommendation for us. More paperwork and fees—but on David's 18th birthday, we went to court, and we were granted legal guardianship of our son. Again we had asked people to pray that it would be an efficient process, and it was.

Norris had advised us that without the guardianship, David could get married, sign his name to buy a car, apply for credit cards, etc. With the guardianship, his signature by itself is not legal. We have had many opportunities to reinforce to him that he cannot buy a car, join the military, get a credit card, get married, etc., on his own.

We thought David might balk at the idea of guardianship. We prayed about how to explain it to him so that he would understand that it was for his protection and not for his limitation (although actually it certainly does limit him, from making bad mistakes that could be very serious to him and have ramifications for all of us).

One weekend, when we were visiting him in Utah having lunch in a Panda Express, we brought up the subject. David was used to the idea that he had a team that worked together to make decisions for and with him. Dan explained that with the guardianship, the team would continue to make decisions regarding his life, even though he was turning 18. David was sure the team would be more lenient than we would be as his careful parents, and that it would mean he would get to do all the things that he felt he had been denied all these years. That sounded good to him.

We have learned with David to keep the discussions simple and brief and then to move on to another topic. He can ask questions later as they arise.

Walking by faith is strenuous! But why should we ever give up hope when "with God all things are possible." We believe in miracles. We know that signs, wonders, and miracles are happening in our world today. God may surprise us all and show up and touch David's brain and restore those brain cells! Oh what a happy day that would be.

The insights...

<u>A word from the Lord</u>

Before we began foster care, the Lord gave me a clear word that what we were stepping into, the world of foster care and adoption, was not going to be easy.

I have never been a member of Aglow, but I went to an Aglow Conference in Carson City, in 1993 or 1994, before we had started fostering. I had no sooner arrived, than a lady that I did not know came up to me and said that she had a 'word' for me. She seemed pretty excited about it, but for some reason I put her off, and kept putting her off, the rest of that day. Finally she almost insisted that we sit and talk. This is what I remember about it:

The Lord wants you to know that He has a very intense ministry for you. It will push you to your limits, but don't despair. He will be with you every step of the way. There will be times when you will think you are losing your mind. But hold on to Him. He has prepared you for this and He will see you through it.

The lady acted so relieved that she had been able to unload the weight of her message, and I felt badly for having kept her at bay. I felt sure that what she had spoken was from the Holy Spirit, and I had the conviction that it was regarding foster care. I was not deterred in my vision, but realized that I was even more excited about the challenge before me. I took this prophetic counsel seriously and it helped me be steady in the crunch times. God was with me.

You might have noticed that same excitement rising up inside you when a difficult task or a demanding problem is put before you. Maybe now you are realizing that rather than being dismayed in reading about our foster and adoption years, you can hear a summons from the Holy Spirit that is giving you courage, which you would not normally have possessed. You may be experiencing it now, and you may feel surprisingly and bravely interested in moving toward fostering or toward adopting.

If so, seek your own personal word from the Lord. We did not base our decisions to foster or to adopt on one person's 'word from the Lord.' For six years I searched the Bible, cried out to God, and wrote down everything I believed I was hearing from Him. I agonized and sought Him: "What is Your will for us, Lord? We only want to please You and live for You. Speak in such a way that we know it is You. Speak so that both Dan and I hear Your purpose for us and our family."

The Bible says:

'Call to Me, and I will answer you, and show you great and mighty things which you do not know.' Jeremiah 33:3

'And you will seek me and find Me, when you search for Me with all your heart.' Jeremiah 29:13.

Call Him, seek Him, and search for Him with all your heart. Over and over again. He will meet you.

Reasons people adopt

One day, a few years ago, I was thinking about the reasons people might decide to adopt. I kept adding to the list as ideas came to my mind. As you are seeking the Lord and praying, the Holy Spirit may use this list to help you clarify your ideas and motives:

- supernatural experience: *"I had a vision."*
- love for God: *"Lord, what can I do to show my love for You?"*
- obedience to God: *"I hear Your bidding. Yes, I will do it."*
- caring for the orphan is a biblical thing to do:
  Religion that our Father accepts as pure and faultless is this: to look
  after the orphans and widows in their distress and to keep oneself from
  being polluted by the world. James 1:27 NIV
- personal conviction: *"God told me to do it."*
- humanitarian: *"I believe in 'rescue' work."*
- Messiah complex: *"I'm the one that's supposed to save this child."*
- my need:
  - for a sense of personal fulfillment
  - for the attention and acclaim
  - to have a baby or a child that I cannot produce
- long-held dream: *"I always knew I would adopt."*
- thoughtlessness: *"It seemed like the right thing to do."*
- peer pressure: *"I got swept up in adoption fever."*
- societal need: *"I was overcome by the statistics."*
- guilt or pity: *"Nobody else wanted this poor child."*

- to spite husband: *"I'll show HIM!"*
- to spite wife: *"I'll show HER!"*
- to spite others: *"I'll show THEM!"*
- to 'one-up' somebody else: *"This ought to impress them!"*
- pressure from the system–*"If you don't, maybe nobody else will take them!"*
- pressure from sibling, parent, grandparent: (a guilt trip) *"How can you ignore the plight of this poor child!*
- pressure from your own children: *"Mom, PLEASE, I want a little sister!"*
- pressure from society: advertisements or statistics
- inner pressures: *"I didn't want to break up a sibling group."*

You may find that one or even several of these ideas are working in your mind regarding whether or not you will decide to foster or adopt. Some of them are noble, some are prideful, and some are spiritual. Each one needs to be laid down at the Cross; yes, even the spiritual ones. The richness of our lives comes out of our relationship with Jesus. I believe He wants to be considered and that He wants you to seek His opinion. I believe that He wants you to have a testimony of how you submitted your interest in caring for children to Him and how He led you step-by-step to your conclusion. During the process, He may re-direct you. He may show you that your own children need you more than you have realized and inspire you to spend more time with them. He may show you that you are a support person and that you can do more good focusing on your own family and helping a foster family a couple of times a month. He may show you that your nieces and nephews need you so that they don't end up in foster care.

We saw wonderful Christian families torn apart through divorce because they overextended themselves in fostering and adoption.

We saw the children of wonderful Christians get lost and set aside because their parents kept reaching out to other people's children.

We have apologized to our sons for however we over-emphasized the foster children's needs over their needs.

If you are already committed to taking care of your niece or nephew, I believe Jesus will meet you and uphold you as you diligently seek Him. Be committed to taking care of them as unto the Lord— through His strength and with His methods of love and prayerfulness. If you are faltering in your parenting, pray about getting counseling. You might try to set up a support group of other foster parents and take turns supervising the children while the others share their stories and their needs, and pray for one another.

Suggestions and encouragements

A husband and wife need to be in agreement that they want to do foster care and that they want to adopt, and they need to stay in agreement.

When we started the process of getting into foster care, Dan began having second thoughts and the whole idea was put 'on hold' for a few weeks. Because he knew my vision and commitment to fostering, he honored me and sought the Lord in prayer and fasting. He had been worried that it was going to be a huge distraction, and not a positive move for our family. He did not look forward to getting back into car seats, cribs, playpens, and all of the time-consuming involvement that having a baby in the house would bring. As he fasted and sought the Lord, he began to understand that having babies in the house was going to be good for the whole family. The evidence that God was speaking to him was that his attitude completely changed and then stayed changed. It was still hard and it was still time consuming, and there was a rigorous period of adjustment for us all, but knowing that God had spoken personally to each of us, we kept moving forward together.

As I said, we have seen some families seriously overextend themselves. In fact, we found ourselves in a stressful situation when we had our five kids plus five fosters. It is so easy for this to happen. Couples need to stay in communication, and listen to each other, and be willing to make changes for the good of the family. Patience and good humor will be necessary in the interim.

Another temptation to overextend is that fostering brings compensation. At the time that we retired, the monthly salary was $1200 a month per child (as compared to $385 per month when we began foster care). I believe strongly that there should be generous compensation for this work. But it is tempting to want to move to a bigger house with a bigger mortgage, or to buy another car, etc. People can get spread too thin and relationships can suffer. And before you know it, you have your own small orphanage and all of the time-consuming responsibilities that go with it. Been there.

A family's dynamics change dramatically when you have your own baby. But to bring in someone else's baby, toddler, school-age child, or teen—brings untold challenges. If husband and wife are not prepared to love and discipline the child together there will be trouble. Your teamwork needs to be strong or the stress can be unbearable. We found we needed to constantly maintain our level of teamwork.

The project of bringing foster children into your home becomes part of the training and modeling that your own children experience. They benefit from it in the same way as the other things you do as a family. They become a part of the team; they are not shoved aside. This is a family commitment.

An older foster or adopted child may often try to divide and conquer. By that I mean that she will seek to divide the family by causing disruptions and by putting herself in the supreme attention position, or by allying with one of the family members to turn one against another. Foster and adopted kids can be serious attention-seekers and may do just about anything to get it.

A very dysfunctional child will bring disruption, may do physical damage to the home, or harm your own child. You may as well expect unique problems that you have not anticipated. Dan says, "The children are from a different gene pool than your own children and they have very different backgrounds, which profoundly affects who they are and how they behave. Their behavior won't make any sense to you—you will find yourself saying, 'Why do they do that?'"

This is not a decision to take lightly.

Do some soul-searching as you re-read the 'reasons people adopt'. Some of those reasons will not provide a firm foundation upon which to extend your family. If your reasons to foster and adopt are superficial, the results will be beyond your capability to handle. Your family will have an artificial façade that cannot withstand the fierceness of the storms that will come against it.

What storms?

- babies that cry half the night (or all night), night after night with the resulting fatigue that is inevitable
- your own children becoming dissatisfied, unhappy, and rebellious. It may take months to move a problematic foster child out of your home

- working with biological parents that are very disagreeable or downright dangerous
- adopting a sweet child whose personality later changes with puberty
- coping with your own failure, insecurities, fears, feelings of helplessness and hopelessness, as well as anger and resentment

This is an endeavor that will force you to grow—or crush you.

I don't want to do to you what has annoyed me. I don't want to assume that you do not pray or read your Bible. I do not want to assume that you have not given this serious thought and prayer. I will not assume that about you.

I am speaking now to the person who has <u>not</u> put this to prayer or discussed it with God.

I believe God hears all conversations directed His way. Talk to Him. You might say: "God, I don't talk to you much, but I am really interested in helping children. Would you please help my husband and me make this decision? Please give us a strong conviction and agreement if we are to proceed. Please give us a strong caution if we are not to proceed. Help us to know it is You that is directing us!"

I suggest that you read your Bible and ask the Holy Spirit to speak to you—more than once or twice! Get really serious about it. Think about individuals or couples that you would use as personal references. Talking to them might be helpful, especially if they know you well.

If you do not have people to use as references, you will not be able to do this job. In Washoe County seven references are required, with only two being family members. This is not a job that is done in a vacuum. If you do not like people very much, working on becoming a friendly and congenial person is a good initial goal for you.

If you have already adopted, and are feeling pinched and have the urgency for escape—there is always hope and help in Jesus Christ! He is the God of the impossible. He is FOR you, and He is FOR your adopted child. Cry out to Him with all your heart. It may seem that your situation is beyond desperate and irreversible. My Bible says that *He always leads us in triumph* (2 Cor. 2:14), so press in to Him, but also get professional help. The people He provided for us in the village were consistently top quality professionals. I pray that you will surrender completely to Jesus, pour out your heart to Him, and that He will lead you clearly to the next step.

Go to your county website. In Reno it is: www.fostercare@washoecounty.us

It lists foster parent requirements, characteristics of foster parents, and orientation and training dates. Washoe County requires 27 hours of initial training for foster parents, and four hours of in-service training per year. You will need to submit to a criminal background check for yourself and for anyone living in your home who is 18 or older. There is also a child abuse/local law enforcement screening. You must provide a physician's statement about your medical condition. There will also be expectations about the state of your home.

If you are interested in adopting a local child, you can be approved to be a 'fos/adopt' home. This is the abbreviation for 'foster/adoptive' family. In this capacity, children will be placed in your home who will possibly be coming up for adoption. The primary goal of the system in Reno is to return the child to his biological family, and you will need to cooperate with that. But the child may be available for adoption if no family members step forward who are willing to raise the child, or if they do not fulfill the county's requirements, or if the family placement fails.

It will probably seem like a daunting undertaking. Even in the initial stages, this calling is not for the meek or the weak. Keep praying. Talk to God about what you feel you are gleaning from your questioning and your searching. You could keep a journal that records your conversations with God, what impresses you as you read your Bible daily, what people have said that is encouraging or discouraging, and the highlights of the classes that impress you. You could make a 'pro-and-con' list.

I believe that if you follow these suggestions, you will have your answer in time, and I pray right now that God will clearly lead you each step of the way as you submit yourself to His Lordship.

Highlights from John Trentalange's philosophy

We received so much help and encouragement from John. We received our second wind of motivation, a renewed philosophy of parenting, and concrete advice that we were able to put immediately into practice.

1. Don't be task oriented, be relationship oriented. Remember: keeping the relationship intact is the goal. If we are driven to complete the specific task we lose focus on the relationship.

2. Time in – Most of us set the disruptive child aside and give him 'time out' for disobedience or rowdiness. John suggests 'time in', because much of the time the disorderly child is causing a ruckus because he is looking for a connection. "It looks like you need some 'time in' with Dad, David. Let's go out back and work on those weeds together."

3. The good things in life, like our children, are worth hard work.

4. Be emotionally present, be calm, be clear and consistent, and don't give confusing messages. The messages we need to deliver to David are deeper and stronger than words. They are about caring and commitment. We give negative messages through our body language and actions—such as, if we walk away yelling "go to your room!"
   The positive messages we want to deliver will be communicated by staying in the conversation, not yelling, not leaving, and what he will <u>hear</u> is:
   - ✓ "I will always love you in spite of your behavior."
   - ✓ "I am here for you." [*we are really conveying: "nothing you can do can overwhelm me."*
   - ✓ "I am not going anywhere." [*we are really conveying: "nothing you can do can push me away."*]
   - ✓ "Certain behaviors that you do have consequences, but I want to connect to you in a positive way."
   - ✓ "I really like it when you act like this, it makes me want to spend time with you."

5. People need incentives to motivate them towards desirable behavior. When children wake up in the morning, the good things that are built into the day are their incentives. There need to be enough incentives in life so that even if some of those incentives are lost as a consequence of bad behavior, there are still other incentives and life is still good. If everything is taken away, the message is rejection. Things that are taken away need to be restored fairly quickly—within three days to a week.

6. "Your behavior is showing me...." The first thing that we implemented from our counseling with John was the phrase *"Your behavior is showing me...."* This phrase is always used in a quiet controlled manner, never by yelling or by demanding.

    For example: "Your behavior is showing me that you do not want to watch that TV program tonight." or "Your behavior is showing me that you have lost interest in earning money for taking out the trash. You still have to take out the trash, but I will not be paying you for it if you continue in that disrespectful attitude." Then the child gets a chance to change his behavior.

7. Team meetings: This concept was such a Godsend. I mentioned that a child's goal may be to 'divide and conquer.' John told us to get David used to the fact that Dan and I made our decisions as a team. When David would press me for a decision about something, instead of buckling under the pressure and getting stressed and giving in—or getting mad—I would say, "David, I'll talk to Dad about it and get back to you."This is an amazing way to stay in control in a very nice way. If he got angry and yelled— "just tell me NOW." I could say calmly, "I tried to get Dad on his cell phone, but he is with clients. He will be home at 8:00 and I will be happy to talk to him about it then." I wouldn't have to get into a power struggle. I just re-iterated that I would get back to him about it. I was able to stay in self-control and not lose it if he became angry and started yelling. I would stand firm on my boundary that Dan and I make the decisions in the home based on our working together as a team.
    David got used to having to wait for decisions to be made. It was a great lesson in delayed gratification, which is a challenge for everyone.

8. John suggested we remember: (from my notes on 11-18-06)
    My value is in obeying God.
    My value is NOT in whether David obeys me or is nice to me.
    It is my job to love David.
    It is not my job to get love from him.
    Jesus loved; He was not always loved back. He was not a failure
    He was obedient.
    My value is based on God's response to me.
    My value is not based on David's response to me.

I need to stop wanting things from David: love, respect, kindness.

I am committed to David, not to his choices.

Focus on what we are giving David, not on what he is giving us.

No one chooses to be a parent of a child with disabilities. Go ahead and grieve this.

ACCEPTANCE and PEACE are the signs of grief being over.

David is our ministry, but the ministry is not what gives us value. Think about Noah, Moses, and Jesus. Each of them obeyed what God asked them to do, but they were not valued by all of the people around them. In fact, in many people's eyes they were failures. In keeping our eyes on the Lord, we walk in obedience to Him and get our significance from that. We do not get our significance from what people say about us.

The honeymoon stage

Here is a letter that I wrote to Michelle Molina Price, the social worker who with Haley had brought David into our home. This was written in 1994, three weeks after David had arrived.

I am sorry I missed your call yesterday. I have been wanting to give you a report on this precious child you directed our way. He is a wonderful boy, Michelle. We have seen David brighten up before our eyes. There are so many prayers going up for him, and God is working in his life. He is a happy happy baby, very curious, always reaching out to explore his world. Also, very persistent. His disposition is wonderful. He is patient and uncomplaining, though he lets us know about the condition of his diaper and whether he is hungry or tired. He is easily satisfied, not spoiled or over-indulged. The hardships he has faced in many ways have given him a more pleasant personality. That is God working everything for good, we believe. He will go to strangers easily, studies them seriously. Those who talk to him and cuddle him and fuss over him a little are rewarded with a <u>beautiful</u> smile. People stop me everywhere I go to ask me about him and to comment on what a beautiful boy he is. I tell them that he is our foster baby—he is excellent advertisement for your program! I am being very careful what I say about him, realizing that "this could be David's mother I am talking to."

When I wrote this note, I was in euphoria (or what is commonly called the honeymoon stage of fostering). I was so thrilled to see the changes that our love was making on this needy little baby boy. I also felt like I was contributing to society by intervening in his very sad life and 'saving' him. He had been on the track of falling right through the cracks—and we had intruded into the downward spiral his life had been taking, had reached into it, and had pulled him out.

All of this was true. I was not misinterpreting what our intervention had done for David. The delusional part was that I expected little David's progress to continue at this rate– and that he would become normal at warp speed. I expected that he was well on his way to being an ordinary boy, and that his challenges would fall away, fade away—and he would be free of them in a short time.

This expectation was inaccurate and misguided, and I was on shaky ground.

The other reason for my delight was that I was ecstatic that our sons were having this experience of giving and loving. They were learning to focus on extending themselves out of their comfort zone and they were enthusiastically 'giving themselves away' to our guest, our soon-to-be little brother.

From this place of exhilaration, I could never have imagined that I would be grieving the dream rather than seeing it fulfilled.

<u>It is a covenant relationship</u>

From the honeymoon to the grave! From euphoria to grieving the dream. And then the dream dies very dead, and yet we keep on walking.

So why go to all of this effort? Because I am in a covenant relationship: I am committed to the adopted child, and to the Person who called me to this relationship. I will not walk away from it. God has placed me here on earth and in this relationship to be part of His redemption story, so that the rejected, brain damaged child understands what the unconditional love of God is like.

When our lives show what God's love in a difficult situation can do, people pay attention and some of them want that kind of love for themselves.

It is a common story: anyone who walks through difficulty and relies on Jesus Christ comes out a better person and there will be fruit. We can find testimonies galore.

The plot may not unfold as you had envisioned at the outset, but God gets some consideration. The thrust of the attention may be: "They must be crazy, I'm glad it's them and not me! I wonder how this will turn out?"

As we persevere through the years, I believe that *He who calls you is faithful, He will surely do it. 1 Thessalonians 5:24 NIV* He called me to this relationship with David, and He will be faithful to me as I walk it out—as my Father, my Savior, my Healer, my Comforter, my Helper, and more.

I mentioned in the beginning of the book that this adoption experience may be more of a faith walk than you ever imagined you could do. But didn't God hear you say in a surrendered time, "Lord, how can I serve You?" Friend, that you are walking by faith makes God happy because, *Without faith it is impossible to please God. Hebrews 11:6*

Counseling with David Turner MFT

Let's shift to February 2011—seventeen years after I wrote that thank you note to our social worker, Michelle. David was in the youth residential treatment center in Utah. We were preparing for his return to Reno in June, when he 'aged out' of the facility because he was turning 18 in four months.(Remember that David was transferred to another facility and did not in fact come back to Reno for fourteen more months.)

I previously mentioned that in anticipating David's return to Reno, Dan suggested that we get professional counseling in order to be ready to deal with our son again. Even though he would not be living in our home, we were still very shaken by our most recent years with David and did not want to fall back into past feelings of sadness and discouragement. We wanted to approach the prospect of being involved in his daily life with a fresh perspective.

David Turner helped us see that we had experienced:

1. The loss of a child. The child we adopted had morphed into another person that we tried unsuccessfully to deal with but felt like we lost him in our attempts to help him.
2. The loss of self-efficacy. Self-efficacy is a person's belief in his or her ability to bring about change, or to succeed in a personal situation.(4) A person with strong self-efficacy sees new and challenging problems as tasks to be mastered. A person with a weak sense of self-efficacy avoids challenging tasks, believing the tasks are beyond his capabilities.

David Turner's example was Peter in the Bible. He had had incredible self-efficacy. He was the guy that was 'all in.' Yet later, he wept bitterly, and realized that his zeal wasn't worth anything.

Through our experience with raising David, we had traded our strong self-efficacy for inadequacy and we were now living among our friends and co-workers in the belief that we had failed.

3. We were living in 'loss of sense of self' as measured by what we **do**.
4. We were experiencing loss of being creative and courageous.
5. We were experiencing loss of what we had considered our 'mission.'
6. We were deeply grieved by the loss of our youth church.
7. I was experiencing the loss of being a **star** in foster care.
8. I was experiencing loss of physical mobility. I had been used to walking daily which had become increasingly more difficult because of pain in my hip. Although I had inherited my hip problem from my Dad, I surmised that the disintegration of my hip was partly the result of resentment and bitterness landing in my physical body. Emotional stressors can become physical pain. I was continually having to deal with my disappointment in who David was turning out to be.
9. We were advised by David Turner to ask the Lord: "What is Your redemptive purpose in all of this?"

<u>Thanks for helping me cope:</u>

I have some very faithful friends who have been unwavering in their commitment to me, friends that I cherish: Jackie S, Bonnee, Janet, Diane, Vera, Sandy, Patty, Jackie C, Kathy M, Kathy B, Lucy, and Karen M. A great support was my long-time friend JoAnn A, who has gone to be with the Lord. I have known each of these women for a minimum of 18 years, two of them for forty years. My awesome sisters, Marsha and Connie, have stood by me steadfastly, unwavering in their support, love, and friendship.

I met with three teens, Charisse, Katelyn, and Juliana, once a week for three years, in a mentoring group. They are now 21, 22, and 23. I am so proud of these girls. Maintaining my connection with them, and being valued by them, has been a tremendous 'pick-me-up' over the years.

I was in a book club with my friend, Renee, which brought lots of laughs and was always uplifting.

I have been a volunteer at the Sparks Library, shelving books and media materials one to four hours a week for five years. The librarians, aides, and other volunteers there have been like angels for me. These men and women have not realized what their appreciation of me, and their friendship, has meant to me. My splintered life was set aside during the hours I worked in the library stacks. My joy was in knowing that I would receive cheery hellos and appreciative thanks from them every week.

I have attended a weekly women's Bible study, for the last 5½ years and made many precious friends and received lasting emotional healing. Thank you to each of the women on the prayer team who prayed faithfully and powerfully and often for me.

At the time of publication, and over the last several months, David's behavior has regressed. He falls back into anxiety, anger, blaming others, and has been cutting himself again. Robert has encouraged us that it is not uncommon that as behavior is being extinguished there is a resurgence of symptoms. I want to thank David's therapist, Jennifer, and David's work supervisor, Stephanie, for their heartfelt support of David (and me) through this awkward period! Thank you for your unwavering solidarity. Thank you for caring about David.

Part IV - The Good News about adoption

<u>Pep Talk</u>

The foster care experience can be positive and fulfilling, which is what it was for me. If you are doing foster care and it is not positive and fulfilling, but only dreary and strenuous, and it has been like that for a long time, you may want to devote yourself to some serious prayer as to whether you are in the right helping profession. Ask Jesus to revive you or to re-direct you. Ask people to pray for you.

Even though foster care was positive and fulfilling and literally 'a dream come true' for me, I needed help from the Lord every single day. In photos during that time, I look very tired, but I also look ecstatically happy!

This book was conceived with four goals:

1. to proclaim the excellencies of Him who called us out of darkness into his marvelous light (1 Peter 2:9)

2. to advise people to take fostering and adoption very seriously and to stay in a close personal relationship with Jesus throughout their experience in it

3. to strongly recommend that the couple who is fostering be strongly joined together in their commitment to each other and their biological children, and that they stay in open and honest communication with each other and with the Lord

4. to encourage the church family to be available to assist the families who are fostering or adopting

<u>It's Time</u>

Our time on earth is short. Even if we were not going to some day give an account of our lives to the Lord, it would just make sense to live out our years here in some significant way. Many people want to live a meaningful life, a life that counts, and one that leaves the world a better place. Many people find meaning for their lives by investing themselves in enriching other people's lives.

If God is in the work you are doing 'for Him', you have the satisfaction that you are being obedient to The One Who Matters. He will help you to stay humble, so you don't feel like too much of a hero, which could be a stumbling block. He will be there for you whenever you turn to Him, and you will find that you are being held in His everlasting arms.

If there are problems in your home, think about what Mother Teresa said, that loving the world starts in our homes. *"But before we are able to live that life outside, we must live it in our own homes. Charity begins at home."*(5)

It's time. The Bible says: *Your people shall be volunteers in the day of Your power.* Psalm 110:3The day of God's power is here. The Holy Spirit is being poured out upon all flesh (Joel 2:28) and we, His people, have the privilege of stepping forward to be involved in His work on the earth.

If you are looking for purpose or meaning for your life, ask Jesus what it is that He would like you to do.

1. We all have gifts from the Holy Spirit.

Having then gifts differing according to the grace that is given to us, let us use them. Romans 12:6.

If you have been a Christian for awhile, you probably have determined what your gifts are. Often the things we like to do indicate our gifting: teaching, childcare, attending sick people, organizing and/or administration, or perhaps hospitality. There are also inventories that you can take which determine your preferences and strengths through a series of many questions. They can be found online.

Your friends or co-workers might point out that you seem to have an administrative gift, or that if they got real sick they would like you to take care of them. You can also pray and ask the Holy Spirit to lead you and confirm what you think your gifts are.

2. There are good works that Jesus wants us to walk in.

For we are His workmanship created in Christ Jesus for good works, which God prepared beforehand that we should walk in them. Ephesians 2:10

It may, or may not be, foster care or adoption, but you will be able to partner with Jesus in something He already has in mind for you to do.

The world is full of hurting people. You may be one of them right now. That means you will need some healing before you reach out to help someone else who is needy.

One thing we do know: "Jesus is the answer for the world today, above Him there's no other, Jesus is the way."(6)

There will come a time when He says, "Honey, it's time for you to extend yourself to others."

God believes in the family

I was thinking about the concept, 'it takes a village to raise a child.' It has been used as the title of a couple of books, and is commonly known to be an African saying.

But I propose that 'it takes a family to raise a child.'

If the only input in a person's life is the village, no matter how sympathetic, astute, caring, and practical the village may be, there is going to be something missing. There is no substitute for the deeply influential connections that are built into family life.

The family is God's idea. He didn't start with a town, He started with a man and a woman and their children.

It is the family that helps the child process everything he is hearing from the village—especially if he has limited thinking capacity. David calls us almost every night to tell us about his day and to get our input on his experiences in the village. In many ways he is maturing. He is becoming proactive. An example of this is that he wanted to change to a different Chrysalis home after several months of living in the first one. I initially protested because we really liked the house manager, Rosie, and her staff, and I felt that he was safe there. But within a few minutes I came to my senses. WOW! David is making an adult, proactive decision that it is time to move to another home. I need to support him in this.

The family and the village worked together successfully.

It is the family who advocates for the child. Dan and/or I were present at every appointment with every villager that met with David as he was growing up in our home. We have stood up for David, we have dialogued where David could not have understood what was going on, and where he could not have discussed or evaluated things on his own. We often felt that we had a better idea than the person in the village of what would be best for David.

This first year that David was back in town from Utah, I started out being 'Mother Bear Mom' and jumped in with both feet to be David's advocate. After a few months, the Lord showed me clearly that I was to back off and let the house manager take David to his appointments and she would report to me. In the beginning, when he was ill, I met them at the doctor's office. If he went to the ER, I was there. (David goes to the ER often.) But, God showed me that David could only progress in moving into adulthood as I stepped back. The family needs to know when to let the child-becoming-an-adult take more of the reins. The Lord helps us know these things.

It is the family who is there with the young child 24/7. The family keeps on loving, forgiving, and providing nurturing. The family helps to work out the problems and settle the disputes. The family is supportive when others get weary or give up.

The villagers go home every night. They have given their daily hours away, and they go to their own homes and to their own families or to the place they live alone or with roommates. And in their families, they receive their own comfort and replenishment.

We have come to love the village. The village came around us and helped us in ways that we had never imagined we would need.

We have accessed invaluable village assistance in Medicaid, SSI, and court-appointed guardianship. We sing the praises of amazing therapists, doctors, nurses, and receptionists. We are so thankful for the probation officers, educators, coaches, scoutmasters, tutors, music teachers, doctors, lawyers, judges, social workers, treatment program staff, counselors, pastors, and other wonderful people God put in David's and our lives. This is real. This is not an exaggeration. It has been a magnetic attraction of genuinely caring individuals to us.

The church is where God's families meet. It is where singles step into family interconnectedness, and divorcees and widows are accepted. In the local church, relationships are built that become trusting and supportive. We look for one another each week, and we look out for each other by praying and keeping in touch. When doing foster care, having the support of the church is a great under girding influence. Foster parents need respite care for their foster children so they can get a break and keep their marriage strong. They could use some free time to do something fun with their own children so their family bonds can stay strong. It is helpful for church friends to offer meals, lawn care, rides to sports activities, and even be available to share with house cleaning and laundry.

In our experience, our church friends stepped in right from the beginning and prayed and got excited with us as we went through the initial steps of approval by the Department of Child and Family Services.

The ladies in our church gave a baby shower for David soon after he came to us and supplemented his very meager wardrobe. Some of their children made a banner welcoming David. Everyone celebrated his arrival and he got lots of attention.

Dawn and Jackie put fresh paint on dismal bedroom walls and wallpapered the kitchen before we moved into the 2400 square foot house. A few years later, Jinny helped me paint the family room. When the mother of one of our foster children was nearing the end of her pregnancy, the ladies in the church gave her a luncheon and a baby shower, and everyone overwhelmed her with gifts. Cherisewed some outfits for David when he was young. Jackie and her husband bought shoes for one of our sons. Joe and Helen remembered David's birthdays with gifts and hugs when he was young.

We thank our pastors and their wives and their congregations for loving and supporting us during our fostering years and in the succeeding years. Your support was invaluable. Thank you!

Part V - Epilogue

The God of the Bible is very personal and very faithful and very loving. He is also prophetic. God speaks to people to tell them future events, to encourage them, to warn them, to correct them, and for other reasons. He gives visions, words of knowledge, and words of wisdom. He also highlights our Bible reading, especially if we are seeking him for direction or insight into something we are going through, and that is called a **rhema** word from God.

Do you passionately want to hear His voice? Talk to the Holy Spirit. Every time I sit to read my Bible, I write in my journal, SPEAK LORD (as the boy Samuel said when he heard the Lord call his name in 1 Samuel 3:10). Then I read, expecting to have verses highlighted by the Holy Spirit for my edification and instruction, and I write what I hear from the Lord in my journal.

I have described the vision I had, and I have explained my meeting with the woman coming up to me in the Aglow conference. God wanted to speak to me, and both of those encounters with Him were hugely encouraging. In Part VI of this book, you can read "The Vision and the Visitation" which is another encounter I had with Him.

There are two more awesome prophetic experiences that God gave us that I want to include.

In 2001, Eric Johnson from Bethel Church in Redding, California, visited our home with his youth group. He was calling out words of knowledge and he spoke a word of healing: "I don't want to embarrass anybody, but somebody here is having a really hard time with a learning disability, with math and reading, and God wants to heal you." David was at Old Oak Ranch at a kids' camp that week, but nobody else in the room acknowledged that they had a problem like what Eric had described. So Dan spoke up and said that the word must be for our son, David, who was not present. Healings of this type take place commonly at Bethel Church. We have heard testimonies of healings of Dyslexia, ADD, Obsessive-Compulsive Disorder, and Bipolar Disorder and many others. We have remembered and claimed this 'word' for David, and we are still waiting, agreeing with it, praying, and expecting it to come to pass.

In 2007, when we were living in the Red Rock house, Dan and David had been on a camping trip. When they returned David walked into the kitchen, and I saw peace on his face, and he looked completely healed and in his right mind. He said, "Hi, Mom. We had a great time. I'm going in to take a shower. See ya later." I was stunned.

Dan came into the kitchen and, still in shock, I said, "David looks healed." Dan said, "I saw and experienced the same thing yesterday at the campsite."

A few days later, while we were in church, Lora told us that she was looking at David standing against the wall in the back of the church and he was standing up straight, clear-eyed, and apparently completely healed. She was contemplating this, and when she looked again he was back to his normal appearance. She understood that to be God opening a window to show us what He was going to do.

In His sovereignty, God pulled back the veil for me, for Dan, and for Lora. We received hope at a critical time that David would be healed, and it encouraged us greatly. We needed it, because the months at Red Rock were some of the worst times for David. We felt that God was giving us something tangible to hang onto. He was showing us His power to heal. He was giving us the ability to work for something that was good and inspiring us to walk by faith to attain it.

God does not play games. He does not tease. We take Him very seriously.

God is not a man that He should lie, nor a son of man that he should repent. Has He said, and will He not do? Or has He spoken, and will He not make it good? Num. 23:19

To declare that the Lord is upright, He is my rock, there is no unrighteousness in Him. Psalm 92:15

Have you not known? Have you not heard? The everlasting God, the LORD, the Creator of the ends of the earth, neither faints nor is weary. His understanding is unsearchable. Isaiah 40:29

We cannot put our God in a box and think we have ever figured Him out. We seek Him with all our hearts as much as we can in our flakey humanity. In our work, we may get derailed, but we get up and keep going. We worship Him in our church services, and in our living rooms with all our hearts, and promise Him our devotion. And then, when He asks us to do something for Him, we are willing and prepared to say yes. Of course, later, we may be screaming—*God what is happening???* HELP!!!! But He is there, encouraging us, under girding us, and strengthening us.

He gives power to the weak, and to those who have no might He increases strength...but those who wait on the LORD shall renew their strength.... Is a 40:29.

Since 2006, I have been collecting verses for David's healing. I go through periods of praying them, and find that it is easiest to be disciplined when I take them on my morning walk and meditate on them, which I do sporadically.

I have personalized the verses, inserting David's name. Speaking verses out loud, proclaiming them to the spiritual realm, is prophetic! Believing that what I do not see with my eyes, yet believe in my heart, even though weakly, is prophetic! I am calling what is not as though it was real. (Romans 4:17)

And David continued to grow and become strong, increasing in wisdom; and the grace of God was upon him. Luke 2:40

Do not be afraid any longer; only believe and David shall be made well. Luke 8:50

For if you forgive David when he sins against you, your heavenly Father will also forgive you. But, if you do not forgive David of his sins, your Father will not forgive your sins. Matt.14:15

And Jesus went about all Galilee, teaching in their synagogues, preaching the gospel of the kingdom, and healing all kinds of sickness and all kinds of disease among the people. Then his fame went throughout all Syria; and they brought to Him all sick people who were afflicted with various diseases and torments, and those who were demon-possessed, epileptics and paralytics, and HE HEALED THEM. Matt 4:23-24

Thus says the Lord who made you and formed you from the womb, who will help you. Do not fear, David, my servant...whom I have chosen. Is a 44:2

When evening had come, they brought to Him many who were demon-possessed. And he cast out the spirits with a word, and healed all that were sick, that it might be fulfilled which was spoken by the prophet Isaiah, "HE HIMSELF TOOK OUR INFIRMITIES AND BORE OUR SICKNESSES." Matt 8:17

For You formed David's inward parts; You covered him in his mother's womb. I will praise You, for he is fearfully and wonderfully made; marvelous are Your works, and that my soul knows very well.[Lord, I forgive his parents who tampered with Your formation and I trust Your redeeming power.]

David's frame was not hidden from You when he was made in secret and skillfully wrought in the lowest parts of the earth.

Your eyes saw David's substance, being yet unformed. And in Your book they all were all written—the days fashioned for David, when yet there was none of them.

How precious....yes! How precious also are Your thoughts to David, O God! How great is the sum of them! If I should count them they would be more in number than the sand! Ps 139:13-18

Do not rejoice over me, my enemy; when I fall, I will arise, when I sit in darkness, the Lord will be a light to me. Micah 7:8

I believe we have been proactive for David and for the foster children the Lord has prompted us to advocate for. We have a clear conscience that we have walked extra miles with David. We have not pushed into realms where the Spirit was not leading.

The Bible tells us to count the cost when we embark on a project. We have encountered deep humiliation, insults, pain, and trauma. Our marriage has been tried and tested. We took a lot of time and energy from our own sons. Hours and hours of our lives have been invested in other people's children. People have pulled away from us, and invitations to dinners and outings have diminished.

We are still contending for David, keeping in close relationship, giving him guidance, and hoping and praying that he will make good choices. He has been given a chance for a life that is very different from the one his biological parents were living. We keep our eyes on Jesus, knowing that if David veers away, we will have God's solace and His perspective.

As Tom Smith, the horse trainer, said in the movie Seabiscuit, "You don't throw a whole life away because it's banged up a little."(7) Or a lot.

We have a testimony of the reality of the living Lord Jesus Christ that no one can take away from us. *And they overcame him by the blood of the Lamb, and by the word of their testimony, and they did not love their lives to the death. Rev 12:11*

He has heard my cries of desperation over these 26 years [I am including all of the years of holding on to the vision, plus all of the fostering and adoption years up to the present time]:

> "What are You doing to us?"
> "This is way over the top and too much, Lord!"
> "I feel like I am losing my mind!!"
> "HELP ME JESUS!"
> "Is this how God treats the people He loves?"
> "I've had enough, get me out of here!!"
> "I mean it this time, I have REALLY reached my limit!
>> Get me out of this!!"

All of the "I'm at the end of myself!" exclamations God heard. He met me every time. And every time, He exchanged my brokenness for His perseverance, and my faithlessness for His faithfulness. He walked with me and He lived through me. He is my champion.

Inasmuch as there is none like You, O LORD (You are great, and Your name is great in might), who would not fear You, O King of the nations? For this is Your rightful due, for among all the wise men of the nations, and in all their kingdoms, there is none like You. Jeremiah 10:6-7

And for the sorrow, I proclaimed Isaiah 61:23: *He gave me beauty for ashes, the oil of joy for mourning, the garment of praise for the spirit of heaviness, that we might be trees of righteousness, the planting of the Lord, that He might be glorified.*

I praise Him for His faithfulness.

Recently we experienced a shift in our praying. Dan was musing on the message in the story of Elijah on the top of Mount Carmel in First Kings 18:42-45. Elijah had received from God the promise of rain for the water-starved nation. So Elijah prayed. He sent his servant to look toward the sea for clouds. The servant reported, "There is nothing." Elijah was bowed down on the ground and his face was between his knees. Elijah was very seriously and desperately praying. He sent the servant six times to look for a sign of rain. Elijah continued praying intensely for, we assume, a significant length of time. The seventh time, the servant went to look for signs of rain, he reported that he saw one cloud, as small as a man's hand, rising out of the sea. Then the sky became black with clouds and wind and there came a heavy rain. And the promise of God was fulfilled.

What Dan felt the Lord was saying, prophetically, was that we have received the promise of David's healing—we saw it for ourselves at Red Rock and Lora saw it in church. It is promised, it will happen. We must do our part, which is to pray, pray, pray. We chose the minutes before bedtime and have been seriously praying every night for God's promise and our son's miracle.

Another prophetic revelation came to me last month. I was re-reading this manuscript AGAIN, and I felt insecure, AGAIN, about being so open about our lives but especially about David's life. At my Bible study, I went to the front of the room for prayer and asked for a fresh filling of the Holy Spirit, with no other request and nothing else on my mind. Before she prayed for me, Carol said: "The Lord wants you to know, '**It's okay. I know the rest of the story.**'" Carol had no idea what the words that she spoke referred to. All she knew was that those words had come into her mind as I was standing before her and she believed they were a message to me from God. I knew what the words referred to. God was letting me know that it was okay to proceed, that I could trust Him with this book and what is contained in it. I was to forge on, trusting Him. Isn't He wonderful?

Here's one more special prophetic word from the Lord.

One night, eight years ago, (March 25, 2007), when Dan and David and I were in a campground in Quartzite, Arizona, I could not sleep. I felt God wanted to speak to me. I sat at the small table in the motorhome and wrote what I felt that I heard the Holy Spirit saying to me:

I needed you to walk David through this because he is a chosen vessel of mine.
I knew I could count on you two.
You are chosen vessels for this purpose.

Think of Ananias meeting Saul on Straight Street,
Think of David playing the harp for King Saul,
Think of Jesus' earthly life for your sake.

Can you do this for Me?
Can you be My witnesses of obedience, for others to gain inspiration?
Can you show that denying self and taking up the cross to follow Me is worth it and possible in this day?

I call My people to challenges.
I call My people to courageous ventures.
I call My people to faith walks.

Let us not shrink back. Let us press in and press on, fixing our eyes on Jesus. He has called us to walk by faith in Him through challenges and in courageous ventures. Fostering and adopting qualify as challenging and courageous ventures! Take His hand and go for it, because Jesus is Faithful!

In the United States, in 2013, there were 397,122 children in foster care and out of those 101,666 were eligible for adoption, according to the Congressional Coalition on Adoption Institute.
www.ccainstitute.org

Every child is a precious gem, each ones needs a future and a hope. Jesus is asking, "What then will each of these children turn out to be? Who will help them get there?"

Salvation is available!

If you are not a Christian, please feel free to become one! The door to Jesus' heart is open wide to the person who is sincerely repentant and realizes his/her need of a Savior.

Humble yourself and pray to Him.
Psalm 66:19-20

Jesus came to seek and to save those who are lost, and we all are or were.
Luke 19:10, Matt 18:11

The Bible says that all have sinned and have fallen short of the glory of God.
Romans 3:23

The Bible also says that God desires that none should perish but that everyone should come to repentance.
2 Peter 3:9

So, there is room for you! And we want you to join us in this Christian family.

No sin, no past issues, are too big to keep you out of the Kingdom of God—if you are sincerely sorry for the bad things you have done, and if you believe that Jesus died on the cross for your sins, and if you want to do life according to the Bible's way. Romans 5:8

I also believe that in salvation it is good for a person to give his entire life to the Lord, so that God may have full access to you and step right in to direct you into the good plans He has for you. He has a future for you that has hope in it! Oh, such good news! Jeremiah 29:11

PRAY THIS PRAYER to become a Christ-follower, a Christian:
Dear God, I admit I am a sinner. I need Your forgiveness and I believe that Jesus Christ died in my place paying the penalty for my sins. I am turning from my sin to You. I accept Jesus Christ as my personal Savior and Lord. Thank You that the Holy Spirit is filling me now and taking control of my life. I invite You to help me in every area of my new life. Thank You for loving me and staying with me always. Thank You for taking me to heaven someday in the future. In Jesus' name. Amen.

An additional, prayer to God:

Thank You that You know the plans that You have for me and that they are good plans. Please fix what I have messed up and give me the patience to wait for You to work everything together for good. Fill me with love and peace and joy! Thank You. Amen.

Dan and Georgann's prayer and goal:

O God, You have taught us from our youth; and to this day we declare Your wondrous works. Now also when we are old and gray headed, O God, we know you will not forsake us until we declare Your strength to this generation, Your power to everyone who is to come!

Psalm 71:17-18 (personalized)

Footnotes:

1. Magdalena: Released from Shame, dvd, produced by the Jesus Film, 2006 www.magdalenamovie.com

2. Robert Davidson, writer and composer, *The Steadfast Love of the Lord.*

3. PRN refers to the Latin term *pro re nata,* which means, "as the thing is needed." www.safemedication.com

4. self-efficacy definition is from www.about.com by Kendra Cherry. It is Albert Bandura's concept from his social cognitive theory, 1994.

5. **Heart of Joy,** by Mother Teresa, edited by Jose Luis Gonzalez-Balado, Servant Books, 1987, page 52.

6. lyrics and music by Andrae & Sandra Crouch, 1975. Find it on youtube: Andrae Crouch Jesus is the Answer

7. **Seabiscuit: An American Legend,** by Laura Hillenbrand, Random House, NY; 2001.

Part VI - Articles of Interest
- with an Introduction from Dan

In the interest of making this more helpful and more than just a narrative, we have separated out several topics here that can be read without reading the rest of the book. These sections may be read in any order, or may be skipped over. Pick and choose what you are interested in or have questions about. If you read everything, there will necessarily be some redundancy here and there in order to make each section able to stand alone.

I have been a carpenter, draftsman, pastor, and now I am a Marriage and Family Therapist. I made the career-changing decision to study counseling partly because of my experience as a Pastor. Many people were coming to me for counseling, and I did not really have the understanding or skills to be very helpful. As I studied over the six years that it took me to get the degree, I came to understand myself better, and I came to understand our son David better from psychological, cognitive, and emotional perspectives. What follows in the sections that I have written is partly from my academic learning and partly from experiencing it firsthand. These are not scholarly papers. They are intended to be very reader-friendly, practical, and personal. What I have done is to give a sketch of what you are dealing with, not an exhaustive examination of each subject. I have included some bibliographies for further reading if you want to investigate any particular subject further.

1. Fetal Alcohol Syndrome – Dan

FAS is the official acronym most commonly used for Fetal Alcohol Syndrome. You will also see FASD, which refers to Fetal Alcohol Spectrum Disorders, because the ways in which FAS appears to affect children's lives manifests itself in a wide spectrum of disorders from learning disabilities and behavior problems to physical appearance and physical disabilities. ARND is another acronym, which stands for Alcohol Related Neuro Developmental Disorder. This is concerned with how brain functions have been affected by prenatal exposure to alcohol. Suffice it to say that FAS has many different ways of showing up in a child's life.

"In 1973, Fetal alcohol Syndrome (FAS) was identified as a birth defect... FAS is the most frequent cause of mental retardation...central nervous system (CNS) dysfunction... the brain is the organ that is the most vulnerable to prenatal alcohol exposure (Goodlett & West, 1992)... and CNS effects can last a lifetime (Dumas & Rabe, 1994)." (Streissguth, 1999, p186)

The above quotes are from a 14-year study at the University of Washington School of Medicine and published in the Psychological Science Magazine, May 1999. I do not intend to present an academic and comprehensive description of FAS in this book because many resources are now available to do that. A list of resources follows at the end of the chapter.

What is revealed in even the early studies on FAS is alarming, and having raised a son who is profoundly impacted by FAS, I am intimately in touch with the tragedy that follows the life of a person whose mom consumed alcohol during pregnancy.

In the above study, FAS is identified as a birth defect, and the conclusion is also that the dysfunction in the central nervous system is permanent. I tell people it is like being born without an arm; you're not going to grow a new one. The direct effects of the alcohol in the unborn child are: decreased transport of nutrients through the placenta, impaired blood flow in the placenta, and a direct toxic effect which leads to cell death (loss of brain cells, neurons, in the brain) as well as an impairment of normal neuronal migration patterns in the fetal brain. Neuronal migration refers to the process that takes place in the developing baby's brain while still in the womb. Brain cells, or neurons, are generated in the base of the brain and have to migrate to their final destination and place of functionality as the baby grows. This is obviously a very important process, especially for the frontal lobe of the cerebral cortex, or logic center, right behind the forehead, to which the baby's neurons must travel the farthest. And, given this, it is no surprise that, in FAS children, it is the thinking, the logic, that is so profoundly effected. According to Susan Doctor, our local and nationally recognized expert on FAS, 250,000 neurons per minute develop during the fetus' development of the central nervous system, and when alcohol is in the bloodstream of the fetus, all aspects of that development seem to be affected.

Alcohol gets into the fetal bloodstream through the placenta. In the development of the baby, the last organ to fully develop is the lungs.

The second-to-last is the liver, responsible for removal of alcohol from the bloodstream, so the baby is relying upon Mom's liver to remove alcohol (and other toxins) from the blood. Alcohol that gets into the baby's bloodstream takes almost twice as long to be processed by the not-yet fully-developed baby liver as for the Mom, so there is longer exposure for the baby than for Mom.

A child who is born with FAS will likely be at risk to have one or all of the difficulties covered in the following paragraphs. As I have listed each one, I have given a quick account of our experience with our son David. Keep in mind when reading these, that David tested at the worst level, level 1, of five levels, when he did the FAS assessment, so his difficulties are on the more severe end of the scale.

(1) Attention deficit disorder. ADD is an inability to focus and concentrate for reading, studying, learning, working, relating, etc. This can be a serious learning disability. Apparently, with this disorder, people experience everything going on in the environment with the same intensity. You may be in a room now where you can hear freeway noise, some one else's radio playing, or people may be walking past. There may also be other things going on, but you are able to shut most of that out, in order to focus and read this. People with ADD experience all of those things equally, and shutting them out is difficult, if not impossible. Our son, David, has to work with or play with someone else, or he gets stuck and does nothing. His brothers took him snowboarding several times when he was 11 and 12 and he had a good time, but when I took him, and was not actually boarding with him, but was watching from the lodge balcony, he just stood around, and could not get himself into actively having fun. He just watched other people. When he is assigned a work project, like, "please rake these leaves up and put them in the garbage can," unless someone is with him, he will not get more than a few rake-strokes done before his mind is off somewhere else and his body follows, and the job is forgotten.

(2) Memory problems. What is learned one day, like how to do an arithmetic skill, or how a certain chore is to be done, is not retained for the next day. Many, many repetitions may be required if the child is to learn the procedure at all, and it may

never be retained if it is too complex. David did learn how to add and subtract after about three years of work on how to carry to the next place value and add a column, or how to borrow from the next place value to subtract. Multiplication tables were completely out of the range of his capability. Multiplication as a concept was not something that he ever understood. Although he can do it on the calculator, he is not sure when to multiply or when to divide, nor is he able to really understand what the answer denotes once he gets it. It is all far too abstract for him.

(3) Language delays. Depending on the exact parts and functions of the brain that have been affected by prenatal exposure to alcohol, language development may or may not be influenced. Some children will speak with obvious speech impediments all their lives, and others may never be able to remember and use words beyond the basic needs for communication. David had some difficulty in this area, and spoke later in age than his brothers, our biological sons. His enunciation was a problem and Special Children's Clinic speech therapists worked with him. To his credit, however, David now, at 21, has a very good vocabulary and is articulate to the point that most casual acquaintances are not aware that he has severe learning disabilities. Some therapists call the type of brain function that goes with FAS "Spotty Intelligence." One aspect of a child's intelligence may function very well, and others are almost missing altogether. David can use the word, "ambiguous" fluidly and accurately, but if I ask him to write down a phone number, it is going to take a while. He still might get some of the numbers backwards or in the wrong order, or just skip some and not end up with seven numbers.

(4) Poor abstraction. Concrete ideas like "put the glass on the counter" are much easier than more abstract concepts like, "please put away the glass," or, "clean up after yourself." Or, in trying to teach the alphabet, if the teacher says, "This symbol is an 'M,' and it says mmmmm," that is an abstract idea that does not make sense to a child with extensive damage to the frontal lobe of the brain. This inability to understand abstracts affects a broad spectrum of skills that we take for granted that a child will be able to learn, like the alphabet, phonetics and reading,

number symbols, and arithmetic. It also affects the ability to make good judgments about what is a good idea and what is not. Anything that requires a many-layered collection of considerations will not be processed well. David learned to ride a bike pretty well by age eight. I took him out for a ride. Near our house was a vacant lot where there were some dirt mounds and holes that the neighborhood kids had been using to jump their bikes. David, without a trial run, asking me about it, or even taking a look at it from the side, just assumed he could do anything the other kids had done. He attempted a jump over a pit about six feet deep and about eight feet across. He sailed out over the pit and, far short of the level landing spot, crashed face-first into the bank on the other side, and could have broken his neck. Fortunately, he had a helmet on, which saved him from even worse injury, but he was injured badly, and we took him to the hospital. They took one look at him in the E.R. and whisked him into a room calling "Code Blue" on the speaker system. He bore some scars on his face for years as a result, and it was the incident that most clearly illustrated to us the severity of his thinking deficits. We had to realize, and accept, that he is not capable of making good judgments.

(5) Difficulty understanding social cues. This is an aspect of difficulty with FAS that bears a lot of similarities with insecure attachment problems to be covered in a later chapter. Understanding social cues is a skill that we normally do all the time without even being aware that we are doing it. We constantly, subconsciously, read others' faces, body language, and intonation whenever we interact with others. We recognize other's intentions; we know whether they are interested or not, and if we recognize that they are not interested in what we are saying, we may stop, or change the subject. FAS people often do not do that automatically. David gets going on a subject and will continue on and on, never noticing that his respondent is not paying attention any more. Or he will begin talking with someone not noticing that the individual is distressed, busy, or upset about something. David will begin trying to interact without seeing that the other person is in no shape to be interested in him or in

whatever he is interested in talking about. Being able to read the interest, discomfort, pain, sadness, anger, or a shift in attention in another's face and demeanor may not be a normal function of the person with FAS. You may have to explain yourself to him or her in a very concrete way, stating why you can't talk right now and when you will be able to.

(6) Consequences. Even severe consequences often do not compute; they do not translate in the normal way into change of behavior and choices. People with FAS do not really link the consequences in life to the poor choices that gave rise to them, and will continue making those poor choices in spite of consequences that would teach anyone else not to do those things. Designing relevant, immediate consequences is part of any good parenting, to extinguish certain behaviors, but for David, the consequences, although he did not like them, usually did not deter him the next time he thought about doing that behavior. He would proceed with the behavior, and when the consequence happened, he was angry with us for doing that to him. No amount of explaining seemed to be able to help him understand that the consequence was there because of a choice he made, not because we were trying to be mean to him. (Although now, at 21, David is much improved in consequential thinking.)

(7) Antisocial and delinquent behaviors. These are quite common in FAS young people, but may not be directly the result of neurological deficits. An anger that simmers just below the surface all the time may be the real cause of the delinquency or rebellious life. That chronic anger is an understandable response to the frustration of having constant difficulties in the family, difficulties in peer relationships, and also from schooling that is frustrating, loaded with failure and perhaps including the mocking of peers. I can see the young person concluding, "So if I cannot succeed in doing well, let's see if I can excel at doing badly, being a disappointment to my parents, or getting people really mad at me." There is satisfaction in notoriety if one has concluded that one cannot get any praise for doing well. In David's situation, I know that he was frustrated by the difficulties of his family relationships, and it did not help that he sometimes wondered

why his family of origin had abandoned him. It is not untypical for an adopted child to wonder when his adoptive parents are going to abandon him too, especially if he has the perception that he is a problem in the family. (Children in general can easily go to that perception that they are the problem when there is any difficulty in the family.)

In regard to peer relationships, David never was able to get any good friends in the neighborhood. There was always some upheaval between him and the other children his age that was of gargantuan proportions, enough to stop any further play or relationship for long periods of time. He did not seem to have the tactfulness necessary to negotiate through and around divisive things that normally come up between friends. It always became a big argument and David would stomp out. One of the commonly recognized features of FAS children is that they tend to be friends with younger or older people, not children their own age. This was certainly true of David.

David was homeschooled, so we managed to dodge that bullet of school-mocking and constant academic failure, and we know that was a great saving grace for him. Later on, as a teen, both his therapist and Dr. Able, who evaluated him for FAS, stated that David was probably spared a good deal of the discipline and/or expulsion that he would have experienced in public school. And they were amazed at what he had been able to learn in homeschool, given the learning disabilities that he had. These therapists said that David's self concept was kept positive by not being subjected to what would have happened to him in public school. In homeschool, we just kept working with him, and we avoided things like returning papers to him with big red F's on them to repeatedly announce his failure, but he still was frustrated by just not being able to really get it. The older he got, the more school became a battle because he had little success, very slow progress, and subsequently it was no fun for him. Consequences that we put in place for when he opposed cooperating in school did not motivate him to get down to work. He just became angry with us for making him pull weeds with Dad, or for losing his reward for schoolwork. (We sometimes paid him per page to read, but if he refused to cooperate in reading, of course he did not get paid. That did not compute for him; he just got angry with us. He perceived us as the bad guys who were taking things from him, rather than seeing that it was his choices of behavior that resulted in the consequences.) Often, the progression in terms of mental health problems goes like this: failure at school, leads to antisocial behavior, then steps up to oppositional defiance, and eventually conduct disorder; and about that time, the young person breaks the law and a Probation Officer is then assigned to be a part of the young person's life. (This is not necessarily a bad thing because, in our experience, the P.O. is truly on board to help re-direct the youth.)

All of these dire consequences of prenatal exposure to alcohol vary significantly from case to case, depending on when in the pregnancy the drinking took place, how long, or how often, and how much. Susan Doctor has done a lot of research on the various effects of alcohol on the developing baby and the subsequent problems that arise from FAS. She explains that one of the most commonly impacted parts of the brain is the frontal lobe, or logic center.

The ability to understand and make sense of sequences takes place in the frontal lobe. Most of us do sequences on automatic pilot. This includes things like, when we go to the store, we go to the vegetable department first and buy all the veggies, then to the bulk foods, then the deli, etc., through the store in a sequential order. But if sequences don't make sense to a person, then that person is back and forth all over the store, and may go to the vegetable department three or four times. Sequences also include the concept of cause and effect. I know that if I eat green apples I will get a stomachache. If sequences don't make sense to me, then I may continue eating green apples and never understand why I get the stomachache because the sequence of cause (eating green apples) and effect (stomach ache) does not connect. Therefore, for the person with FAS, consequences don't make sense because consequences are a matter of cause and effect. Normally we think, "If I do this, then that consequence is going to happen, and I don't like that consequence, so maybe I won't do the action in the first place." But if I don't understand sequences, then that whole reasoning process is lost. Furthermore, many tasks of life and at work are sequential. First we do this, then we do the next thing, and so forth, so the work place is not friendly to people who cannot do things in the right order, sequentially.

Time organization is in the frontal lobe. Planning and scheduling become a difficult or impossible task sometimes for people affected by FAS. Abstractions are difficult for the person with FAS, as mentioned earlier, again a function of the frontal lobe. Therefore, metaphors are often lost on the person with FAS. They do not understand the implications of an instruction like, "Don't behave like a sheep." (Implying that one should not just follow the one in front of you mindlessly.) It may be taken too literally, which is puzzling to them because they haven't said, "Baa," lately, and they know they are not a sheep.

2. Parenting the Child with FAS – Dan

We need to talk about the differences in the way one parents a child with FAS. If we do not make some allowances for this child, we will be frustrated and blaming the child for behavior that happens for reasons that are beyond anyone's control, and certainly beyond the child's control. If a child is suspected of being FAS, or of having prenatal exposure to alcohol, then the paragraphs that follow include some of the basic ideas from Susan Doctor that parents need to keep in mind. I relate these as a matter of personal experience combined with the notes I took at Susan Doctor's lecture series on FAS that we heard at a foster parent-training seminar.

The older the child gets, the wider will be the difference between what we want from our child and what we get. Mentally prepare yourself to adapt to a wide spectrum of differences that surface particularly at school age and in adolescence. In infancy, the effects are more difficult to notice, but as the child matures, and particularly in adolescence, parents really begin to have to make some adjustments to the parenting style that they might have used for a child without FAS. School is a place where the difficulties begin to emerge, partly because the child is then subject to chronic, consistent failure (unexplainable and frustrating to the child). All of us experience failure. It is inevitable, but the angst of failure is worsened by also being called lazy or stupid or rebellious, when it is really more a matter that the teacher and/or parents do not understand the brain of the child. We homeschooled David, as I have mentioned, and that was helpful not only because he was not labeled, diagnosed or singled out as deficient among his peers, but also because he was able to learn at his own very slow pace, and was able to maintain a fairly good self concept because he got more positive reinforcement than negativity combined with punishment. Public or private schools, with rooms full of students, cannot give the time and repetition necessary to teach the severely FAS brain in a way that the child can retain the material and get understanding.

Safety, structure, and stability of the home are essential.

Structure and routine can be very helpful to the child or adult affected by FAS. If he or she knows what to expect because of the daily routine or the structure of the household, that reduces the anxiety that can so easily drive a 'fight or flight' response in an FAS child when the unexpected happens. An FAS child is much more likely to over-react or panic (go into fight or flight mode) when faced with sudden changes than a normal child. Fight or flight is a response from a part of the brain called the Amygdala, a lower order of the brain that it is not logical; it is a reaction, like a knee-jerk reaction. Fight or flight, once initiated, is accompanied by several immediate biological changes, including a dose of adrenaline, a spike in blood sugar, and a rise in Cortisol (a stress-related hormone) in the bloodstream. Fight or flight is a necessary reaction when we are being chased by a bear, but not very helpful if it is actually a non-threatening event.

You certainly have had the experience of being suddenly and severely frightened, but then you discovered that you were not really in danger a few seconds later, and you were left physically trembling and mentally shaken. That is because the Amygdala very quickly initiated a fight or flight response, but a few seconds later our frontal lobe came to the rescue and was able to figure out that we were not really in danger, and although we are shaking, we are in the process of calming down already. For the FAS child or adult, however, the frontal lobe cannot come to the rescue, or is much slower at figuring out whether the danger is real or not.

Consequently, for an FAS child, such incidents become a severe, out of control reaction that makes no sense to those who have a fully functional frontal lobe. And in the same way, a seemingly simple change in routine, like, "dinner will be late," can become an apocalyptic event for a child whose Amygdala is saying, "You are not going to eat tonight; fight or flee!" To this child, survival is at risk. And that child may decide to run away, or start a fight about when he or she gets to eat. It all seems like a huge overreaction to the parent who sees the real situation in the way a healthy frontal lobe sees it. Parents need to understand the very real fear that the child is experiencing and respond with calming, holding, explaining, and time, so that the child's brain can become calm and push the "reset" button. Shouting, "Calm down! It is not the end of the world!" will not help in any way. In fact, it will probably intensify and prolong the reaction.

Parents need to keep a steady routine, and if it does need to be changed for some reason, give the child clear, concrete notice as far in advance as possible, and help the child work through it. Sudden changes to the expected normal routine or not knowing what is going to happen are frightening to the child with FAS and will result in bad reactions.

Acceptance of the things that the child cannot do well will also be helpful. In general, if a child can't learn calculus, we can accept that. We can tell ourselves that life goes on. If a child with prenatal exposure to alcohol cannot seem to learn how to read, or spell, that can be much harder to accept because we have the mindset that life does not go on without reading and spelling. The process of coming to acceptance is becoming able to tell ourselves that life really can go on, and learning what the options are for the future and what the adjustments are that will have to be made. If the parents have exhausted all options and tried all the teaching styles available, as parents we would do well to accept what it is that the child can or cannot learn, rather than either putting impossible pressure on the child, or being dismayed and disappointed in our child. It is very easy for us parents to conclude that the child is being manipulative or lazy or rude, or any number of other unacceptable behaviors, when it is really a matter that the child's brain is not functioning in the way ours do. Parents need to ask themselves whether the child really can do this or not. It becomes even more tricky when the child really is being manipulative, lazy, etc., and great care needs to be given to take the time to discern which is happening. For example: David could not remember how to carry numbers in adding a column of numbers (three, plus four, plus six, is thirteen; write down the three and carry the one). You remember the mantra from first grade so well you don't even have to think about it. It was sorely tempting to believe that he was just trying to get out of schoolwork. Yesterday he could do it. Why can't he do it today? He really did forget. And he would forget day after day, month after month, and we kept trying different approaches, but gradually he could remember it and do it, even over a weekend. Berating him for being lazy, etc., was not going to be helpful in that situation.

Focusing on the things that the child can do well affords many reasons to validate the child, applaud, compliment, and encourage the child. David has a gift for music that is something we encouraged. Piano lessons were helpful for a while, but his brain was not doing well with learning how to read music, so we had to let that go, accept that, and just let him have fun playing by ear. Baseball was way too complex for David. He liked being around the team, but could not remember what he was supposed to do. However, he did become quite good on the computer with Microsoft Flight Simulator. He learns so much in his own style that he learns well by just letting him do trial and error. With the Flight Simulator, we just let him crash a lot, and after a year or so, I was amazed. He could line up with the runway and land a 747, flaps down, wheels down, correct speed, correct rate of descent, the whole complicated process. He gets a lot of compliments on that ability. Another thing David can do well is spot things in the outdoors before anyone else. When we are hiking he is usually the first to spot the deer, wild horses, or mountain sheep, and he gets a lot of accolade for that and is proud of that capability. When we are driving down the freeway, he will point out some things that no one else has noticed, usually things out of the ordinary. He will see the broken sign, or a detail about a building or a passing car that is unusual, or the llama in a field full of horses. So we make it a point to say, "Wow Dave how did you see that?"

If you are adopting a child with FAS, what I am trying to give you are a few of the things that you will want to take into consideration. Adoption is not guaranteed to be all you hoped it would be in the best of circumstances, and if the child has had prenatal exposure to alcohol, any exposure at all, you may find your expectations drastically challenged as time goes on. You will want to educate yourself as much as possible. Attend seminars, lectures, support groups, etc., and read books and look on the internet. I include here a few helpful resources.

BOOKS:

The following are available from Groundwork Press, which you can find on line at www.groundworkpress.com

Living With FASD: a Guide for Parents, Third Edition, by Sara Graefe

Living With Prenatal Drug Exposure: a Guide for Parents, by Lissa Cowan and Jennifer Lee

Adoption Piece by Piece - this is a three-volume set, but each book is available by itself.

> Volume I : Lifelong Issues
> Volume II : Special Needs
> Volume III: A Toolkit for Parents
>   (A description of the topics in each book is available on the website.)

SCIENTIFIC STUDIES:

Streissguth, A. P., Barr, H. M., Bookstein, F. L., Sampson, P. D., & Olson, H. C.. (1999). The Long-Term Neuro cognitive Consequences of Prenatal Alcohol Exposure: A 14-Year Study. *Psychological Science, vol. 10, no.3, May 1999.*

Jirikowic, T., Kartin, D., and Olson, H. *Canadian Journal of Occupational Therapy. Vol. 75, no.4, Oct. 2008.* [This is fairly academic, but the discussion at the end is sobering.]

ON LINE:

Dr. Susan Doctor has not written any books, but has a few articles available on line if you search for "Susan Doctor FAS." She also has conducted seminars, which you might be able to find out about on line and attend.

Another good website with all kinds of helpful materials including a good DVD on FAS and parenting children with FAS is called: **FASD Support Site** and it can be found at: fasd.brighttomorrow.com

Another comprehensive resource on line is from the Government bureau of Health and Human Services. It can be found by doing a search for **Child Welfare Information Gateway** and clicking the tab on publications.

3. Attachment Theory – Dan

When a baby is born, there is a great amount of care that is necessary even just for survival. Some babies are well cared for, and some miss out on the cuddling, cooing, and interaction of good baby care. Attachment Theory says that the kind of care a baby gets in infancy and up to age five, determines how well that child will be able to form deep, warm, trusting, and lasting relationships as an adult. It says further, that the child who has successfully attached to a caregiver is then able to go on in childhood and attach successfully to others even if there is a change in who the caregiver is. (The caregiver is usually Mom, so I will refer usually to Mom, although I know that Dads, grandparents, aunties, etc., sometimes are the main caregivers.) The baby that gets consistent tender loving care from Mom for the first year, for example, can continue to thrive if, for some reason, Mom is no longer there, as long as the care given by the new person is on the same level of attentiveness, responsiveness and sensitivity as Mom. If there is a familiar quickness of response when baby calls for help, and help is given in a loving way and in the way that is asked for (cuddle when cuddle needed, diaper change when that is needed, and burp when that is needed, etc.) then the baby will be able to transfer the attachment to the new caregiver.

Early researchers and developers of the theory, John Bowlby and Mary Ainsworth, defined three levels of attachment, or attachment styles. Optimum attachment is seen in a child raised in the best conditions. He or she will develop a <u>secure attachment</u> with Mom (or whoever the care-giver is), meaning that this person is the trusted, safe one to whom to go with a need, because he or she is the one who is always there and is responsive and sensitive. This caregiver is the attachment figure. This child has fairly consistently from birth been able to call for help and get it pretty quickly, get the right help at the right time, and get it in a loving way. In addition, this child has experienced plenty of interaction face-to-face, smiling, talking, playing, and connecting with Mom. Pain, hunger, and discomfort have all been met with a response that soothes the angst, calms the baby's emotions, and models how to handle crisis. Psychologists call this "good emotional regulation."

A less desirable level of attachment is called <u>anxious ambivalent</u>. This child is worried (anxious) about whether needs will be met or not, because about half of the time, Mom does not show up to help. Maybe Mom leaves baby with a not-so-attentive babysitter, or she is somehow preoccupied and does not respond to baby's cries for a long time, if at all, and when she does come she is angry or rough in how she provides for baby. This baby did not experience very much cooing and giggling and playing with Mom. This baby is ambivalent, that is, unsure, whether Mom is safe and trustworthy or not, because sometimes she is and sometimes she is not. Pain, hunger, and discomfort were not calmly soothed, but sometimes went on for long periods, causing the baby to escalate in panic, rage, or fear. These patterns of emotional regulation cause, later in life, what is called emotional dysregulation, in other words, panic, fear, and over reaction in situations that are only mildly painful, uncomfortable or frightening.

In the worst-case scenario, there is no consistent care giving. Baby has to cry for a long time to get fed or changed, and baby's needs are not met in a loving way, but abruptly and coldly. There has been no interaction in a playful loving way with anyone. This attachment style is called <u>anxious avoidant</u> because, besides being worried about how baby's needs will be met, baby has concluded that caregivers are untrustworthy and unsafe people. This baby actually avoids trusting contact with adults, pushes away, and is unresponsive and unaffectionate. This baby is in survival mode, having concluded that if there is a need, baby better take care of it herself or himself if possible. As soon as these children are able, they will begin to steal food and hide it to be sure that they can take care of their needs. Lying for them is very common, and it is not a moral issue to them, it is a survival issue. If, in their minds, they need to say some words to make sure they get what they think they need, it does not matter whether those words are true or not, they will speak them to attempt to get what they need. These children seem to be taking responsibility for their care giving into their own hands as much as possible.

Bowlby and Ainsworth laid the groundwork for attachment theory. Attachment Theory is a theory; it is not an exact science. It suggests how we become loving human beings (or not) as a result of conditions during our infancy. Daniel Sonkin, a licensed Marriage and Family Therapist with thirty years of experience, has done a good deal of research about attachment theory. At the risk of being repetitive, I am going to give an additional explanation of the theory as Sonkin explains it.

Think of babies being born asking the question, "Is anyone there who is attentive, responsive and sensitive?" Babies cannot take care of themselves, and someone must be there who is going to respond to the baby's calls for help, and who is going to be sensitive enough to figure out what is needed. If the baby gets a "yes" response most of the time to calls for help, then the baby develops that <u>secure attachment</u> style that Bowlby defined.

When the baby asks that question, "Is anyone there who is attentive, responsive and sensitive?" and half of the time the baby gets a "no" answer (no one shows up to give care) then the baby develops an insecure attachment, that which Bowlby referred to as <u>anxious ambivalent.</u>

If baby gets a consistent "no" when asking the question about whether anyone will take care of baby's needs, this leads to what Bowlby calls an <u>anxious avoidant </u>attachment style. Ultimately, these children seem to become self-reliant, even in infancy, as much as possible, and they actually avoid getting close to anyone. This is probably where our son David was when he came to our home. He was not interested in others, seemed to be wrapped up in his own little world, and when we held him, rather than put his head on our shoulder, or lean against us, or even make eye contact, he would stiff-arm us and keep his head as far from us as he could, and mostly look away, outward, not at us. This was at nine months old.

I believe that attachment theory explains a lot of what we experienced with our son. It is a theory, and therefore not every case fits into it exactly. There are always the outliers that defy explanation or do not fit into a theory, so if any of the following scenarios are in contradiction to your personal experience, do not throw the whole theory out on the basis of one case.

Here are three examples of a single common situation as experienced by children with the three different attachment styles. A <u>securely attached</u> child, when left at a day care or with a strange babysitter, will cry, but usually not for very long. Within a few minutes, the baby is apparently thinking, "Well, Mom (or other care-giver) always comes back, so I know she'll be back soon. Mom doesn't leave me with dangerous people or in dangerous places, so I'm probably okay here with this person; I might as well make friends and play until Mom gets back." And he or she does. She settles down quickly and plays happily. When Mom comes back, she is delighted to see her and give lots of hugs and smiles, and goes with Mom happily.

An <u>anxious ambivalent</u> child, when left in an unknown situation, will cry and will not stop crying for a long time. If you have ever worked in a daycare, you will know that some children can cry for hours and may never really settle in to play. Apparently what is in that baby's mind is, "Oh my gosh, I don't know if this place is safe because Mom has left me in unsafe places before, and I don't know if this person is nice or not, because some of the people she has left me with were not nice, and I don't know if she is coming back because she has left for days or weeks before, and this is very scary." Then when Mom does come back, the child is part glad and part angry with Mom. Sometimes these babies will hit Mom, or push her away, or run away. Or sometimes they will cling desperately to Mom, weeping. They are apparently angry that Mom left them again in a situation that was frightening to them.

Then there is the child with the <u>anxious avoidant</u> attachment style. This baby does not cry when left in a strange place with a strange person. This child has apparently concluded, "Well, no use crying; no one is going to show up to help anyway, so I better figure out whether this person is safe to play with or not. I don't know if Mom is coming back or not, so I better find my way around here." He or she will go play in a corner often, rather than interact with anyone. In research, these children were hooked up with monitors for stress, heart rate, etc., and found that this <u>anxious avoidant</u> child is actually pretty stressed, but is just not showing it outwardly. When Mom, or the caregiver returns for the child, there is little or no acknowledgement of her return, no hugs of joy, and no anger for leaving, just resignation.(David did not cry when Hayley and Michelle left him with us that first day.)

People contemplating adoption should not omit considering the implications of attachment theory. Even if the child goes to the adoptive family straight from the hospital, never knows that he is adopted, and never experiences some of the lack of love and care that classically insecurely attached children have to experience, attachment theory applies because <u>you</u> are an attachment figure, and you come loaded with an attachment style of your own which profoundly effects your thoughts, feelings and actions as you interact with your child. Having an idea of how attachment develops is crucial to being a good Mom or Dad. <u>And</u> if your bundle of joy comes to you from anything other than the hospital at birth, your knowledge of attachment theory can be helpful in creating, for that child (who may have had detrimental experiences) a sense of security and safety (a <u>secure attachment</u> style) very early on. It is in those early years that it is easiest to form a <u>secure attachment</u> style. In that first year in particular, the brain is developing and learning at breakneck speed. One of the things that the baby brain is formulating is the child's attachment style; how to relate to other people around, and how to categorize some as safe attachment figures, and some as not so safe. A child who has experienced any level of trauma, terror, neglect, or violence will already be forming the beginnings of a very untrusting attachment style. Children who have heard a lot of yelling or experienced violence (even when they were in the womb) may be born with an aversion to Dad, if he was the one yelling or being mean. He is unsafe. All males may be seen as unsafe to that baby. You, adoptive Dad, may have to be super mellow and super patient to overcome that. Or, if Mom was in a chaotic or highly unstable lifestyle, the baby can be born with some serious questions about Mom, females, and caregivers in general. The more you can know about your adoptive child's experience even in the womb) the better equipped you will be to understand and bring healing to any damage done to the attachment style of your child.

Being a Parent who is Building Secure Attachment

One of the huge variables in dealing with children is the gene pool of their families of origin. That is the part of a child's being that comes from <u>nature</u>. The other big part of a child's being is that which comes from <u>nurture</u>, that is, the influence that you exert as a parent, and how your family was for the child, obviously, that is going to affect how the child turns out. Neither nature nor nurture is the whole story, in fact they appear to be fairly equally balanced in the final picture. This segment of the book is about the nurture part, that is, what you do. Who your child is by nature will often dictate the kind of nurture you should give to be the most effective. In other words, be aware of who your child is, and proceed with caution. Parenting is not a "one-size-fits-all" procedure. If attachment theory is to be taken into account, there are some sound guidelines that can be helpful:

Developing a <u>secure attachment</u> can be seen essentially as developing a secure and trusting relationship. That seems simple enough: do not do anything untrustworthy, and be as stable and consistent as possible. Every interaction that your child has with you will either move attachment towards insecure or towards secure, depending on how you are perceived and how you manage to come across to the child. Additionally, how you are perceived by the child may already be loaded in the insecure direction, depending upon the history of this child's interactions with care-givers. If your child is already at risk of being on the insecure end of the spectrum, it is essential that his or her experience of you should consistently be loving, compassionate, and favorable. This doesn't mean the child gets everything he/she wants, it just means that administering structure and boundaries is always done in a loving way, i.e., no yelling, no harshness, and no corporal punishment. John Trentalange, the attachment specialist who helped us the most, gave us the term "constant object." He said that we, as parents, had to be constant objects to David, meaning that every time David experienced us, he saw someone who was on his side. The overall message of the constant-object-parent to the child is: "I am here for you unconditionally. You can't overwhelm, scare, or change me. I will not feel rejection or withdraw from the relationship." Out of this understanding we developed the ability to not take things personally when David was misbehaving or directly attacking us. If we got our feelings hurt when David insulted or injured us, and withdrew from the relationship, then David did not see the constant object; he saw the changeable object. We had to be able to say, "Gee I'm sorry you feel that way about us, but that doesn't make us love you less." To oppositional behavior we had to be able to say, "Oh, too bad you chose to act in this manner, maybe tomorrow you will be able to make a choice that will have a better outcome for you." We began to be consistent, never turning against him no matter how hard he tried to make us the bad guys. Even in enforcing consequences for behaviors we found a way to stay out of the punisher role so that we could remain that constant object for David. More on that in the paragraphs ahead.

There is a way to be a constant object without being a liberal pushover and spoiling your child. Giving in to a child's demands is not what I mean by favor. Gently, lovingly, confidently, and firmly establishing and maintaining boundaries of acceptable and unacceptable behaviors is favor. Here is what I mean:

If a parent sets no guidelines on what a child may do (in misguided attempt to love), if a parent has no structure or system in the home that establishes what the child may eat, or when, or where, or no rules about how things are to be done in this home, then that is liberal parenting, and the message to the child is, "You are not worth the effort required to establish some guidelines for our lives together. Do whatever you want." That child <u>will</u> do whatever he or she wants, and will not believe that you love her or him. These children long for some structure in their lives and envy children who have to be home at a certain time for dinner, or whose parents want to know where they are.

On the other extreme is too much structure, too much control, too many demands and too little flexibility. Parents who try to run a family this way run a high risk of experiencing rebellion during their children's adolescence, or of the children asking to be emancipated: "Get me out of here!" Children need to be able to make their own choices, especially when they begin to become adults and start to carve out their own independence.

Maintaining a balanced parenting style of both love and structure is one of the central dilemmas of parents. For the child for whom you are working to form a secure attachment, or heal a damaged attachment, you must provide, and enforce, the structure with lots of love and without any yelling, finger wagging, put-downs, or corporal punishment. Any harshness will be perceived by an insecurely attached child as proof that you are untrustworthy (remember that they have already begun to conclude that care-givers don't really give good care and are basically untrustworthy). If you get down in her face and loudly chew that child out, she will conclude, "I knew I couldn't trust you." If you afflict physical pain or corporal punishment of any sort, you will be seen as just another of what has already been experienced as dangerous caregivers. If you are the enforcer of punishment, saying, "Since you have disobeyed the rules, I'm taking away your phone for a week," then you are affirming the insecure child's conclusion that you are not really there for her.

Avoiding the role of the enforcer, the punisher, is an essential for parents of children with insecure attachment. You can't be the bad guy, the vindictive one, the one who wields the mode of punishment. And yet there need to be consequences in place that can extinguish certain behaviors and encourage others. John Trentalange gave us the best plan that I have heard of for accomplishing this. It is to set up a system, and let the system be the enforcer. It is a family system for establishing the behaviors that are deemed non-negotiable. The system says that there are certain good things that flow to our lives every day as a matter of being part of this family. (These may be things such as walking the dog together, having a cell phone, having a TV in your room, being able to watch certain TV shows, playing certain games, having certain freedoms, having friends over, buying things, earning money through work, and so forth.) However, the system also says that when the non-negotiable behaviors are simply forgotten or defiantly ignored, that causes the guilty party to lose some of those good things that otherwise automatically flow to the family members. (Non-negotiable behaviors may be things like doing homework, maintaining attendance at school, respectful language to everyone, non-violence, feeding or grooming the pets, cleaning up after the pets, obedience the first time without complaining, clear standards of cleanliness, and so forth. It is a good idea to consider these carefully; making the bed may be negotiable, but brushing teeth may not be.) It may be a good thing to get the family involved in creating this system. Sit everyone down together to design a system. Discuss what the non-negotiable behaviors are and how they are defined. Discuss what the consequences are (what is lost) for ignoring those non-negotiable responsibilities. You will find that your children will sometimes devise more strict consequences for certain behaviors than you would.

Once the system is created, the system is the enforcer. Then you, the parent, can say, "Oh Johnny, you didn't feed the dog this morning before school. That's too bad; our system says that you will lose the chance to go to the park with the dog this afternoon because of that. Maybe tomorrow you will remember to feed the dog and then you'll get to take the dog for a walk." You see, you are still giving favor to the child, pulling for excellence, pulling for success, rooting for him or her to do well, and of course celebrating when he or she does remember to feed the dog. You never have to get angry and yell. You never have to punish. You never have to leave your role as a secure safe person, a constant object, an attachment figure. This is good parenting for any child. The only reason we get away with yelling and harshness at all is if we have securely attached children who already perceive us as safe and secure. Securely attached children can receive a punishment or listen to a harsh scolding and say to themselves, "Gosh, I must have really done something wrong, I'd better shape up," because they have the perception that the parent is trustworthy, safe, and would not be out to hurt them, whereas the insecurely attached child has a perception that the parent is probably not trustworthy and likely to be out to hurt them, so harshness only strengthens that conclusion.

Allow me to address some specific behaviors that are fairly typical for children with attachment problems, and I will offer my personal theories about them. Lying and stealing are often a chronic problem. I believe that these behaviors come from the insecure attachment mindset, namely that the child believes he or she has to take care of himself or herself; no one else is going to do that for him or her. Again, remember that these children are in survival mode. There is a level of intensity in how they perceive situations because they believe them to be a matter of survival, not just a matter of preference. There are things that happen that would be a minor problem to a securely attached child, for example, "No, son, you are not old enough to have a pocket knife," to which a securely attached child will say, "Awww, when am I going to be old enough?" The same restriction given to a child in survival mode may give rise to a mindset (not spoken out loud) something like, "Well, I'll just get one somewhere else then, because I need a knife. This is something that I must have, and Mom and Dad have no idea how important it is." And without any consideration of the rights of others, because, when it is a genuine issue of survival, we don't consider the needs of others, that child will steal his brother's pocket knife, or whatever other source there may be for such items. In fact he may steal pocketknives routinely for years. This was our experience with David. No amount of lecturing from us, or shame from having deeply disappointed his brothers stopped the behavior. A month or so after being caught stealing a brother's pocketknife, he would steal another one from a different brother.

One of the other common things to steal is food. Perhaps that is more easily understood as a matter of survival. If, in the first months or years of life, food was not provided regularly, or there was not enough, children get into that survival mode and begin to provide for themselves by stealing and keeping a little food aside, and, even after years of having three square meals a day and plenty of snacks, these children will continue to steal food and hoard it, or get up in the middle of the night and eat clandestinely, as if tomorrow there may not be food in the refrigerator.

Lying and stealing are not moral issues to one who has to survive. We say whatever we have to in order to survive; we take whatever we have to in order to survive. In the mind of the insecurely attached child,

I believe there is the conclusion that, "I have to take care of myself because no one else will." And no matter how incorrect that conclusion may be, it is often unshakeable. The result is a child who is constantly lying and stealing without any thought of what untruth and stealing does to others, or the crushing experience of betrayal it carries. There is no concern for how it influences what people may think of that child in the future. It is not a matter of morality to the child. It is a matter of survival. I think these children really believe it is about survival, not in a conscious way, but it is there, driving what is, to us parents, totally irrational behavior, because we know that they do not have to do this to survive.

Insecurely attached children will often tell wild stories just to be noticed because it is important to be validated. We may say, "She is just doing that for attention." For the anxious ambivalent child, there is no such thing as, "just for attention," it is, to that child, a matter of life itself to get attention. Remember that this child rarely got attention for even the basic needs of life, and to get attention for having done something wonderful is glorious, so making up a story that gets that kind of notice is part of the program, never mind that when it is found out to be a lie, everyone is upset. In the meanwhile, it was great to have everyone's attention and approval. David would commonly tell grandiose stories, either to get sympathy or to get praise. He told one of our friends that he had just found out that his biological father had died, and, this friend, after weeping with David and praying for him, told me about it and was pretty confused that David would tell him something like that, knowing it was not true, just to get the attention. Other times David would make up stories about accomplishments, such as records he had set in running, that were patently not true, and it did not seem to matter to him when the truth came out. He apparently had achieved his goal of having significance in someone else's eyes for a few minutes.

There are many therapists now that understand attachment or specialize in that kind of therapy. In many cases, the children need therapy, and the family needs therapy together so that the relationships can be improved. These children can learn to trust and can do well in life with proper intervention. If parents refuse to change parenting mode from strictness, power and intimidation, children with attachment disorders generally will not do well. Parents will be frustrated, may conclude that they are inadequate, and may also escalate the punishment in an ever-increasing spiral until real damage is done both to the children and the parents. It can get very ugly, and the damage done can last a lifetime.

Punishment will not extinguish behavior that is driven by the need to survive. Our need to survive is basic and powerful, and children in that mode of thinking tend to stay there until a long, long period of consistently repeated experiences has formed a new expectation in their minds that says, "I am going to be taken care of by my parents. My survival needs are met in this family." Great patience and understanding is called for from parents of these children. Understanding the source of these behaviors can give us empathy for the children, and patience is needed to outlast the warped way in which their minds have been formed to distrust their parents, of all people. We parents absolutely cannot take it personally when we are lied to or stolen from. It is not about us. We do need to talk about it with our children and provide adverse consequences for their behaviors, and provide instruction and direction for proper behavior, and we must model behaviors that we want them to emulate. We have to be patient and live in hope that they will eventually change, and not blame ourselves for the mistakes they are making, or be embarrassed by that behavior. Do not tell your children that they have embarrassed you. Your reputation then becomes more important than the child, and may even give the child the impression all he or she is good for is to make you look good.

This has been a fairly quick summary of the theory of attachment, and how it becomes meaningful when we adopt children who are insecurely attached. Hopefully this has been helpful in illustrating how very real the damage is to the child's way of thinking when babies do not get loved and cared for in a consistently attentive, responsive and sensitive manner with lots of playing and communicating with the parents.

Here are a few references that may be helpful if you would like to learn more about attachment theory.

Ainsworth, M. D., Blehar, M., Waters, R., and Wall, S. (1978). *Patterns of Attachment.* Hillsdale, NJ: Lawrence Erlbaum.

Bowlby, J. (1969). *Attachment and Loss: Volume 1 Attachment.* New York: Basic Books.

Bowlby, J. (1973). Attachment and Loss: Volume 2 Separation anxiety and anger. New York: Basic Books.

Damasio, A. (1999) *Body and Emotion in the Making of Consciousness,* Orlando, FL: Harcourt Inc.

Masterson, J. F. (Ed.). (2005). *The Personality Disorders Through the Lens of Attachment Theory and the Neurobiologic Development of the Self: A Clinical Integration.* Phoenix, AZ: Zeig, Tucker and Thiesen Inc.

Karen, Robert (1998) *Becoming Attached: First Relationships and how they Form our Capacity to Love.* Oxford: Oxford University Press.

Rholes, S.W., and Simpson, J.A. (1998). *Attachment Theory and Close Relationships.* New York, NY: Guilford Press.

Siegel, D. J., and Hartzell, M. (2003). *Parenting from the Inside Out.* New York, NY: Jeremy P. Tharcher/Penguin.

Trentalange, John (2014) *Transformational Living: Everything You Need to Know to Live a Happy and Purposeful Life.* Mustang, OK: Tate Publishing Enterprises LLC

4. Becoming Whole and Free of Shame – Dan

Parents of adopted children often find themselves in a relationship with the adopted child that is tragically different from what they imagined it would be when they first began, and confusion sets in. That confusion takes many forms, but stems from the very natural questions that arise as a parent, namely, "What am I doing wrong? What is wrong with me? What is wrong with this child? Why can't I feel happy with this relationship?" and, "Why do I feel disgust, shame, even dislike for this child, when this is supposed to be such a wonderful redemptive work, to give this young person a forever family?"

It is important that the parent is able to rise above the natural responses of shame, condemning self, or blaming the child. The short story is that there is no one to blame; it doesn't do any good anyway, and there is no cause for shame if your child does not become what you dreamed of when you signed up for adoption. Our natural response to pain, insult, unhappiness, and injury is to look for blame. It never helps to place blame, in fact, it usually makes things worse, but we generally do tend to go looking for someone that is the one at fault.

Let us consider some other ways to think our way through the disappointments of parenting. If a rock falls off a cliff and injures someone, we do not look to blame someone, because there is a lack of possible culprits. It just happened. In an adoptive parent's relationship with his or her child or children, there are many things that can arise to cause problems that can be as crushing as a falling rock. And if they fall, it does no one any good to place blame on someone for the damage, especially on yourself if you are the parent, or on the child. Some of the rocks on the cliff are: (1) This young person comes to your family from a different gene pool than you. He or she may not ever get your sense of humor, your way of thinking, or your reasoning for why things are the way they are in your home. It is undeniable that a good percentage of who we are and who we become is genetic, not just formed by upbringing. Coming from a different gene pool, a child may not match very well with the rest of the family, and this can result in friction, disagreement, and dislike. (2) Attachment problems, as addressed in a previous chapter, can cause huge distrust and misunderstandings between well-meaning parents and a child whose past has left etched into his or her character some traits that are difficult or impossible to completely overcome. (3) Pre-natal exposure to alcohol (FAS), also discussed in a previous chapter, gives rise to learning difficulties, inabilities, and tendencies that parents do not understand, and can lead to parental judgment of the child in the belief that this child is making choices maliciously just to cause problems.

None of the above "rocks on the cliff" are the parent's fault. None are the child's fault. Let us consciously avoid placing blame on the children or ourselves. Nonetheless, we the parent, are left with emotional pain. What we do with that pain will make all the difference. Acceptance is the goal if we are not to be left living with bitterness, anger, self-condemnation, or sadness for the rest of our lives. You have probably heard of the "Serenity Prayer," which goes, "God grant me the serenity to accept the things I cannot change; courage to change the things I can; and the wisdom to know the difference." Acceptance of things we cannot change requires first realizing that these are unchangeable things, and any efforts to bring change will be something like beating our heads against a wall, unproductive and painful. Acceptance does not mean you decide that it is a wonderful thing that your child has an apparently unchangeable distrust of you, or that he or she lives with brain damage from FAS. Acceptance is something that only you can create for yourself. It is an understanding that allows you to go on with life free from the pain that is caused by that unchangeable tragedy. Life does go on. A choice must be made to go on without the sorrow, anger, or bitterness. Who wants to live with that for the rest of your life? One hears people say, "It ruined my life." Well, I hope you are not one who is predisposed to let your life get ruined. I have a good friend who lost his sight at age 42. He is now 58 and I have learned much about acceptance by spending time with him. His life goes on. He counts his blessings. He works hard at having a full life. He has a great sense of humor. He has friends. He did not allow it to ruin his life. He went through a very dark time before coming to acceptance, but he made it, and consequently I, and a lot of other people, get to have his friendship. He is not holed up in some dank emotional basement refusing to live. So parents of children with unchangeable issues must learn to come to acceptance.

Georgann wrote a little in the main body of the story about "grieving the dream." Grieving is basically the same whether we are grieving the loss of a dreamed-of relationship with an adopted child, or the loss of a loved one through death. There are books written on this, most notably, Elisabeth Kubler-Ross in 1969, *On Death and Dying,* but allow me to summarize the idea. Grieving is the process, to put it briefly, of working through the natural responses of denial, anger, bargaining, sadness and/or depression, and finally coming to acceptance. Grief theory contends that we have to spend that time in denial ("I can't believe this is happening to me"). And often we have to spend some time in anger, probably looking for someone to blame. (These emotions run through us in no particular order, and we may move back and forth between them for a while.) Bargaining is the stage in which we think through the 'If only..." thoughts, and we wish we could do something now to make it better. We may even try to make a deal with God that if we do some certain thing, He will fix our pain. Additionally, inevitably, we are going to be sad, and that is not a bad thing. We tend to want to get over it quickly or avoid being sad altogether. Our culture tells us that it is bad to be sad and that we should go have a drink, get high, or bury ourselves in work or recreation so we don't have to feel sad. Actually, the way through sadness is to be sad as long as we need to be. We fear that if we allow ourselves to feel sad, we will never stop. But the reverse is true. Eventually you can be mostly done with being sad. Memories will still come up and refresh the sadness but it will no longer be overwhelming when you have spent enough time there. It is vitally important to allow this process to take place and not get stuck in anger, denial, or sadness. We must be able to move on to acceptance. Give yourself time and space to do this. Do not consider yourself weak if you are overwhelmed by these difficult emotions.

"Free from shame" is part of the heading of this section. Shame is a particularly difficult emotion to deal with. If I feel shame, it plagues me and presses in on me relentlessly. Shame is the belief that there is something wrong with me. (It is distinct from guilt, which is the knowledge that I have made a mistake.) Often shame comes from the belief that others think badly of us, which is so easy to believe as a parent, particularly if our children's behaviors have impacted other people's lives.

Our tendency to believe that others think badly of us is somewhat contingent upon the level of shaming that we experienced in our childhood years. People who have been shamed much hear shame everywhere. This may require some good counseling to rise above that constant internal voice of condemnation. If you are a person who feels shame constantly, I would recommend getting a good counselor to help work through that in order to get free.

Shame may come from criticism. Maybe we have actually heard the criticism of others. Some people love to be the "Monday morning quarterback." They do not have a clue what we have tried, or what kind of person our child is. The voice of these people I can fairly easily silence in my own head by telling myself basically that they do not know what they are talking about. The criticism they give is irrelevant.

When there is a percentage of criticism that is true, it is hard to take, no matter what the source, nor how "constructive" it is meant to be. It takes a big person to own up to mistakes or to be brave enough to listen while a critic explains more clearly what he or she means. On the other hand it also takes a big person to stay respectful yet stick with your principles with someone who criticizes and you cannot agree.

When things began to be discouraging in our relationship with David, there was a distinct tendency to take on shame and bitterness. Bitterness, for me, took the form of anger, first at David, then at myself for being angry at David, because parents aren't supposed to be angry with their children. Then that became shame that I could not be a wonderful adoptive parent with a glowing story of success; instead I was just angry. I was angry that I could not succeed, angry that David was so uncooperative, angry that he was so ungrateful, and angry that there seemed to be no end in sight. I was doomed to a future of endless disappointment.

It was at this point that I was finally able to begin to "grieve the dream." I gradually became able to accept the facts of David's diagnosis. I began to accept the things I cannot change. And I began to take solace in the truth that Georgann and I had really given it our one-hundred-and-ten-percent. There are no regrets if you have given it your very best. I can accept the mistakes I have made. I can live with the criticism of those who think we should have done better or differently than we did. And I can live with David and love him just as he is, celebrate every inch of progress, and encourage him in every setback. I am not ashamed of how we have done or with how David is now. I know who he is. I know who I am. I know what is possible and I know what is impossible. Part of the healing and movement towards wholeness also comes from all those who stand amazed, and say, "You guys have really done an amazing job with David." It is sometimes my tendency to want to diminish their encouragement with comments that bring out the imperfections, but I have learned to say, "Thanks for the encouragement," and allow myself to be encouraged.

5. Covenant Relationships – Dan

Most of our relationships in life are basically contract relationships. A contract basically says, "I will do this for you if you do that for me." And the contingency plan is, "If you do _not_ do that for me, then I do not have to do this for you." We get into contract relationships for what we can get out of them, and if we do not get the pay-off then the relationship is ended. Contracts are based on a task. Contracts are temporary; they end when the goal is reached.

Covenant relationships are very different. Covenant relationships are not based on what we get out of them, but on what we can put _into_ the relationship. We love enough to invest in the enrichment of someone else's life. The classic covenant relationship is between parent and child. We have children because we want to invest ourselves into another human being. Covenant relationships are not temporary, but for life. They are not task oriented and therefore there is no plan for how to get out of the relationship if the task is not achieved or the desired benefit is not received. There is no safety plan; we still stay in the relationship, for what we can put into it. Covenant relationships can be summarized by the statement, "I am here for you, no matter what." This is the ideal, of course, and we are fallible humans, so covenant relationships unfortunately are not always forever. Sometimes they change to become about the benefits instead of about the investment, and they end. Sometimes the "no matter what" is so unimaginably big that the person who has promised to be there, just can't do it, so it ends, tragically. It is always difficult when a covenant ends or is damaged with distrust or suspicion.

Parent-child relationships, sibling relationships, and marriages are covenant relationships. The marriage covenant is unique in that it is one that we create very carefully by choice. Parent child relationships often surprise us as we get smitten by a discovery, "I'm pregnant?" Or, "You're what?" Then we have a good nine months to prepare ourselves for being parents in a covenant way.

Adoption is no less a covenant than natural childbearing. It is forever, and it is meant to be about the investment of ourselves into a child, not the pay-off of what this child can do for me, mean to me, or to prove what I am capable of. "I am here for you, no matter what," is the wonderful ideal that we long to give to the orphan child. Children need someone to be there for them no matter what because there are lots of "no matter whats" that come along, lots of mistakes. Parental support is the avenue to growth. In contrast, parental condemnation and conditional love that is only there when the child performs well will be contractual and not make an investment in the child.

Here is the miracle of covenant relationships: both parties come out better, stronger, more wholesome, more loving, more confident, more courageous, and more likely to continue to succeed. Here is the devastation of covenant relationships: when a covenant relationship is broken, the damage goes really deep. These are the most hurtful things that can happen to us. Dr. Daniel Brown, a Pastor, who wrote the book, "Unlock the Power of Family," says that he realized through his pastoral counseling that people who came into his office shattered and in need of help, got that way because of broken covenants. It did not happen at work or at school, it happened in the family. So, the family, that was designed to be such tremendous encouragement to us, became the means of destruction, discouragement, and rejection.

It is vitally important to consider these ideas about covenants when considering adoption. All of these ideas are explained very fully in Daniel Brown's book, and I would strongly recommend your reading it if you want to adopt.

When we considered adopting David, we sat down with our four biological sons and explained that if we added David into the family, it would be forever. We said, "No matter what happens, on Thanksgiving and Christmas twenty years from now, David will be invited. Long after Georgann and I are gone David will still be your brother. We are in this for what we can do for David, not vice-versa." We do not get to end this because it did not turn out the way we wanted it to. We get to become stronger and find a way where there seems to be no way. And David gets to have a forever family that he was not blessed with from infancy because of his biological parents' human fallibility. Our sons all agreed that they were in this for life.

It is covenant; it is powerful; and without it a child never has a chance at a truly secure attachment.

6. Button Pushing – Dan

Danny Silk, a Marriage and Family Therapist who is on staff at Bethel Church in Redding, CA, helped me tremendously with this concept. We have all heard the saying, "He or she pushes my buttons," which seems to indicate that there is an unsolvable problem and I am helpless when my buttons are pushed. Danny Silk says that it is our responsibility to disconnect those buttons. It is like a button by the elevator door: push it and the elevator shows up and the doors open. But, if someone has taken the little plate off and cut the wires off and then put it back on the wall, then someone can push the button all they want and the elevator will not show up. Only you can disconnect your buttons. It is actually your responsibility to disconnect those buttons, especially for your children. You must disconnect them or you are walking around with a big button that your angry child can push at any time and watch the show.

So here is how you do it. You become aware of your reactions to your children and notice the reactions that you don't like, the ones you want to change. Those are the ones that are ignited by a "button." You are disappointed in yourself, but you say, "They just know how to push my buttons." Let me be blunt: that is just an excuse for your bad behavior. Begin to pay attention and look deep inside to determine why that particular thing, that "button", is so upsetting to you.

For example, David used to tell me (and it was a "button" for me), "You don't know crap about being a Dad." And I would get angry, scold him, tell him how wrong he was, and send him to his room. But it happened all the time, no matter how negative my reaction was, he continued to push that "button." So with Danny Silk's advice in mind, I looked inside and realized that (a) I know that I am a good Dad, four sons before had turned out fine, so it was not true. (b) I <u>did</u> have some serious questions as to how good a Dad I was with David because it did not seem to be going too well, so I did not want to be accused of something I did not like about myself. (c) With my reaction, I gave away the power to be who I wanted to be, (a good Dad) and became a distracted, enraged, unhelpful person, doing more harm than good to the relationship. (d) Every time I reacted that way, David was in control of me, and that felt like power to him. I did not really want to reinforce that notion of what power is to him.

Then with all of that in mind, I was able to say, when he said that, "Gee Dave, I'm sorry you think that about me." It completely deflated the situation. And then I would proceed to go back to what we were talking about, usually something he wanted to distract me from; a consequence, or whatever he wanted to change around. He might smolder a little bit, but I remained calm, no longer angered by that "button." And it did not take long for him to stop saying that because the button did not give him the desired result any more.

You will discover from time to time that your child will discover a new button you did not know was there. If the child gets you angry by doing the same thing over and over, that is a new button he or she has discovered and you need to get to work and uncover those wires that empower the button. Heal yourself, go to counseling, go to prayer, or talk to your spouse. Listen carefully (these are usually sensitive issues that you take very personally, so it requires some fortitude to let someone help you unwrap it). Eventually you will become a person who does not have any "buttons" and the home will become noticeably calmer. You will be very glad to be free; and you will teach your children that self-control is real power, and that button-pushing is just manipulation.

7. Telling David About His Biological Parents - Dan

Some adoptive parents choose to keep the adoption closed, meaning there is no communication with the biological parents, and others choose to do an open adoption and take the risks involved in allowing some level of communication with the biological parents while the child is growing up. This is an important decision, as we will see. Either way, inevitably the adopted child and his or her parents will face the dilemma of whether to contact the biological parents. The dilemma is basically whether this is a good idea that will be good for everyone, or at least good for the adopted person (some biological parents flatly do not want to ever be contacted again). Part of the dilemma also is the question of whether to just find out who they are, or whether to re-connect with them on some level if they are willing.

Usually at some point, the child will be told he or she is adopted. It is a pretty difficult family secret to keep if the adoptive parents choose to keep it forever. Family secrets seem to be predictably damaging, whether they ever get divulged or not. Everyone holding that secret has to wrestle with whether to be faithful to the wishes of the one who wants the secret kept or to be faithful to the one who might need to know. When the child is told, a seed is planted that says, "Who were they?" and that seed grows with the child until it blossoms and perhaps bears fruit; hopefully it is sweet.

We chose the open adoption route with David's father. We never met or contacted the mother. She just was not in the picture, and her parental rights were terminated soon after David came into our home. We met David's father and had his full cooperation and approval in regard to the adoption, and we had no intention of keeping the information that David was adopted a secret from David. That was a long time ago, and I am not sure whether it was blithe idealism, or perhaps more carefully thought-out idealism, but it was certainly a level of idealism which I do not hold to so firmly now. Nevertheless, David's father was in and out of our lives for a few years, usually when he needed something, and although I do believe it was good for David to have a visual recollection of him, there was not really a relationship there. David was about six the last time we saw his father, and then he sort of disappeared. We have not been able (and we have not worked real hard at it) to find out whether he is still alive, or where he is. The reason that we have not tried hard to keep in touch with David's father was simply that the more we saw of his life, the less we valued his example and influence for David. That was the risk we took in doing the open adoption, and as it turned out, we were grateful that he was not in the picture any more. There is however, still a significant connection for David to his father. I am not sure it is all bad, by any means. It may be just enough to satisfy his curiosity. But any time David thinks he has seen his father it creates emotional shock waves that he needs to talk about for a while, and we question again what to do about it for the future, if anything.

The recommendation, early on, of our social workers was to tell David, "Your Mommy and Daddy could not even take care of themselves, and so they certainly were not able to take care of you." In other words, "It had nothing to do with you not being worth keeping and loving." Talking to David in that manner seemed to be sufficient until he got into his teen years, and then his curiosity deepened with questions like, "What if I were still with them? What other children did they have? Should I try to find any of my biological family when I am old enough? I wonder if my father and mother are still alive?" And David still vacillates between wanting to find them and being afraid of what he would find out if he did. We parents vacillate too. Who knows whether it would resolve some things for David or whether it would be somehow shocking to discover who his biological parents were. We can theorize, we can guess, but never know for sure.

When David turned 18, we did give him the copies of the letters that his father had sent to us while he was in prison when David was still only two or three. There were three or four letters, and they were all very positive, and he stated that he knew he had made the right decision to let David be adopted. I know that was helpful for David.

Given David's emotional patterns, we have not been eager to stir up anything upsetting because he gets so distraught when he faces disturbing new facts or challenges to his identity and family of origin. Some young people might be more matter-of-fact or logical about such discoveries, but for David the pattern is more towards major emotional upheaval. Maybe facing the emotions would ultimately be helpful, or, conversely, maybe it would scar him for life. I can only imagine. We have left it basically up to David at this point, trusting that God will be able to protect and guide him in the best way at the best time. At 21 now, as David continues to mature, we are more hopeful that David will be able to navigate this minefield well.

Our personal identities are quite strongly based on the concept of our origins. Alex Haley's story, "Roots" is one of the high-profile examples of the importance that we put on our origins. People's interest in genealogies is usually more than a casual curiosity. I have heard of adopted people, growing up knowing they are adopted, and they are at peace with that identity until they suddenly find out something about their biological parents and other full or half siblings, and it shakes them to the core. Immediately it becomes for them a deep need to make contact, to understand, and to resolve questions.

Many variables enter into the picture when there is that deeply felt-need to connect, to discover. One of the most important, perhaps, is the question of the socio-economic class of the biological parents, as crass as that sounds. Adoptive parents are usually in a fairly good place financially, usually are not drug or alcohol abusers, have good life-skills, and live pretty well. Very often the biological parents are on the opposite end of that spectrum. Suddenly discovering origins in a different socio-economic status, and perhaps visiting with biological family and getting an up-close and personal experience of that could be a challenging discovery to resolve in terms of identity, "Who am I, really?"

Another variable to consider is the mental capabilities of the adopted person. How well does this person handle emotions? How well can he or she think through the concepts of identity and what that means for the future and the present? I think this is the reason most state laws prohibit people involved in a closed adoption from making any efforts to discover biological origins until the adopted person is at least 18. Maturity does help one to process these sorts of weighty revelations and come to an understanding of the true basis of identity. I am not sure that 18 is really a very good standard. Older, up to 25 or 30, might better prepare one for coming to grips with such things than just turning 18 would. Legally, however one can usually begin the search at 18 years old, and adoptive parents' choices as far as helping or hindering that process then are more limited. Adoptive parents might be privy to information that they will have to decide whether to divulge or not. Adoptive parents may choose to be involved in the search or not if they have concerns about how this is going to fare for the young person.

There are clearly no pat answers to how to proceed with this delicate but inevitable situation of what to do with the possibility of discovering more about and/or reconnecting with biological parents. There are stories on both sides: some find the new connection and new understanding miraculously helpful. Others have wished they never found out what they found out, and would rather have lived unenlightened, blind to the reality of origins in favor of the reality of their life's experiences. Others decide not to take the risk, and do life based entirely on what they already know and leave it at that. Much prayer and Divine guidance are needed.

8. A Look at Adoption in the Bible – Dan

One of the most consistent themes throughout the Bible is the expectation that God and the people of God will take care of the orphan and the oppressed (widows, strangers, and the poor.) I have highlighted in pink in my Bible every verse in which "orphan" appears, and it is throughout the books of the law (e.g. Duets 24:17-22) it is in the Psalms (e.g. Ps. 10: 14-18) and the prophets (e.g. Is. 1: 17, 23, Jer. 5:28, Zech. 7:10, Mal. 3:5). Israel's failure to take care of orphans and widows was one of the big problems that God had with Israel before they went into captivity, and one of the reasons for that time of judgment. In the New Testament, the clarion call, specifically, is in James 1:27, "Pure and undefiled religion in the sight of our God and Father is this: to visit orphans and widows in their distress, and to keep oneself unstained by the world." Not so specifically, John puts out the general call in the very convicting verse, I John 3:17, "But whoever has the world's goods, and sees his brother in need and closes his heart against him, how does the love of God abide in him?"

So we have much scriptural evidence that this phenomenon of adoption is in the heart and character of God. None would question that. Adoption is not just a New Testament concept. It is clear that God always intended to give to His people the position of sonship. In Exodus 4:22, for example, God declares, "Israel is My son." Then Paul, in Romans, Galatians and Ephesians, talks about it, using the actual word, "adoption," as a part of the definition of what happens when a person who has been previously alienated from God becomes a child of God. That person is now declared to be in the family of God, and is placed in the position of a son or daughter of God. Paul writes in Rom 8:15 that we "have received a spirit of adoption as sons by which we cry out, 'Abba Father!'" Vine's Expository Dictionary of Biblical Words presents the view that the spirit of adoption is the Holy Spirit producing in us, "the *realization* of sonship, and the *attitude* belonging to sons." That makes sense to me.

Are you thinking about adopting a child? It is probably your heart's desire that your adopted child gain, "the <u>realization</u> of sonship [or daughterhood]," and that he or she gets "the <u>attitude</u> of sonship [or daughterhood]," and of course you want your adoptive child to be on equal status with a natural born child, that is, the <u>position</u> of sonship [or daughterhood]. God, in the way He deals with those previously alien to His family, gives us a good model of what adoption is meant to be, and He demonstrates the heart of adoption in that He makes a way for us to become unquestionably and forever His.

I interpret God's view on adoption to be that it is central to who He is in relationship to mankind. It is His basic way of operating in this fallen world. He doesn't give us a handout, or a new set of clothes, or a pat on the back; He **adopts** us. He is into this relationship one-hundred percent. It is the standard solution to the problem of being without a Heavenly Father. We don't join Big Brothers & Big Sisters (no disrespect to that admirable work), He **adopts** us. We don't just get to come over for dinner often; we live with Him in the Father's house. It is the pinnacle of what can be done for a stranger. It is unsurpassed in its totality of involvement, sacrifice, risk, and hope. Without any guarantees, it holds the greatest chance of success among all the things one could do to help a stranger.

An interesting legal detail that we discovered in adopting David, and it has been mentioned before in this book, but bears repeating, is that David's birth certificate that he was issued when he was born was destroyed, and his new birth certificate lists Georgann and I as his... parents. No one could ever tell by looking at that document that David was ever anything other than completely one of our biological children. It looks just like his brothers' birth certificates. The legal position of the adopted child is every bit as secure as that of the natural-born child. It says something powerful when a society (the U.S.A.) gives away such a clear legal status. The legal world, not known for compassion, empathy, or any warm fuzziness, gives a mandate of equality and complete acceptance to the adopted members of our society. No more questions asked, never to be brought up again that this child is adopted. She or he is a Smith or a Whomever, period.

One day, I was under a kitchen sink fixing a leak in the home of a family, which had just finalized the adoption of several children. One of the new adoptees, this little, three-and-a-half foot tall girl came and stood by my feet with her hands behind her back. (We had gotten to know each other a little on previous visits.) She announced, quite confidently, "I'm official now." With my head still in the cabinet under the sink, I queried, "Official?" And just as confidently, she said, "Yes, I'm an official [her new last name.]" As I pulled myself out from under the sink, I looked at her, and this little wisp of a thing, this little nine-year old girl, was just as bold as a lion. She was delighted. She knew I would be delighted along with her. And it was as if she knew the world would be delighted with her for the rest of her life.

9. Notes From our Therapy Sessions with John Trentalange - Dan

As we have written in other parts of this book, we were very significantly helped by our family therapist and attachment specialist John Trentalange. He was a licensed therapist in Colorado Springs at the time we first met with him. He specializes in attachment. After some careful shopping on line and talking to John and other therapists, we chose John and have been much helped by him. John now has a book out called *Transformational Living.* The book covers all of the following topics in depth.

The following paragraphs are excerpts from my notes taken during therapy sessions with John. I have left them in the first-person, as it fits in with our story of raising David, but of course they are principles that anyone may apply to any other similar situation. I have included in brackets my own expansion of the ideas presented.

The first principle was, "Slow down." Your lives are far too busy. David needs full-time parents who show interest in him, have time for him, and can engage with him to teach, to model, and to direct his life. What can you cut out of your life to give him more of yourselves? [At that time we had been doing foster care, pastoring a church and I was going to grad school for counseling.]

I, the adoptive parent cannot derive my value from the way David responds to me. [In other words, my significance, or how I view myself, cannot be based on what David says he thinks about me, or how he treats me in response to my parenting efforts.] My value comes from how God responds to me. Value is not based upon outcome. God judges our value based on our obedience, not on the outcome. Our point of obedience before God is to love David; it is not our job to get David to love us; that always has to be his choice alone.

We are here to do a job, not to get rewards. Stop wanting rewards from David (his respect, his cooperation, etc.). We have expectations of what he is supposed to be. John gave us homework to do: list your expectations of David. What is your dream for David? (I wrote out a page and a half of things like, "I expected that raising David would be a totally fun and rewarding experience (and some of it was, I don't want to be all negative here). That it would pay off marvelously because he would respond so well to all our care and generosity. That he would run and jump on me when I got home and give big hugs. None of these things, nor the rest of what I written down at that time were coming to pass. I'm hurt, I'm exhausted, I'm annoyed – this is because of unmet expectations. This is the grief work: grieve the dream. It is a loss, like a death. If we do not grieve the loss, then we are stuck in wishing it were still some way that it is not. Being stuck, wishing things were somehow other than they are, means being stuck in denial, being angry, sad, guilty, or depressed. Grieving is a conscious process that we have to will ourselves to get through sometimes. It involves expressing our feelings of anger and sadness, and sharing it with someone who can empathize. Basically, it is the process of coming to accept what we cannot change; acceptance of the way it really is, instead of pain because it is not what we wanted. It is the only way to peace in the reality of the situation.)

David is our ministry, but our ministry is not what gives us value. This was particularly pertinent for us because we were ministers and got a lot of commendation for it.

From a journal about how hard it is for me to receive love: "I am fighting to get love from David, but when others give it I resist." [This was an area of personal discovery for me. For doing some deep thinking about what love means to you, how you know when you are loved, and what your emotional need is for love can be helpful, as it was for me, in regard to this project of loving an adopted child. If I am parenting an adoptive child because I want to be loved, something is backwards there.]

How emotionally present are you when together with David? [This is part of the "slow down" message. Several things can impact our ability to be present for our children. Busyness is a big one, and the other is disappointment in the child. If we allow disappointment to build up, we defend ourselves from further disappointment by not being as engaged as the child needs us to be.] He is aware of that level of how emotionally present we are. He is very attuned to our mood. We have to work at not caring. 'Not caring' here means that we <u>do</u> care about David rather than caring about whether he respects us or treats us well. This means paying attention to our focus. Either we focus on the child or we focus on how the child is treating us. You can't do both. [If we focus on how David is treating us, and he has not been treating us well, then we are likely to be withdrawn, sharp, abrupt, or distracted. If we care too much about how he treats us or how he behaves, we take it personally and wind up in a bad mood all the time.]

Messages that we need to deliver to David in ways that are deeper and stronger than words: (1) "I always love you in spite of your behavior." (2) "Nothing you do can overwhelm me." (Stay connected to his heart, but disengaged from his behavior.) "Love is always there." (3) "I am not going anywhere. Nothing you do will push me away. This kind of behavior has consequences, but I am not leaving."

Debrief with David when it is going well: take a minute to say, "This is fun. I enjoyed that." Start by doing it <u>after</u> the activity, then later <u>during</u> the activity.

There is a lot of spiritual warfare in this business [the business of adoption and working to heal the attachment style of a child]. The Enemy does not want people securely attached. Figure out the lies you have believed and renounce them. [Lies like, "You are not good enough to do this. This child is out to get you. You got a broken kid; it's hopeless. There is nothing good in the future with this child." We can believe some pretty grim things that are flatly not true.] Ask the Lord to reveal to you your own wounds that need to heal. [No matter who we are, we come into this with baggage. You have probably heard the saying, "Hurt people hurt people." Your hurts from the imperfect way you have been parented or the imperfect ways life treated you, often can be the things that set you up to be a person who hurts others, oddly enough, rather than to be a person who wants to protect others from what you have experienced.] Look at your engagement with David; what is going on in your engagement? [This is a review of your mood around him, your expectations of him, what you want from him, and what you are working to accomplish with him, and within him.]

Close proximity. Gentle holding, on his terms, in tune with his timing and his choosing, is heartbeat-hearing. Attachment begins in the womb listening to Mom's heart. [The womb may have been the most secure attachment experience that the child has ever had. Holding, rocking, and staying (not leaving) have healing influences, perhaps because they approximate that early womb experience.]

In regard to suicidal talk or threats: [Going to counseling about this is always a good idea, so that you have some backup and some professional help with this scary and complicated situation, especially with teenagers. One myth about this is: that talking about it will make it more likely to happen. Just the opposite is true. A similar myth: that giving attention to suicidal talk/threats will reward the behavior and make it worse. Okay, maybe true, but ignoring the behavior is much more likely to amplify it, and for children, trying to get attention is not an invalid goal. Redirecting the child to develop a different means of getting attention will be part of the help you can give.] One of the primary red flags you are looking for if a child is talking about suicide is, does he/she have a plan? A thought-out plan of how to do it indicates much more danger than some vague idea that life is not worth living, but both are a serious cry for help and there is a need for the parents to pay attention and get some help. [John was able to be helpful in our specific situation so that we had an understanding about what was going on, and we knew about what the options were each time we faced that situation. That is why I recommend counseling, because hard and fast rules about this touchy subject are not likely to be applicable to what you are facing. A professional counselor can talk you through your specific scenario and will be very helpful.]

Children with attachment disorders have no internal structure, so they need an external structure initially. The goal is that the highly structured external world, provided by parents, teaches him about schedules, values, and responsibility. Over time this becomes internally wired so the child can operate in the mainstream and be able to live a normal life. Children have to internalize their external world. A token system is often used to motivate kids to behave in certain ways. It is used as an external influence until the child develops an internal reward system. The goal is always for the child to internalize it. [Ultimately we want children to learn to do the right thing just because it is the right thing, not because they will get punished or rewarded by an external system.] Structure for David helps him know what is next. Knowing what is expected of him is a set-up for success. Lack of structure in the home equals chaos in the brain of the child. Chaos appears then in organization problems in thought or writing. Children thrive in a structured environment [routine, schedule, rules, values] but too much structure tends to communicate that the parent does not trust the child.

Structure creates and enhances self-identity, the understanding of where you end, and I begin. Structure is external boundaries that mirror internal limitations (we are all limited and finite) and the external structure helps David find out what God made him to do and be, what his talents are, and what has to happen first before he can do the next thing. Self-identity is about security and safety. An internal structure allows David to explore the world and take healthy risks.

A child's environment consists of:
(1) Mental and physical wellness of the individual caregivers of the child.
(2) Mental and spiritual wellness of the marriage. Children are highly spiritual.
(3) Physical environment (is it child-friendly?)
(4) Messages to the child; what is important, for example, the car or the child?
(5) Routines; preferably maintained daily within an hour.
(6) How are the Mom and Dad communicating, especially in front of the children?

Every power struggle is the adult's fault. If you truly know who you are, 95% of power struggles will not happen. [I can be challenged by David, and I won't be shaken. It is my own insecurities that can shake me up.]

Understand power: if David wants something from me, I have all the power. If I want nothing from David, he has no power over me. David needs to be convinced that what we have for him is valuable.

Do not give David a chance to say, "Dad said...," or, "Mom said..." because we have already talked about it. We have had a team meeting. Make all instruction to David specific and concrete; there will be fewer arguments because he understands.

Brain food: good books, science, Bible, math, English, work ethic, skills.

Brain starvation: TV, drugs, alcohol, no thinking or learning.

Body food: nutritious food, exercise, water, washing.

Body starvation: junk food, no food, filthiness, dehydration, alcohol, drugs, sugar.

Heart food: love, good touching, good thoughts (that open the heart.)

Heart starvation: hatred, bad touch, bad thoughts (that close the heart.)

Incentives are rewards that feed the healthy things. Without incentives we starve.

This is a brief summary of what we took many counseling sessions to understand and begin to implement, but hopefully it is helpful, particularly in the context of this larger narrative of our experience. I highly recommend John's book, especially the chapters: Power, Control, and Attention; Learning to Discipline Without Emotion; and The Subject of Power Struggles.

10. Facing Some Hard Things About Fostering & Adoption – Jessica Lemaire, MSW

Our oldest son, Tim, and his wife, Jessica, have fostered and adopted. Jessica was a social worker with Child Protective Services in Reno for 5 years. These are her insights:

1. Love is not enough. You can't love these kids into something they do not want. I can take them in to my home, do everything I can to help them, and see their behavior change, but it is

disillusioning, because it is not necessarily lasting. Whatever I do may not change things for the child.

2. Expectations. We have expectations of success, but really the kids are going to do what they are going to do.

3. Exhausting—because of the pain. We listened to parenting tapes with two couples that were our best friends. Their kids were not adopted, had no attachment issues, no abandonment issues, no FAS. The parenting tapes conveyed, "If you are not doing things THIS way, you are wrong." My feelings rose up—"Why aren't my kids like Erin's and Angel's?" We can't help but compare our kids to our friends' kids.

4. Exhausting—because you never get a real break.

5. Exhausting—because of the waiting. It can take years to determine if the foster child you want to adopt is going to be available for adoption because the system has to check out all of the child's family members as possible placements. This means that people who are just fostering, but looking to adopt a particular child are waiting months and even years for the call that will tell them that their child is available finally to adopt.

6. Loss and grief. When an adoption falls through for any reason and is not brought to completion, the loss and grief is like the child had a terminal illness and then he died. All of the months of waiting and hoping and yearning to finally bring the child into the family through adoption, and then having him removed because social services has discovered a relative who will take him.

7. Loss and grief. When a person is fostering, how often does a person have to give up or lose that many kids? [For Tim and Jessica it was 8 children who came through their house as fosters and then moved on to other placements or back with their parents.]

8. Anger. Kids put you in awkward positions, embarrass you, and say things that are not true.

9. Hopelessness. When the full realization comes—that a significant number your child's brain cells were dissolved with the alcohol his mother drank while he was in the womb—it is a hopeless feeling. You have to come to a place of acceptance.

10. Joy. As you watch your child make progress in his growth and development and in his personality. There is joy as you see that he is really connected to your extended family and they to him. There is authenticity in our extended family and they have been willing to be committed to our adopted son. I remember the day that our friend Lindsey said: "Quinn and Tim really do look alike!" I realized that it was the shared mannerisms that Quinn had picked up from his Dad.

11. Short leash. It is a challenge to keep your child on a short leash or he may do something impulsive. [One morning when Tim & Jess got up the stove was on. When they talked to Quinn, he said he had gotten hungry and had been cooking himself some quesadillas at 4am and had neglected to turn off the burner.]

12. Empathy for your child. It is harder for your adopted child than it is for you as his parents, and your heart aches for him. Quinn lived with his biological Mom for 4 years. She became unable to care for him. At first she made some contact, but that was a long time ago. He has been concerned about her for years. Now he asks, "Is she dead?" It is really important for him to get some information. He is a teenager now and could work on processing the truth. Realize that you are not your child's only Mom, and try not to be threatened by his having a relationship with her.

11. Interview with David About His Experiences with FAS – David Lemaire, age 20

What do you think are the main struggles for you of the effects of FAS? -- For me, I would say, the main effects of FAS are keeping a positive mindset and knowing that there will always be certain things that I can never do. I think of the things I can do instead of the things I can't. Because I have been talking to one of my staff a lot about different things that my life has thrown at me--what I mean by that, I have had so many things in my life that have changed since I have grown up. I don't always know all the time how to handle those things. If I don't handle it appropriately it doesn't help me at all. But if I do handle it in an adult fashion I learn about the things that are different about me and I can use it to better myself and help others. There are certain things that are different about me, but there are certain things that other people can benefit from.

Can you be specific? One thing that I can benefit from is my ability to understand what other people are going through that have the same effects that I do. I can really understand what they are going through and help them with their issues. I have found in the past that I have had a lot of difficulties with people telling me that I can't do things when I know I can do them. This goes into a situation I have been talking to Richard [Chrysalis house manager] about. It seems people are telling me I can't do things and they are taking pity on me because of my disabilities. The staff helped me to see that there are more things that I can do. I know what I am capable of and not capable of. I would benefit from making my own meals and doing my own laundry. People always try to help me with them, but I like to be independent. They say, "Pick up this piece of clothing and put it over here." They try to micromanage my room cleanup.

Now I clean my room every night. Do my laundry on my own. Cook my own meals, do my own dishes. I like to live my life like an ordinary person. I don't like being rushed.

One staff has an issue—if you don't do it in the second he wants it done he will keep on bugging me. He backed off.

What about reading? I've been finding that in the past I had a very difficult time reading, all that time you guys spent teaching me in homeschooling, it may have seemed at the time for all of us that it was doing no good for me. But everything is starting to fall together. Now I look at a book and I can understand what half the words mean. And I've been able to write things non-phonetically. Remember how hard it was for me to spell a word? Words I had problems with in the past are suddenly coming clear. Math is a different thing, not coming together yet.

Tell us about when you arrived at Copper Hills [David's first placement in Utah, a lock-down facility, age 17] – When I first got there it was like a surreal dream. I realized for the first time that I was a long way from home. Never had that feeling before. I got checked in and said goodbye to you guys—it didn't really register at first that you guys were really leaving. For the first time, I felt alone. Felt scared, frightened. Didn't know what to do.

What about your angry episodes there? I didn't get angry the first 2 weeks. Then something snapped. Everything people said and did pissed me off, and from there I started getting into more and more trouble, and it escalated from there.

They told me in the beginning, that after the honeymoon stage my true colors would show. I said, "This is my true colors." "No David, just wait." When the honeymoon stage ended I realized I was a different person than I thought I was. I thought I was going to stay under the radar and make it out of there in 3 months, but it didn't work. Shortly after that I started going off the wall. I got into restraints every day. Everything they asked me to do I would give them the finger. At first I did not go after anyone, I was intimidated. One day I said something to one of the peers and I got a butt whooping. But it never ended good for me. It always ended up being a bad situation.

How about Benchmark? [This was David's second placement in Utah, age 18, also a lockdown facility] – At first I was angry but I settled down. I had no time-outs at Benchmark. I had tons at Copper Hills.

What do you think was going on at Copper Hills? -- The problem was that I was more confused.

What about electronic things—like your DSI and games? When it comes to electronics I don't have that much problems with electronics. I understand them quite well. It's easier to write on computer than paper.

I have a hard time with game system controllers—you have to coordinate your hands, and on the new ones, both analogs move, there are more buttons, you have to memorize stuff and it is very difficult for me. My brain won't process all that.
One side rotates the view. Push up. Not like a Nintendo 64, which is easy.
PS2 is harder, and so are x-box, ps3, ds, dsi, wii.
Wii is very hard. The wands have toggle, all wireless.
You can tell the people who have FAS, you can see the things they have difficulties with.

What do you think are the typical things that you notice that tells you that someone is FAS?

A lot of people that have FAS also have a hyperactive attention disorder. It is difficult for them to sit and hold a conversation. One

friend forgets what he is going to say, his brain runs ahead of him. He is five sentences ahead of what he is going to say.
I have to say, "Whoa, slow down."
He skips stuff.

How about your biological parents?
With my bio parents, it is hard to tell because sometimes I feel like I hate them and I'm mad about what happened with the FAS, but other times I get mad at myself because I feel it's more my fault that I have FAS. Staff says I can't think that way. In a way they (my bio parents) did me a favor, because who knows where I would be right now. I could be in a ditch somewhere. I know that the family I am in is 'there for me,' I am safe. I truly know what family means.

I don't know anything about my Mom. It's so hard for me not to get mad at her for drinking when she was pregnant with me. Maybe she was going through something hard. There are so many things I have done in the past that people have given me a second chance on, that there's no reason for me not to give her a second chance. I wish she could have been here to hear me say that.

What do you want to say about what you have figured out about those angry years?
I realized that a lot of it had to do about me not knowing what was going on in my life. It was frustrating for me, I was lost in a desert and couldn't find my way out. When people tried to help me I felt pushed further into the desert.
It was all just one big threat to me.
I took that I could not do the math and stuff as a bad thing. Math itself became a bad thing because I couldn't do it.

What about Marcella and Serena? (our neighbors when he was 8-10 years old) Were those frustrating relationships?
I didn't know how to react to people. At that point I had no social skills and it was very difficult for me to have a friendship.

How did you learn social skills? Watching other people and getting prompts from you guys.

What is it that is most helpful to you in making a friendship?

The most helpful thing in making a friendship is to know a little bit about them. Is this going to be a smart idea to get into a relationship with them? Is it a stupid idea to get into this relationship?

What about the new kid at Chrysalis?
I am having second thoughts.
He's a little bit astray.

What are some of the things that you think are natural interests for you?
I would say a natural interest for me would be to fit in with other people, go to parties, do what every one else does. Be normal.

What about camping and outdoors?
Oh, ever since I was real young, like seven or eight, the outdoors has been a part of my life. If I could live out in the middle of the desert-- out in the middle of nowhere, hearing the sound of the breeze going through the air, the sound of the birds chirping, no road noises-- I would think to myself, "I have a good life." I can understand why my grandfather lives out where he does. He has peace and quiet, time to himself to be able to reflect. He loves his life. If I could have that I would be happy.

What about if you were alone?
Alone? Never thought about someone else out there with me—sort of picture my self as a wild man living out there.

What are the things that lifestyle would eliminate that are problems now?
It would eliminate my fear of being looked down on. I feel that I don't fit in. I could fit in out there.

What are some of the things you wish you could do?
I would like to travel the world, be able to see things that are out there. I've been to Nepal, India, England, Canada, but I know there are other things I could see: Australia, Africa, Brazil, Thailand, China, just to be able to see what there is to see.
I have always been fascinated about how different people live their lives. Native Americans live their lives in a peaceful, calm manner. They didn't fight unless bothered. It seems we Americans look for fights. Native Americans seem like they were very peaceful people, more in tune with the earth and how it worked.

12. The Vision and the Visitations – Georgann

Our foster care adventure was a "God Thing." God gave me a vision of babies when I was just minding my own business raising our sons and trying to be a good wife and Mom. There came a season when my faith in God to bring the vision to reality took a dive. I faltered in carrying the vision and my doubts became mountains. Jesus came to me to verify that He was truly with me and to encourage me to continue in faith. Here is an article I wrote about it:

Our family lived in upstate New York during 1986-88. Dan was attending Elim Bible Institute and working part-time. I attended a few classes, but my focus was on homeschooling our sons, participating in the homeschool group, and babysitting some of our friends' children.

After we had been there almost two years, I woke up one morning realizing I had had a vision of babies—babies wearing blue hospital-type gowns and seeming to be superimposed over one another. I was impacted and I was happy. It was more than a dream; there was something living and supernatural about it.

I prayed to find the meaning of the vision—was I to bear more children? I was 42 years old so it did not seem very likely, and besides Dan had had a vasectomy. Yet I knew that nothing was impossible with God. Was God going to be adding more children to our family?

Over the next few years I seriously sought to find the answer to this question, but God wasn't revealing His plan about how it would all work out. What He did do was to keep the vision alive with many nudges and divine promptings: nonchalant comments that people would speak, baby-related questions that someone would ask me out of the blue, and stirrings in my heart when I heard a story of families with a multitude of children. These would come with that sense of surprise that often accompanies the Spirit when He wants me to understand that He is present. As I spent time in the Bible, my awareness of the Father's heart of compassion for the orphan and the needy, the broken-hearted, and the destitute began to expand, and my desire to be of some service to babies was deeply stirred. This was a mystifying time in my life, but I kept seeking God with a sense of wonder.

From New York we went to San Francisco, Pasadena, and then Carson City and lived for a time in each city. I was burdened by my thoughts of having another baby, wanting so much to know what God would have me do. One weekend, Dan and I went to a seminar to hear a Christian speaker whose reputation we knew to be sound. I saved the notes I took notes on his message: "You are being challenged by the Holy Spirit to do things you have never done before....Be aware that there is a great struggle to get through to obey God once you have heard from Him....Do what God has called you to do and you will be a happy Christian."

His words lined up with what I was experiencing with the Lord. 1) I was being challenged to step out of my comfort zone and being led by God by means of a heavenly vision into something that seemed outlandish and yet wonderful! 2) I was experiencing a great inward struggle to see how the pieces of the puzzle fit together so that I could obey Him—but I felt He was not giving me concrete instructions! I didn't know what He wanted me to DO! 3) I was surrendered, I knew that I wanted to do whatever God had called me to do and that I would be happy in it—but what was it, and what did it have to do with babies???

Because the message related so amazingly to my life experience, I decided to go up for prayer to see if through this man, God might give me further insight and direction as to how He was going to bring the baby vision to pass. I wrote in my notes that I was praying: "Speak, Lord, Your servant is listening." I fully submitted myself to hearing from the Lord. I explained the baby vision to the man of God, and he said very blithely and confidently something like, "*Oh, God does not mean babies—He means new Christians. You will be nurturing and bringing along new believers in their new faith.*"

I was shaken and then I was devastated. I knew that the focal point of the vision I had experienced was about caring for infants. I believed that the Spirit had been impressing on me the desire to take care of helpless children and orphans. The man had given his word with such positive conviction that my world rocked as if I was in a level eight earthquake. Friends of mine knew this man, and trusted him. He was known as a sound teacher who moved in the prophetic. I was thrown off kilter.

I wrote in my journal my frustration that the prophet had disaffirmed my own personal experience with God. His contradiction caused me to feel that I was wrong and that he had the correct insight.

I remembered the impression I had had from the vision was that I would be caring for a newborn (or possibly more than one baby), and I knew that God had been reinforcing this in many many ways in my day-to-day life for years. I wrote in my journal: *God, I have no desire to desire what You are not putting on my heart. If I am believing wrongly, please take it (the desire for babies) away.* Proverbs 28:14 Blessed is the man who always fears the Lord, but he who hardens his heart falls into trouble. *Help me to always fear you and to not harden my heart. ---Yet, it occurs to me, maybe my acute disappointment is Holy Spirit grief! Maybe the speaker spoke out of turn and the Holy Spirit is grieved by the pain the man caused me.* I was plunged into the agony of my soul, and I went to bed that night in deep despair.

At 4:15am, I opened my eyes with a start and looked into the hall and had an impression of Jesus there. He said, "This child shall be a light among the nations." I saw the bottom of His robe and His legs and His feet in His sandals. There was nothing mystical or shining, no aura, no finery. His robe was simple and plain. There was a light outside the bedroom window, a star. I bowed to the ground and said, "My Lord and my God, my Lord and my God". I said it again and again. I went into the living room and bowed down on the floor. "Oh that my Lord would come to me." Doubt came. I heard, "Luke 1:47". I looked it up in my Bible: "and my spirit rejoices in God my SAVIOR"—it was Jesus. I danced. Doubt came back. I heard, "Romans 8:31" "What then shall we say in response to this? If God is for us, who can be against us? He who did not spare His own Son, but gave Him up for us all, how will He not also, along with Him, graciously give us all things."

I went back to bed at 5:30am. I woke Dan up and we prayed, then I explained it to Dan, though as I spoke it sounded ridiculous, but Dan said that his spirit witnessed it was true. Then he said something like, "I feel immersed in your love. Surely you have encountered the Lord." (from my journal, 2-19-91)

I believe Jesus came to me that night because He saw that a surrendered daughter of His was seriously crushed and in a dilemma of her faith.

I wrote in my journal the next day: *Last night's experience was un-sensational. I was so challenged all day by my rational flesh arguing with my mind. I was only able to truly believe that the visitation had been real because of my Spirit responses of worship ["my Lord and my God!"], and the scriptures that God gave me, plus Dan's verification several times that he believed I had been with the Lord. These three concrete things enabled* *me to keep believing I had encountered Jesus. When I went to my daily devotions my psalm for the day was Ps 20:1 May the Lord answer you when you are in distress! v4 May He give you the desire of your heart! Wow! He HAD answered me in my distress! And the vision He had planted in my heart had become the desire of my heart! With my <u>will</u> I said: "Blessed be the name of the Lord, let it be done to me according to Thy will."*(from my journal, 2-20-91)

The next night (2-21) I was heavy and discouraged--with spiritual warfare, I know now. I cried out in desperation: *"Come to me Jesus! Come to me, Jesus!" He came. I KNEW He was there. I perceived Him; I did not see Him.*

The next night (2-22) *at 4:15am, Daniel (son) woke up, and after he went back to sleep I decided to stay up, though I was very sleepy. I called out, "Come to me again." I realized that all of yesterday's faith was gone. HE DID! I was startled by an impression, very fleeting, of Jesus standing there holding what appeared to be two babies superimposed upon one another. "My Lord and My God" was my immediate response again. I will rejoice in the Lord God my Savior.*

I felt that in these visitations and scriptures and words and impressions, Jesus wanted to emphasize His concern for me, and my mental health! I believe He wanted to reinforce my conviction in what I knew was real between us and to negate the word that the man had brought to me. He wanted me to stay on track and not get derailed. <u>I was in a faith walk with Him. I was to keep my eyes on Him and keep walking.</u> I had gone forward for prayer at the seminar, wanting more revelation and more concrete disclosure from God so I could get myself closer to getting that baby!

He had cautioned me three years previously to keep the vision to myself, which was probably because people would not believe me or understand. I was to carry it between Him and me. I had gotten impatient and thought that going to a man of God was not breaking the rules. But God did not relent and pamper me in my desire for some control, so He did not give the prophet some of His inside information to humor me.

God always has purpose in having us walk by faith and in having us wait for His timing. Yet, He was right there to comfort me and encourage me to carry on at the time when my faith was crushed.

It would be two-and-a-half years before the meaning of the baby vision would be revealed to us.

Ten days after the first visitation, we received a telephone call from a man in our denomination, asking Dan to be the interim pastor in a church in San Francisco. We lived there for one-and-a-half years. I kept seeking God about the baby vision, and He kept tugging at my heart and building my faith in His commitment to loving the needy and the orphan.

We completed our interim pastoring assignment in SF, handing the church over to an energetic young pastor and his family. We came back to Reno. A few weeks after we were settled in, our pastor was teaching one Sunday morning and said it was time for the congregation to move out into the community and serve. Dan looked at me with firm assurance and said: "It is foster care!"

My 6-year faith walk was over—and it was time for the baby vision to become reality. God had kept the vision burning in my heart, and Dan had come to share it. There would still be a lot of adjustments to bringing other people's children into our home. But as a family, He had prepared us for the task in many practical ways and we were of the same mind about this next adventure. Plus, we were back in our home church with our tried and true friends. We had rented a large ranch-style house outside of town, and we were ready to settle down to helping some people who were less fortunate than we were.

We called the Department of Child and Family Services, picked up the paperwork, and began the foster care journey that would last twelve years.

Note: A person God is using to give prophetic words is fallible because he or she is a human being. I learned something very important for myself about being very thoughtful and prayerful about giving 'words' to people and about receiving 'words'. I hold no offense or grudge toward the man who spoke to me so authoritatively that day. Though I was shaken and in some dismay for quite a while, I worked through it. All of our experiences mature us, if we stay in forgiveness and keep ourselves from bitterness.

Another note: To be perfectly honest, I was for the entire 6 years that I carried the vision unsure whether God was speaking about me giving birth to another baby or whether He was going to bring us a baby to rescue. That kept me (and Dan) humble, and a little koo-koo. It is another story for another time.

13. Bible Verses About the Orphan and the Needy - compiled by Dan & Georgann

It was the Word of God that impacted us, gave us His attitude, and kept us steady. God's heart in the Old Testament and the New Testament is clearly supportive of His people extending themselves for those who are alone and for those who are needing care. In studying the Bible for ourselves, Christians learn God's values as we seek Him and sit with Him on a regular basis. Please note that there are promises for us as we obey the Lord.

These verses are from the New American Standard Bible, unless otherwise noted.

Deut. 10:18 He executes justice for the **ORPHAN** and the widow, and shows His love for the alien by giving him food and clothing.

Deut. 14:28-29 At the end of every third year you shall bring out all the tithe of your produce in that year, and shall deposit it in your town.

And the Levite, because he has no portion or inheritance among you, and the alien, the **ORPHAN** and the widow who are in your town, shall come and eat and be satisfied, in order that the Lord your God may bless you in all the work of your hands which you do.

Deut. 15:11 "For the **POOR** will never cease to be in the land; therefore I command you, saying, 'You shall freely open your hand to your brother, to your **NEEDY** and **POOR** in your land.'

Deut. 16:10-12 Then you shall celebrate the Feast of Weeks to the Lord your God with a tribute of a freewill offering of your hand, which you shall give just as the Lord your God blesses you;

And you shall rejoice before the Lord your God, you and your son and your daughter and your male and female servants and the Levite who is in your town, and the stranger and the **ORPHAN** and the widow who are in your midst, in the place where the Lord your God chooses to establish His name.

And you shall remember that you were a slave in Egypt, and you shall be careful to observe these statutes.

Deut. 24:19-21 When you reap your harvest in your field and have forgotten a sheaf in the field, you shall not go back to get it; it shall be for the alien, for the **ORPHAN**, and for the widow, in order that the Lord your God may bless you in all the work of your hands.

When you beat your olive tree, you shall not go over the boughs again; it shall be for the alien, for the **ORPHAN**, and for the widow.

When you gather the grapes of your vineyard, you shall not go over it again, it shall be for the alien, for the **ORPHAN**, and for the widow.

Psalm 82:3 Defend the **POOR** and the **FATHERLESS**; do justice to the **AFFLICTED** and the **NEEDY**.

Proverbs 19:17 He who has pity on the **POOR** lends to the LORD, and He will pay back what he has given.(NKJV)

Isaiah 1:17　　Learn to do good;
　　　　　　　Seek justice,
　　　　　　　Reprove the ruthless;
　　　　　　　Defend the **ORPHAN**,
　　　　　　　Plead for the widow.

Isaiah 58: 6a,7 Is this not the fast which I choose...Is it not to divide your bread with the **HUNGRY** and bring the homeless **POOR** into the house; when you see the **NAKED**, to cover him; and not to hide yourself from your own flesh?

Isaiah 58:10 And if you give yourself to the **HUNGRY** and satisfy the desire of the **AFFLICTED**, then your light will rise in darkness and your gloom will become like midday. And the LORD will continually guide you, and satisfy your desire in scorched places, and give strength to your bones; and you will be like a watered garden, and like a spring of water whose waters do not fail.

Zechariah 7:9-10 Thus has the LORD of hosts said, 'Dispense true justice, and practice kindness and compassion each to his brother; and do not oppress the widow or the **ORPHAN,** the stranger or the **POOR**, and do not devise evil in your hearts against one another.'

Matthew 25:35-36 [Jesus said] 'For I was **HUNGRY**, and you gave me something to eat; I was **THIRSTY**, and you gave me something to drink; I was a stranger, and you invited Me in; **NAKED**, and you clothed Me; I was sick, and you visited Me; I was in prison, and you came to Me.'

John 14:18 [Jesus said] "I WILL NOT LEAVE YOU AS **ORPHANS**; I WILL COME TO YOU."

Acts 20:35 "In everything I showed you that by working hard in this manner you must help the **WEAK** and remember the words of the Lord Jesus, that He Himself said, 'It is more blessed to give than to receive.'"

James 1:27 Pure and undefiled religion in the sight of our God and Father is this: to visit **ORPHANS** and widows in their distress and to keep oneself unstained from the world.

1 John 3:17-18 But whoever has the world's goods, and sees his **BROTHER IN NEED** and closes his heart against him, how does the love of God abide in him? Little children, let us not love with word or with tongue, but in deed and truth.

14. One Person's Philosophy of Life – a Friend in the Village

We were talking with a friend in the village recently, one who is in a helping profession. He said he has had an ongoing visualization. It is that when we die we will stand before a Judge and be asked to give an account of our lives. **You were given a mouth, you were given hands. Did you feed yourself or use them to feed others?**

This person left a lucrative job for one in which he would be involved every day in helping others.

Suggested Books and websites:

The Bain Event: Our Adoption Story, Dave and Kathy Bain, 2010. This is their adoption story and can be ordered at Dave's email: Dadbain@gmail.com

The Brain That Changes Itself, Norman Doidge, M.D., The Penguin Group USA, Inc., New York, 2007
Available on Kindle and at www.amazonbooks.com

The Choice, a novel, by Robert Whitlow, Thomas Nelson, 2012, Nashville.
Available on Kindle and at www.amazonbooks.com

The Train to Omaha, a novel, by Diane Harper, Wine Press Publishing, 2012, Washington. Available on Kindle and at www.amazonbooks.com

Transformational Living: Everything You Need to Know to Live a Happy and Purposeful Life. John Trentalange, MA, LPC, BCETSTate Publishing, 2014.
Available on Kindle and www.amazonbooks.com
John can be reached at 719-310-9495.

Unlock the Power of the Family, Daniel Brown, Ph.D., 1994, 2004
www.ctw.coastlands.org

Check this website out for some surprises!!
Famous Adopted Children and Famous Adoptive Parents
You just can't imagine what a child might turn out to be!
www.americanadoptions.com/adoption/celebrity adoption
Georgann's website: www.georgannlemaire.com
Georgann's Facebook: Georgann Lemaire/author

Made in the USA
San Bernardino, CA
18 March 2016